Praise for
Forbidden Gate

Tom and Nita Horn have written an unprecedented exposé, which every person of faith needs to understand. How human-transforming technologies will soon radically alter what it means to be human…and with it…the rules for spiritual engagement, is something people will neglect at their own peril.

—DEREK and SHARON GILBERT, P.I.D. Radio

D1431872

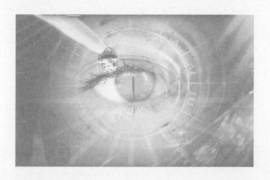

FORBIDDEN GATES

HOW GENETICS, ROBOTICS, ARTIFICIAL INTELLIGENCE,
SYNTHETIC BIOLOGY, NANOTECHNOLOGY, and
HUMAN ENHANCEMENT HERALD

THE DAWN OF TECHNO-DIMENSIONAL
SPIRITUAL WARFARE

THOMAS AND NITA HORN

DEFENDER
CRANE, MISSOURI

FORBIDDEN GATES
HOW GENETICS, ROBOTICS, ARTIFICAL INTELLIGENCE,
SYNTHETIC BIOLOGY, NANOTECHNOLOGY, and
HUMAN ENHANCEMENT HERALD THE DAWN OF
TECHNO-DIMENSIONAL SPIRITUAL WARFARE
Crane, Missouri 65633
©2010 by Tom and Nita Horn

All rights reserved. Published 2010.
Printed in the United States of America.

ISBN 10: 0984061193
ISBN 13: 9780984061198

A CIP catalog record of this book is available from the Library
of Congress.

Cover illustration and design by Steve Warner.

Scripture quoted is taken from the Authorized King James Version,
with interior quotation marks added by the editor for clarity of
reading and with deity pronouns capitalized.

CONTENTS

SECTION ONE
SPIRITUAL WARFARE 101

SECTION TWO
THE BATTLEFIELD UNTIL NOW

Acknowledgments

So many are deserving of acknowledgment without whose friendship, inspiration, assistance, and research this book would have simply been too challenging.

Many thanks are extended in particular to David Hitt, Terry James, Sue Bradley, Derek and Sharon Gilbert, Carl and Althia Anderson, Joe and Katherine Horn, and James and Donna Howell for their tireless encouragement and support.

To our editor and wonderful friend Angie Peters, we express such great appreciation for your diligence in making us better than we are.

Finally, to the many thousands of friends who visit our Web sites and constantly express their love and support, please know how much your affection lifts us up in these critical times.

Foreword

By Terry James

Strange things are afoot at this moment in the world of biological science. The intrigues are made more mystifying by quantum leaps in artificial intelligence.

Adherents of a new spirituality meld and merge secretly with the dark, advancing menace posed by the matters involved. That threat is incalculable to mankind. It is an evil intervention that must, by its very supernatural essence, provoke the judgment of the God of heaven.

Authors Tom and Nita Horn have applied their decades of research and hands-on experience in the sphere of the struggle against "spiritual wickedness in high places" (Ephesians 6:12) to produce this volume of scintillating revelation.

They force to the surface of these troubling days truth about swiftly advancing technologies that, in combination with unseen, otherworldly factors, increasingly challenge the Christian worldview.

For example, they write:

It is an understatement to say that technology often works hand in hand with unseen forces to challenge our faith or to open new channels for spiritual warfare. This has been illustrated in thousands of ways down through time—from the creation of Ouija boards for contacting the spirit world to online pornography gateways. But the current course upon which GRIN [genetics, robotics, artificial intelligence, and nanotechnology] technology and transhumanist philosophy are taking mankind threatens to elevate the reality of these dangers to quantitatively higher levels. Some of the spiritual hazards already surfacing as a result of modern technology include unfamiliar terms like "i-dosing," in which teens get "digitally high" by playing specific Internet videos through headphones that use repetitive tones to create binaural beats, which have been shown in clinical studies to induce particular brain wave states that make the sounds appear to come from the center of the head. Shamans have used variations of such repetitive tones and drumming to stimulate and focus the center mind for centuries to make contact with the spirit world and to achieve altered states of reality.

More broadly, the Internet itself, together with increasing forms of electronic information-driven technology, is creating a new kind of addiction by "rewiring our brains," says Nora Volkow, world-renowned brain scientist and director of the National Institute of Drug Abuse.

This generation now finds itself in the time "like the days of [Noah]" Jesus Christ prophesied for the end of the age nearly two thousand years ago: "And as it was in the days of [Noah], so shall it be also in the days of the Son of man" (Luke 17:26).

One doesn't have to search too deeply through biblical Scripture into the antediluvian time of Noah to find out the primary problem with that generation of earth dwellers: "The earth also was corrupt before God, and the earth was filled with violence. And God looked upon the earth, and, behold, it was corrupt; for all flesh had corrupted his way upon the earth" (Genesis 6:11–12).

Sin certainly had caused the degradation of the human condition in the sense that immorality pervaded all of that pre-Flood society. However, the declaration that "it was corrupt; for all flesh had corrupted his way upon the earth" implies contamination of a sort exponentially beyond the spiritual. The "corruption" involves physical degradation at the genetic level. Humankind's genetic makeup had been corrupted—contaminated—in its most basic construct: at the DNA level.

How can this assertion be verified by the biblical record? We look a bit further into the Genesis account: "And God said unto Noah, 'The end of all flesh is come before me; for the earth is filled with violence through them; and, behold, I will destroy them with the earth'" (Genesis 6:13).

The earth dwellers, with the exception of Noah and his seven family members, were obviously in a condition that made them impossible to reach with the message of redemption. The Genesis account almost certainly tells that their "corruption" made them unsalvageable because they were beings that were beyond human. The implications of the scriptural record are staggering.

> There were giants in the earth in those days; and also after that, when the sons of God came in unto the daughters of men, and they bare children to them, the same became mighty men which were of old, men of renown.
>
> And GOD saw that the wickedness of man was great in the earth, and that every imagination of the thoughts of his heart was only evil continually. And it repented the LORD that He had made man on the earth, and it grieved Him at His heart. And the LORD said, "I will destroy man whom I have created from the face of the earth; both man, and beast, and the creeping thing, and the fowls of the air; for it repenteth me that I have made them." (Genesis 6:4–7)

We can legitimately ask: What on earth happened? Did God not look at all that He created and say that it was good? Why, then, was it so "corrupted" that He "repented" that He had created man?

The answer in the larger sense, of course, is that sin happened. With sin and the fall of man came entropy, the degeneration of all things on the planet. Science has it as the second law of thermodynamics: All things decay and degenerate.

So, Adam's sin brought death and decay.

In the more specific sense, however, "corruption" of a supernaturally inflicted sort afflicted the very genetic makeup—the

DNA—of humankind when the "sons of God came in unto the daughters of men, and they bare children to them."

The sexual unions produced "giants." The scriptural record couldn't be clearer. Corruption of human genetics, then, apparently was a key reason the earth dwellers were beyond redemption, thus had to be destroyed by the worldwide Flood.

Certain angels who fell in the rebellion with Lucifer determined to produce beings that were without human souls—progeny that, apparently like the angels themselves, were lost forever because they had no chance for redemption and reconciliation with the Creator due to the deliberate decision to rebel. The offspring, Nephilim, were spiritual heirs to their fallen *b'nai ha Elohim* progenitors.

Again, Jesus, the greatest of all prophets, said it will be like it was in the days of these hideous, part-human, part-angelic creatures at the time of His Second Advent. Add to the return of the supernatural interlopers the geometrically progressing advances in computer-enhanced interjection into man's genetic mix, and the prophetic picture comes into stark focus. This is where Tom and Nita Horn shine brilliant investigative illumination, exposing the "spiritual wickedness in high places" of these strange, troubling times in which we live. They spotlight the humanistic and scientific diabolists who seek to spread their domination over planet earth. They particularly direct the light of truth upon the minions who are once again investing all possible effort within their evil supernatural power to mingle their seed with the seed of humankind.

The authors write in regard to how all of this might affect humankind: "How brain-machine-interfacing will multiply this divide between human-to-human relationships via human-machine integration is of substantial concern for several reasons.... The real danger, though it may be entirely unavoidable for some, will be the loss of individuality, anonymity, privacy, and even free will as a result of cybernetic integration."

Transhumans and chimera of sinister species-tampering are not the stuff of science fiction; rather, they are clandestinely present today, according to the findings that burst forth from the authors' exhaustive research. The neo-Nephilim/transhuman hybrids might be as near as the next door neighbor—if not at this moment, almost certainly in the very near future.

READ FIRST!

While *Forbidden Gates: How Genetics, Robotics, Artificial Intelligence, Synthetic Biology, Nanotechnology, and Human Enhancement Herald the Dawn of Techno-Dimensional Spiritual Warfare* includes fresh insights for traditional, tried-and-true methods of overcoming darkness, it also unveils for the first time how breakthrough advances in science, technology, and philosophy—including cybernetics, bioengineering, nanotechnology, machine intelligence, synthetic biology, and transhumanism—will combine to create mind-boggling game-changes to everything you have ever known about spiritual warfare.

How so?

In recent years, astonishing technological developments have pushed the frontiers of humanity toward far-reaching morphological transformation that promises in the very near future to redefine what it means to be human. An international, intellectual, and fast-growing cultural movement known as *transhumanism* intends the use of genetics, robotics, artificial intelligence, and nanotechnology (GRIN technologies) as tools that will radically redesign our minds, our memories, our physiology, our offspring, and even perhaps—as Joel Garreau in his best-selling book, *Radical Evolution,* claims—our very souls. The technological, cultural, and metaphysical shift now underway unapologetically forecasts a future dominated by this new species of unrecognizably superior humans, and applications under study now to make this dream a reality are being funded by thousands of government and private research facilities around the world. As the reader will learn, this includes, among other things, rewriting human DNA and combining humans with beasts, a fact that some university studies and transhumanists believe will not only alter our bodies and souls but ultimately could open a door to contact with *unseen intelligence.*

As a result, new modes of perception between things visible and invisible are expected to challenge the church in ways that are historically and theologically unprecedented. Without comprehending what is quickly approaching in related disciplines of research and development, vast numbers of believers could be paralyzed by the most fantastic—and most far-reaching—supernatural implications. The destiny of each individual—as well as the future of their families—will depend on knowledge of the new paradigm and the preparedness to face it head on.

As outlined in this book, the power operating behind this scheme to integrate human-animal-machine interfaces in order to reengineer humanity is not new. The ancient, malevolent force is simply repackaging itself these days as the forward-thinking and enlightened progress needed for the next step in human evolution.

Facing godlike machines and man's willingness to cross over species and extradimensional barriers put in place by God, traditional methods of spiritual warfare—which Christian institutions have relied on for the last century—will soon be monumentally impacted in nontraditional ways and insufficient when approaching this threshold.

Yet it is possible, according to *Forbidden Gates,* not only to survive but to triumph over the uncanny challenges the impending epoch will present. Overcomers will prevail through a working knowledge of the philosophy and technologies driving the threats, combined with a solid understanding of the authority that Christians alone have. What continues within these pages will lift the curtain on a world unlike previous generations could have expected or even imagined, and will inform believers how the power of Christ can be amplified against heretofore unknown adversarial manifestations.

Thomas and Nita Horn have nearly thirty-five years of ministry experience, with twenty-five inside the largest evangelical institution in the world—including executive-level positions with responsibilities such as exorcism. Their newest book, *Forbidden Gates,* is not only unique in its findings, but is invaluable for equipping serious Christians with the knowledge they will soon need to face the future with exceptional confidence. Because *Forbidden Gates* deals with cutting-edge applications for spiritual warfare, it has been divided into four sections to provide systematic learning:

SECTION ONE: Spiritual Warfare 101

SECTION TWO: The Battlefield until Now

SECTION THREE: The Coming Battlefield—Artilects, Terrans, Transhumans

SECTION FOUR: The "Other" Signs of the Days of Noah

The sections above are laid out to allow even readers with little knowledge of the subject matter to learn how to organize and apply dynamic principles of spiritual warfare, and to directly benefit from this book—soon to be one of the most important books in your possession besides the Bible.

Introduction

By David H. Hitt

L adies and gentlemen, the flight crew has turned on the "Fasten Seat Belts" sign. If you haven't already done so, please stow your carry-on luggage underneath the seat in front of you or in an overhead bin. Make sure your seat backs and folding trays are in their full upright and locked position.

You are about to embark on a journey for which you need no ticket—because you are going whether you like it or not. We are *all* going whether we like it or not.

Science is on the verge of a quantum advance, one that will bring into existence objects and creatures we have never seen before having abilities we cannot imagine. The ultimate objective of this new science is nothing short of revolutionary—to transform and recreate mankind itself. If you are accustomed to thinking of yourself as being at the top of the food chain or the final rung on the so-called evolutionary ladder, you can put those thoughts to rest. You are well on the way to being last year's model.

It all started innocently enough. Decades ago, newspaper articles began to tell the story of scientists' successful experiments with hybrid crops that grew faster and in harsher climates, resisted diseases better, and yielded more food per acre than previously thought possible. Later, TV programs touted artificial insemination and test-tube fertilization, which allowed infertile couples to experience the miracle of life. Not long after that, stories were popping up on the World Wide Web about monoclonal antibodies that promised cures for dreaded diseases, robots that looked and acted human, and the mysterious Human Genome Project—a massive effort to reverse engineer the very operating system of the human body. The most immediately impactful technology was the Web itself—a user-friendly medium for connecting people all over the world not only with each other but to an inconceivably large repository of knowledge.

We all saw these developments and wondered with amazement at the marvels of twentieth-century technology. The dreamers among us began to imagine and write of a coming utopia. However, a few on the fringe began to speculate that something more ominous could be on the horizon.

Undaunted, the new science marched on. Today, we are besieged headlong with rumors of things to come—tales of nanotech machines that fly like insects or swim through our bodies and distribute medicine or destroy cancer cells; drugs that make soldiers stronger, able to fight for days without food or rest and kill without hesitation; smart stores that track and automatically reorder their own inventories; and animals that can grow transplantable human organs or photosynthesize their own food.

Some of this reminds us of science-fiction movies we have seen: grand-master chess computers, doomsday lasers, cutting-edge antibiotics battling drug-resistant superbugs, "6-million-dollar" men (and women), apocalyptic seed banks, lifelike robots, machines that accurately guess what we are thinking and anticipate our wants and needs, utterly synthetic foods, and people who never have to sleep.

But sometimes we are reminded more of horror movies: mass murderers that are seemingly killed over and over again but never really die, zombies inexorably pursuing and killing their prey with no emotion, disembodied limbs that crawl around, everything in our lives being monitored and recorded, psychoactive drug trips involving out-of-body experiences and nightmarish demon and alien encounters, and poltergeist-infested homes that terrorize their occupants and make them do things they could not even imagine.

We are also seeing a cultural divide over the next big step: human engineering. On one side are those who are concerned that mankind is beginning to play God and are fearful of the consequences. On the other side are those who insist that if we can, we must. They see the potential for humans to have new and unexpected abilities: to lift great weights, to increase their intelligence a thousandfold, to see, hear, and know things that are now unseeable, unhearable, and unknowable, to read minds, and to live hundreds of years. They see the frontiers and ask, "Why not?"

Genetic engineering and many other sciences having bioethical implications are being debated around the world, sometimes quietly and covertly, other times vociferously and violently.

So where should a Christian stand in this debate? We know that God alone creates life. At the same time, we know that mankind has long been engaged in the selective breeding of plants and animals, which has gone pretty well for us. Are these new sciences more like creating or more like breeding? At what point do we stop building machines to do our thinking for us? Where should we draw the line?

The cold, hard fact is that the scientists know far more about the work they are doing than the politicians who might pass laws banning it, the ethicists who struggle even to define the issues for debate, the pastors whose livelihoods depend on keeping their congregations more blissful than informed, and the general public—which is woefully undereducated and ill-equipped to comprehend the technology and its implications, let alone its morality.

To make matters worse, behind the scientists stand bankers, ready at the drop of a hat to throw vast sums of money toward the next immensely profitable breakthrough. Standing beside the bankers are the warriors who see tremendous military advantage arising from a mastery of this strange science, and doom for those who have done less than their enemies. And in the shadows behind them are those who see in this new science the power they can use to unify and control the world.

These scientists are not Galileos, Newtons, or Curies toiling away in humble solitude. They are well-paid cogs ensconced in prestigious, well-funded research organizations backed by multinational corporations, governments, and banks—the so-called military-industrial complex. Although some of them certainly have evil intent, most have rarely stopped to consider the implications of their work. In fact, many are downright altruistic. They are convinced that the world's survival hinges on their work and that, somehow, everything will turn out okay. They sleep well at night believing that those who oppose them are ignorant, scared, and likely the victims of their own archaic, narrow-minded religions.

Thus it really does not matter what Christians think should be the future of this science, for the powers that be have already dictated the outcome. And it is not good.

So if this new science is predetermined to bring about evil, how should a Christian react? How can Christians defend themselves and their loved ones? The answer is to do the same things Christians have always done to cope with the obstacles the world has thrown at them.

(1) **Increase knowledge.** Learn the nature and extent of this new science. Get to know how it may manifest itself; the people and organizations involved; the vocabulary; and where to turn for current, factual news about it.

(2) **Increase wisdom.** Learn what God's Word has to say about this new science. We must first understand that the God we serve supremely dominates anything we encounter in our lives. We then must realize that the Bible anticipates every bit of it and tells us exactly how to deal with it.

(3) **Increase awareness.** Learn how to spot when you encounter the fruits of this new science, and know the appropriate steps to strip them of their power.

Regarding the first point, you will quickly conclude that the Internet is your friend. This book will guide you to several notable Web sites that present news and perspectives on the state of the art in the relevant sciences and technologies. Understanding how this science is evolving is the key to identifying how it will impact your life and the lives of your loved ones. This should be your ongoing quest.

Regarding the second point, you will learn that there really is nothing new under the sun. The Bible and other historical writings reveal that some of these same pursuits were undertaken thousands of years ago, in quite different times, but with many of the same results. By reading the chapters that follow, you will come to understand that this "new science" has a very dark side and is likely inspired by an equally dark vision for mankind's future.

Regarding the third point, you will get to know the forces behind what will soon be happening all around you. This book will arm you with practical and highly effective tools to counter every move these forces make. Victory can be yours once you decide to understand the issues and commit to conquer them.

Having said this, it is perfectly human to be scared of what lies ahead. It is a mistake to approach this subject lightly or arrogantly. Christians have gotten into great trouble by challenging evil unprepared. However, fear did not get Christianity where it is today, and fear cannot take it where it needs to go in the future.

So relax. You are in the hands of a skilled and experienced flight crew. The captain and first officer know how to fly this plane, and they know the route your flight will be taking like they know the backs of their hands. All you need to do is climb aboard and ride along. You will arrive at your desired destination with the knowledge, wisdom, and tools you will need.

One more thing: Your eyes are about to be opened wide. Take it from someone who just made this trip.

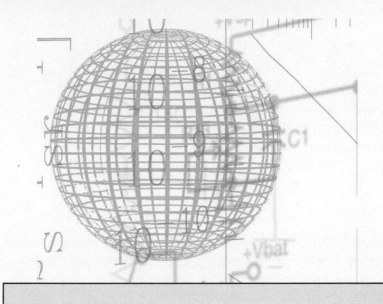

SECTION ONE

SPIRITUAL WARFARE 101

CHAPTER ONE

YOUR HIDDEN ENEMY

Theoden: "I will not risk open war."

Aragorn: "Open war is upon you, whether you would risk it or not."

—from J. R. R. TOLKIEN's *Lord of the Rings*

There is always subtle danger when writers who attempt to discuss evil supernaturalism focus too much on unnecessary and often wildly exaggerated and biblically unsupported characteristics. We've shuddered more than once at so-called authorities on spiritual warfare using their works to fascinate people with everything from the particular names of demons to their size, shape, skin color, hair color, number of digits, and even thickness of saliva dripping from their lips. While such details may seem innocuous enough, or even entertaining in a Stephen King-ish sort of way, this practice can become unbalanced and antithetical to New Testament instructions, even opening doors into the imagination for mental and spiritual danger. It is therefore the goal of this work to help the body of Christ with only the material we believe is necessary to

recognize the battle all believers are engaged in, and to comprehend the nature of the tactics employed by our hidden enemy.
As Theoden learned in the *Lord of the Rings*, we are in this war
whether we want to be or not, so we need to be equipped and
informed.

We shall never forget some years ago, when Dr. David
Yonggi Cho described in vivid detail how he learned the truth
about such unseen intelligence, which among other things operates behind the scenes to obstruct the work of the ministry.

As a young preacher, Cho had gone into a small Korean
community to pioneer a church. Soon he discovered, as is common throughout much of Korea, a temple dedicated to the
city's "guardian god" atop the highest local mountain. When
the priests of the shrine learned that he was planning to start
a missions outreach, they came to him infuriated, demand-
ing that he leave the village. When he refused, they vowed to
return and put to death him and any converts he won in the
meantime.

A few days later, the priests were back—this time with a
mob. The head priest, making sure the crowd was watching,
called out, "Cho! Do you really believe that Jesus Christ is the
same yesterday, today, and forever, and that He can still work
miracles?"

Cho replied, "Yes, I do."

"Then we have a challenge," the priest yelled. "Down in
the village is a woman who has been bedridden for seven years.
She and her child are dying now of disease. If Jesus can heal this
woman in the next thirty days, we will go away and you can
have your church. But if she is not healed, you must abandon
your work or we will return and kill you and your followers."

Cho explained how in the United States, most Americans would never respond to such a dare, but that in those days and in that culture, his failure to do so would have been (in his opinion) to imply that his God was inferior to the temple deity, and would have closed the community's willingness to consider the gospel message.

As a result, Cho accepted the contest, and the following day he traveled with his mother-in-law to the village where he found the dying woman. He suggested to the infirmed lady that if she would pray the sinner's prayer and accept Jesus as her Savior, the Lord might choose to heal her. Instead, he found the woman to be very angry with any god (including Cho's God) who would allow her to suffer the way that she had. After several unsuccessful visits to convince her otherwise, Cho decided prayer alone would be his best alternative for her and her child.

Over the next few weeks, he prayed earnestly for a miracle. He made regular visits to the village and sent messengers to report back any change. To his disappointment, the woman's condition only seemed to worsen.

As the weeks passed and the deadline loomed, Cho grew very concerned. Finally, on the evening of the thirtieth day, he entered his prayer room and reminded God that unless a miracle occurred, people from the temple of the guardian deity would arrive within hours to kill him and his followers. Cho said he prayed throughout that night and into the next morning "with the most passion ever."

Then, at 2 AM, he experienced a powerful vision.

He thought he saw a shadow by the front door, and a strange sound spread along the wall.

Fixing his gaze on the opening, he felt primal fear, black and mindless, roll over him.

His intuition screamed. Something dreadful was coming his way.

Another *thump*, and the front door to his home began slowly opening.

Gooseflesh crawled over his arms as "eerie Oriental music" swept in through the entrance, barely discernable at first, then growing in intensity.

Against his better judgment, he turned his body toward the door.

He held his breath, looked harder, squinted.

The shadow slowed, became defined, an enormous silhouette of something *alive* creeping stealthily toward him.

Remaining very still, a moment passed, then *it* emerged from the darkness: huge, snakelike, an agathodemon from ancient times bearing the body of a serpent and the head of a man. Swaying to the melodious rhythm, the horrendous archfiend appeared wicked and menacing as it slunk along the opening into the room where Cho was. It made eye contact with him, and in heavy modulation that sounded as if each gurgling syllable started somewhere deep underground and passed through boiling magma on its way to his mouth, said, "Cho, if you don't leave this town, you are a dead man. I have been ruling this area all of these years, and who are you to come here and disturb my nest!?"

With that, the being lunged across the room lightning fast, landing on top of Cho and wrapping its body around him like prey, contracting its muscles to quickly constrict the air from his lungs. A baleful laughter, malignant and terrible, tittered from the monster's lips as from pebbled sockets its zenithal eyes glared mockingly down at him.

Grotesque and enraged, the thing opened its mouth wider, exposing a hideous, forked tongue inside a nightmarish cavity lined with jagged molars and angled razor fangs. A phlegmy gurgle more dragonlike than reptilian disgorged a sulfurous stench that distilled through the room, filling the air all around them.

A chill radiated through Cho as seconds passed and the undulating fiend's hide, crusty and wart-covered, tightened around him like a garrote. He could feel his ribs bending toward the breaking point as the sheer force of the brutal creature's strength sent his own tongue curling to the roof of his mouth in pain. His body began reacting to the lack of blood flow, his hands and feet started going numb, and his thoughts raced: *Jesus! I'm dying!*

But at that, something caught his attention. The creature's eyes had seemed to dart wildly about the very moment the name of Jesus passed through his mind. He thought it again— *Jesus*—and this time he was sure. The serpent had cringed, and its grip had weakened *at the very moment he had imagined that name!*

With all the strength he could muster, Cho gasped for a breath of air and opened his mouth in a whisper: "Jesus."

The effect was immediate and dramatic. The sound of the name of Jesus discharged from his lips as tangibly as if a two-edged sword had been thrown into the heart of the being.

He spoke the name again, louder this time, and the demon jerked back, its expression filling with terror, its grip unwinding from his waist.

Slipping from the coil, Cho quickly jumped to his feet and shouted, "JESUS…JESUS…*JESUS!*"

Now the creature reeled, first one way then the other, flailing about as if punch drunk, wailing an otherworldly moan; then abruptly it fell to the floor. Before it could gather its strength and raise up to attack him again, Cho lifted his leg and crushed the humanlike head beneath his foot. Studying it to make sure it wasn't moving, he picked up the front part of the carcass and dragged it toward the entry to toss it outside. As he moved to the opening and pushed the seasoned door fully out of the way, he noticed a large crowd of villagers gathering in front of his home. Cautiously, he surveyed his surroundings, then lifted the agathodemon's face above him and exclaimed, "This is the god you have been serving all of these years, but now you must turn and serve the true and living God!"

With that, Cho awoke to find the serpent-man visitation had been a compelling vision or dream. It was 4 AM, time for early morning prayer at his tent church. With the memory of the threats made against him thirty days earlier still fresh in his mind, he rushed out the door and up the path to meet his tiny congregation. He knew the priests from the guardian temple would not be long in coming, and no sooner had he arrived than a Korean layman started shouting, "Pastor! Come quickly!" Glancing out the tent door, he saw over the hill in the rising dawn what appeared to be the entire city marching up the valley walls.

Cho's palms were sweating and his heart was racing as he stepped outside and watched the throng approach. *Jesus*, he thought, *What should we do? Run? Hide?* Then he noticed something curious. The people looked happy, as if they were rejoicing about something. A moment of silence passed as he considered them, and he thought, *It can't be!* But it was. Leading the crowd, baby in arms, was the dying woman from the village. She ran up to him and said, "Oh, Brother Cho, thank you so much for coming and praying for me last night. The Lord heard your prayer and I am healed!"

Cho stared at her in amazement. "I did not come to your house and pray for you last night," he replied.

"Oh yes," the woman insisted, "You came at two o'clock this morning and stood outside my window. You said loudly, 'Woman! Bc healed in the name of Jesus Christ!' And I arose and found that I was healed, and my baby is healed!"

Then Cho remembered that it had been 2 AM when he had seen the vision and the agathodemon had been destroyed.

With very few exceptions, the entire community converted to Christianity within forty-eight hours. Today, Cho pastors the largest evangelical church in the world, with nearly a million members. It all started in a city delivered from demonic siege.

"THEY'RE HERE"

Undoubtedly when reading the story above, some people will feel hard-pressed to interpret the narrative in any way other than as somebody's overactive imagination. Nevertheless, as Carol Anne so ominously expressed in the 1982 film *Poltergeist*, "They're here." Demons and their militaristic interest in people and geography are ontological facts, according to the Bible. In the Old Testament, demons are seen as the living dynamic behind idolatry (i.e., Deuteronomy 32:17), and in the New Testament, every writer refers to their influence. Extrabiblical texts including ancient pseudepigraphical works like the first Book of Enoch and post-New Testament writings such as the Didache, Ignatius' Epistle to the Ephesians, and the Shepherd of Hermas agree with this concern. Early church fathers also reinforced the belief that evil spirits seek to thwart the will of God on earth through attacks on the body of Christ in particular and against society in general. **Spiritual Warfare 101** begins by taking these facts into account by asserting that not only do visible agents exist everywhere around us, but unseen intermediaries—both good and evil—interlope between spiritual and human personalities at home, in church, in government, and in society. On rare occasions, the general public may catch a glimpse of this ethereal existence. For instance, on April 5, 1991, ABC's *20/20* broadcast the first televised Catholic exorcism. We watched this historic event twenty years ago and thought that, regardless of one's denominational affiliation, it illustrated contemporary demonism.

While deliverance ministry such as exorcism should be carefully administered within the church, demons play an even wider role in society—a role that includes controlling or influencing not only individuals and small groups, but institutions and governments as well. Understanding how and why this is true is defined in demonological studies such as the *divine council* (a term used by Hebrew and Semitic scholars to describe the pantheon of divine beings or angels who administer the affairs of heaven and earth), where experts typically agree that, beginning at the Tower of Babel, the world and its inhabitants were disinherited by the sovereign God of Israel and placed under the authority of lesser divine beings that became corrupt and disloyal to God in their administration of those nations (Psalm 82). Following Babel, these beings quickly became idolized on earth as gods, giving birth to the worship of "demons" (see Acts 7:41–42; Psalms 96:5; and 1 Corinthians 10:20) and the quest by fallen angels to draw mankind away from God. While the dominion of these entities and their goals are frequently overlooked, close collaboration between *evil ones* and unregenerate social architects operates on a regular basis outside the purview of the countless multitudes who are blinded to their reality. Behind governors, legislators, presidents, dictators, and even religious leaders, these wicked spiritual powers move about unrestricted, controlling the machine of ecclesiastical and civil governments as freely as they are allowed. Whenever such principalities recognize a religious or political body that has become a force for moral good, they set about—through a sophisticated labyrinth of visible and invisible representatives—to bring that organization down, one righteous soul at a time.

It is within this concealed arena of evil supernaturalism that unregenerate men are organized. Under demonic influence, they are orchestrated within a great evil system (or empire) described in various scriptural passages as a satanic order. In more than thirty important biblical texts, the Greek New Testament employs the term *kosmos*, describing this "government behind government." It is here that human ego, separated from God, becomes hostile to the service of mankind while viewing people as commodities to be manipulated in the ministration of fiendish ambition. Some expositors believe the origins of this phenomenon began in the distant past, when a fire in the minds of angels caused Lucifer to exalt himself above the good of God's creation. The once-glorified spirit, driven mad by an unequivocal thirst to rule, conquer, and dominate, spawned similar lust between his followers, which continues today among agents of dark power who guard a privileged, "cause-and-effect" symmetry between visible and invisible personalities.

At Satan's desire, archons command this supernatural, geopolitical sphere, dominating *kosmokrators* (rulers of darkness who work in and through human counterparts) who in turn command spirits of lesser rank until every level of earthly government, secular and religious, can be touched by this influence. If we could see through the veil into this domain, we would find a world alive with good against evil, a place where the ultimate prize is the souls of men and where legions war for control of its cities and people. With vivid testimony to this, Satan offered Jesus all the power and the glory of the governments of this world. Satan said, "All this power [control] will I give thee, and the glory of them [earthly cities]: for that is delivered unto me: and to whomsoever I will I give it. If thou therefore wilt worship me, all shall be thine" (Luke 4:6–7).

According to the epistle of the Ephesians, it is this dominion, not flesh and blood, where opposition to God's will on earth is initiated. Whereas people and institutions often provide the "faces" on our problems, the conflict originates beyond them, in this place where unseen forces scheme.

THE MIDDLE GROUND BETWEEN
LIGHT AND SHADOW

Although the hidden region described above represents other-dimensional existence within the *supernatural realm,* the dark strategies fomented there manifest destructive fallout throughout the material world—wars, genocide, terrorism, Christian persecution, broken marriages, juvenile delinquency, occultism, and hundreds of other tangible demonstrations of the infernal influence. Whereas the average person may never understand this assault on his or her corporeal interests as being fundamentally supernatural, Gregory Boyd, in his book, *God at War: The Bible and Spiritual Conflict,* explains:

> God's good creation has in fact been seized by hostile, evil cosmic forces that are seeking to destroy God's beneficent plan for the cosmos…. The general assumption of both the Old and New Testaments is that the earth is virtually engulfed by cosmic forces of destruction, and that evil and suffering are ultimately due to this diabolical siege.[1]

It is therefore the responsibility of every believer to understand the need to put on:

> …the whole armour of God, that ye may be able to stand against the wiles of the devil. For we wrestle not against flesh and blood, but against principalities, against powers, against the rulers of the darkness of

this world, against spiritual wickedness in high places. Wherefore take unto you the whole armour of God, that ye may be able to withstand in the evil day, and having done all, to stand. (Ephesians 6:11–13)

In the tenth chapter of the book of Daniel, the Bible lifts the curtain on this inter-dimensional activity in what is considered to be one of the most important Scriptures having to do with spiritual warfare. This is where the prophet Daniel is found fasting and praying for twenty-one days. He had purposed to chasten himself before the Lord in hopes that God would bless him with a revelation of Israel's future. On the twenty-first day of his fast, while he was standing on the bank of the Tigris River, an angel suddenly appeared to him and said, "From the first day that thou didst set thine heart to understand, and to chasten thyself before thy God, thy words were heard, and I am come for thy words" (Daniel 10:12).

If a messenger was dispatched from heaven "from the first day," why did it take three weeks before he arrived? The angel provided the answer by explaining that a powerful Persian demon had opposed him for twenty-one days. Not until the archangel Michael came to assist in the battle was he free to continue his journey. The book of Daniel also describes similar powers at work behind Babylon, Greece, and Rome, revealing an incredible tenet: Demons can control not only individuals, but entire societies, on a territorial scale.

In Persian theology, the spirit that opposed Daniel and his angel would have been identified as Ahriman, whose legend closely parallels the biblical fall of Lucifer. According to Persian religion, Ahriman was the death dealer—the powerful and self-existing evil spirit from whom war and all other evils had their origin. He was the chief of the cacodemons, or fallen angels, expelled from heaven for their sins. After being kicked out of heaven, the cacodemons endeavored to settle down in various parts of the earth, but were always rejected, and out of revenge found pleasure in tormenting the inhabitants of the earth. Ahriman and his followers finally took up their abode in the space between heaven and the earth and there established their domain, called *Ahriman-abad*—"the abode of Ahriman." From this location, the cacodemons could intrude into and attempt to corrupt the governments of men.

Besides Persian Zoroastrianism and the mythos of Ahriman (and a host of other ancient origin myths for demons), scholars in the field of demonology offer various hypotheses they believe explain the genesis and motivation of these malevolent spirits. What follows is a brief examination of the seven most popular theories.

1. Demons—Spirits of a Pre-Adamic Race?

According to this field of thought, a pre-Adamic race existed on the original earth before it became "dark and void" (Genesis 1:2). These humanlike creatures lived under the government of God and were presided over by Lucifer, the "anointed cherub that covereth" (Ezekiel 28:14). When these pre-Adamites joined Lucifer in revolt against God, a cataclysm fell upon earth, physically destroying its inhabitants. Only the spirits of these beings survived to roam the earth disembodied. This is offered as an explanation for why demons desire to possess humans, as they were meant to be "housed" in bodies of flesh and are uncomfortable otherwise.

2. Demons—Otherworld Beings?

Since little is known about life outside the limited sphere of our planet, a growing body of people contend that intelligent life-forms may have been visiting earth from distant worlds or parallel dimensions since the beginning of time. Some Bible expositors have picked up on this concept, blending it with traditional demonology and suggesting that demons are perhaps entities from another world (or reality) whose structure, like ultraviolet rays, are invisible to the human eye, but nonetheless distinct in atomic design.

Those holding this view note the universal consistency with which extraterrestrials and UFOs have been seen throughout history and that continue to be reported worldwide at a rate greater than six sightings per hour. Eric von Daniken's best-selling book *Chariot of the Gods?* gave international rise to this concept some years ago by speculating that the earth was visited by aliens in the distant past, leaving behind archaeological evidence that gave birth to legends and mythological gods. Unlike von Daniken, in demonology, these creatures are presented as invisible and menacing, the originators of evil supernaturalism.

While authors David Ruffino and Joe Jordan do not believe aliens from outer space are the origin of biblical demons, in their unprecedented new book, *Unholy Communion: The Alien Abduction Phenomenon, Where It Originates—And How It Stops* (available at www.SurvivorMall.com), they claim demonism is actively involved in so-called alien abduction phenomena. These are the noted researchers who, for the first time in history, provided analytical duplication for what over the past two decades a team known as the CE4 Research Group discovered using guidelines for redundancy similar to methods employed by scientists and investigators to illustrate repeatability, and thus "cause and effect." Through more than three hundred actual test cases, "experiencers" (as they are called in abduction communities) witnessed their abuse permanently stopped through *the power of Jesus' name.* This fabulous research illustrates that, regardless of who or what the abductors are, they are subject to the name of Jesus Christ. (Learn more about this unusual research at www.OfficialDisclosure.com.)

3. Demons—Offspring of Angels and Women?

As far back as the beginning of time and within every major culture of the ancient world, the astonishingly consistent story is told of "gods" that descended from heaven and materialized in bodies of flesh. From Rome to Greece—and before that, to Egypt, Persia, Assyria, Babylonia, and Sumer—the earliest records of civilization tell of the era when powerful beings known to the Hebrews as "Watchers" and in the book of Genesis as the *b'nai ha Elohim* (sons of God) mingled with humans, giving birth to part-celestial, part-terrestrial hybrids known as "Nephilim." The Bible says this happened when men began to increase on earth and daughters were born to them. When the sons of God saw the beauty of the women, they took wives from among them to sire their unusual offspring.

In Genesis 6:4, we read: "There were giants in the earth in those days; and also after that, when the sons of God came in unto the daughters of men, and they bare children to them, the same became mighty men which were of old, men of renown."

When this Scripture is compared with other ancient texts, including Enoch, Jubilees, Baruch, Genesis Apocryphon, Philo, Josephus, and Jasher, among others, it unfolds that the giants of the Old Testament such as Goliath were the part-human, part-animal, part-angelic offspring of a supernatural interruption into the divine order of species. The apocryphal Book of Enoch gives a name to the angels involved in this cosmic conspiracy, calling them "Watchers." We read:

> And I Enoch was blessing the Lord of majesty and the King of the ages, and lo! the Watchers called me—Enoch the scribe—and said to me: "Enoch, thou scribe of righteousness, go, declare to the Watchers of the heaven who have left the high heaven, the holy eternal place, and have defiled themselves with women, and have done as the children of earth do, and have taken unto themselves wives: Ye have wrought great destruction on the earth: And ye shall have no peace nor forgiveness of sin: and inasmuch as they delight themselves in their children [the Nephilim], the murder of their beloved ones shall they see, and over the destruction of their children shall they lament, and shall make supplication unto eternity, but mercy and peace shall ye not attain."
> (1 Enoch 10:3–8)

According to Enoch, two hundred of these powerful angels departed "high heaven" and used women (among other raw material) to extend their progeny into mankind's plane of existence. The book of Jude describes the judgment the Watchers received for their actions, saying the "angels which kept not their first estate, but left their own habitation, he hath reserved in everlasting chains under darkness unto the judgment of the great day" (Jude 6).

Unlike these progenitor Watchers who are currently bound under darkness until the Day of Judgment, the spirits of their dead offspring, the Nephilim, continue to roam the earth as cursed entities or demons, according to this theory.

Those holding this view also point to the historical connection between Nephilim and the *Rephaim,* who were associated throughout the ancient world with demons, ghosts, hauntings, the "shades of the dead," and spirits in Sheol.

4. Demons—Spirits of Wicked Men Deceased?

This teaching, still popular with a fragment of modern theologians, seems to have its origin in early Greek mythology. The Homeric gods, who were but supernatural men, were both good and evil. The hypothesis was that the good and powerful spirits of good men rose to assume places of deity after experiencing physical death, while the evil spirits of deceased evil men were gods doomed to roam the earth and its interior. At death, their spirits remained in an eternal limbo, unable to perish yet incapable of attaining heaven. Besides Greeks, the ancient Jewish historians Philo and Josephus held similar views, as did many of the early church fathers.

Hollywood often conveys this idea (that demons are the spirits of dead wicked men) through box office hits such as *Child's Play* and *Nightmare on Elm Street*. In *Nightmare*, Freddy Krueger, played by actor Robert Englund, is the maniacal slasher and indestructible evil spirit of a deceased child molester. In *Child's Play*, a doll possessed by the spirit of a deceased voodoo strangler calls upon Damballa, the serpent god, to give him the power of immortality. Warner Brothers, who in association with Wonderland Sound and Vision produces the popular television drama/horror series *Supernatural*, used our published work on the *strigae* (vicious owl-like affiliates of the goddess Hecate who flew through the night feeding on unattended babies and during the day appeared as simple old women) in the first season of their series in this regard. They invited us to join a panel of paranormal activity experts for the release of the fifth season. The series stars Jared Padalecki as Sam Winchester and Jensen Ackles as Dean Winchester, two brothers who as demon hunters often find themselves pursued by spirits of the wicked dead. While expert input is sought by the screenwriters in order to give series episodes a mode of believability, *Supernatural* blends numerous religious concepts and worldviews inconsistent with orthodox faith and should not be taken seriously.

5. Demons—Fallen Angels?

Of the seven theories we are summarizing, this is the most popular among contemporary Christians. This teaching is based on the assumption that at some time in eons past, Lucifer rose up in great rebellion and declared war on the God of heaven. Somehow he persuaded one-third of the angelic host to stand with him in insurrection (Revelation12:4). At this point, God cast Lucifer and his rebellious angels out of heaven, at which time they became demons. Less in form and nature than they originally were, they brought darkness and chaos upon the virgin earth. Some believe Ezekiel 28:13–19 is a record of this event:

> Thou hast been in Eden the garden of God; every precious stone was thy covering.... Thou art the anointed cherub that covereth; and I have set thee so: thou was upon the holy mountain of God; thou hast walked up and down in the midst of the stones of fire. Thou was perfect in thy ways from the day that thou was created, till iniquity was found in thee. By the multitude of thy merchandise they have filled the midst of thee with violence, and thou hast sinned: therefore I will cast thee as profane out of the mountain of God: and I will destroy thee, O covering cherub, from the midst of the stones of fire.

Isaiah 14:12–14 continues the record on Lucifer's fall:

> How art thou fallen from heaven, O Lucifer, son of the morning! How art thou cut down to the ground which didst weaken the nations! For thou has said in thine heart, "I will ascend into heaven, I will exalt my throne above the stars of God: I will sit also upon the mount of the congregation, in the sides of the north: I will ascend above the heights of the clouds: I will be like the Most High." Yet thou shalt be brought down to hell, to the sides of the pit.

The apostle John records an event in the book of Revelation (12:7–9) that some believe refers to Lucifer's fall. John also tells of other angels:

> And there was war in heaven: Michael and his angels fought against the dragon; and the dragon fought and his angels, And prevailed not; neither was their place found any more in heaven. And the great dragon was cast out, that old serpent called the Devil, and Satan, which deceiveth the whole world: he was cast out into the earth, and his angels were cast out with him.

6. Demons—Several of the Theories Above?

The proponents of this hypothesis believe a singular concept for the origin of "demons" is a mistake, that in fact what is routinely considered "the demonic realm" could be made up of several of the explanations above, and that this might demonstrate the hierarchy of demons as outlined in the book of Ephesians. In this view, "fallen angels" would rank above the "spirits of Nephilim" and so on, with each being part of the army of darkness. Just as privates in the United States military serve under sergeants who serve under majors, Satan's forces consist of wicked spirits (*poneria:* the mass of common demon soldiers comprising Satan's hordes) under rulers of darkness (*kosmokrators:* martial spirits that influence or administer the affairs of earthly governments) and powers (*exousia:* high-ranking officials whose modes of operation are primarily battlefield ops). Above these are principalities or archons (*arche:* brigadier generals over the divisions of Satan's hosts). Satan, who reigns as supreme commander and king, is the "prince of the powers of the air" (Ephesians 2:2).

7. Demons—None of the Above?

Some believe all of the theories above are erroneous and that demons exist only in the imagination. These note how primitive men interpreted inherent diseases such as epilepsy as demonic possession and saw volcanoes and other natural catastrophes as the manifested anger of gods. This illustrates a human psychological weakness, they say, which inadvertently assigns "paranormal activity" to events that men cannot otherwise explain.

While this theory is considered incomplete by most demonologists, it is not without credible points. In addition to ailments that cause people afflicted with disorders such as schizophrenia to experience auditory hallucinations, the human imagination can be persuasive when "filling in the blanks" on unsolved mysteries, sometimes leaving people convinced that undefined activity is the presence of ghostly beings. For instance, people have reported spooky apparitions in areas where strong electromagnetic fields are discovered, suggesting to some researchers that persons who are sensitive to these fields may be confusing the effect upon them by electromagnetic frequencies (EMFs). Some years ago, scientist Vic Tandy's research into frequencies and eyeball resonation led to similar conclusions and a thesis called "Ghosts in the Machine," which was published in the *Journal of the Society for Psychical Research*. Tandy's findings outlined natural causes for certain cases of specter materialization. Using his own experience as an example, Tandy was able to show that 19 Hz standing air waves could, under some circumstances, create sensory phenomena in an open environment suggestive of a ghost. The third of Arthur C. Clark's laws of prediction is also mirrored here, which concludes that "any sufficiently advanced technology is indistinguishable from magic."

CHAPTER TWO

OPEN SESAME!

There is a fifth dimension beyond that which is known to man. It is a dimension as vast as space and as timeless as infinity. It is the middle ground between light and shadow, between science and superstition, and it lies between the pit of man's fears and the summit of his knowledge. This is the dimension of imagination. It is an area which we call "The Twilight Zone."

—Rod Serling

In 1918, famed occultist Aleister Crowley, in attempting to discover how those evil emissaries discussed in chapter one could be extended from their kosmos into man's reality, undertook to create a magical vortex that would span the gap between the world of the seen and the unseen. Crowley's ritual was called the "Amalantrah Working," and according to his records it became successful when a presence manifested itself through the rift. He called this being "Lam" and drew a portrait of it. The startling image, detailed more than ninety years ago, bears powerful similarity to "alien grays" of modern pop culture.

Nearly three decades after the Amalantrah Working, rocket scientist and cofounder of the Jet Propulsion Laboratory, Jack Parsons, and his pal L. Ron Hubbard (Church of Scientology founder) conducted a second ritual called the "Babalon Working" in an attempt to reopen Crowley's gateway. These men were not looking for Lam. They wanted to incarnate the whore of Babalon—a demon child or *gibborim*—through a portal during ritual sex. Parsons wrote that the ceremony was successful and that at one point a brownish/yellow light came through the doorway and something invisible struck him, knocking a candle out of his hand.

It is interesting to note that following Crowley's magic portal (which allegedly produced the alien-looking Lam) and Hubbard and Parson's Babalon Working ritual, Crowley died in 1947—the same year as the Roswell crash and the same year Kenneth Arnold saw his flying saucers and sightings of "aliens" increased around the world. Some believe this is evidence that a demonic portal was indeed breached by these men. While we probably never will know if something truly supernatural happened with Crowley and Parsons, early Christians as well as Hebrews, Assyrians, Greeks, and other ancient cultures believed such dimensional gateways exist and can be opened between the material world and the entities discussed in chapter one. Because physical doorways and windows on buildings were "mirrors" of the unseen gateways and were therefore vulnerable to entry by supernaturalism, those uninterested in making contact with evil spirits placed magic gargoyles on their temples, churches, and castles to scare off and protect from harmful spirits, witches, and other malign influences seeking to manifest. For instance, one of the most widely used symbols by Greeks on their buildings was the terrifying gorgon (such as Medusa), a horrifying female creature whose hair was made of venomous snakes and whose gaze could turn men to stone. To close the doorway to evil spirits in Babylon and Assyria, colossal enchanted creatures built under elaborate ceremonies and blessed by names of good omens flanked the palace entries and towering gates of cities while extra precaution was provided through winged figures holding magic devices cleverly concealed beneath the entryway floors. It was also important in ancient times to defend one's personal property and private residence against fiendish undesirables, therefore apotropaic (an adjective meaning "to ward off evil") devices were placed in home doorways, windows, fireplaces, and chimneys, while charms, bracelets, and talismans were worn upon the body to protect the individuals themselves.

The Hebrew prophet Ezekiel made an interesting statement about such "magic bracelets" *(kesatot),* which were worn upon the body and somehow bound spirits. We read, "Wherefore thus saith the Lord GOD; 'Behold I am against your pillows [*kesatot,* "magic bands"] wherewith ye there hunt the souls to make them fly, and I will tear them from your arms and will let the souls go, even the souls that ye hunt to make them fly'" (Ezekiel 13:20). The kesatot was a magic armband used in connection with a container called the *kiste.* Wherever the kiste is inscribed on sarcophagi, it is depicted as a vessel with a snake peering through an open lid. How the magic worked and in what way a spirit was bound or loosed is a mystery, but a noteworthy verification of the magical properties represented by these utilities is discussed in the scholarly work *Scripture and Other Artifacts* by Phillip King and Michael David Coogan:

In the closing verses of Ezekiel 13 the prophet turns his attention to magic practices whose details remain obscure. Two key terms are kesatot and mispabot.... The kesatot are "sewn" on the arms, while the mispabot are made "on the head of every height," which has been understood to mean "on the heads of persons of every height"....

In modern times, archaeological discoveries and texts from Babylonia in particular have shed further light on what might be involved: G. A. Cooke cited Hellenistic figurines from Tell Sandahannah (Mareshah) in Palestine with wire twisted around their arms and ankles...and a magical text from Babylonia that speaks of white and black wool being bound to a person or to someone's bed.... J. Herrmann [notes] that both words can be related to Akkadian verbs, kasu and sapabu, which mean respectively "to bind" and "to loose"...Herrmann also drew attention to texts in which these verbs were used in a specifically magical sense.... This indicates that, whatever the objects were, their function was to act as "binders" and "loosers" in a magical sense, in other words as means of attack and defense in sorcery.[2]

For people not familiar with the terms "binding" and "loosing," these staple words in spiritual warfare imply that certain influences can and should be "bound"—i.e., binding demons so that they cannot affect our minds, bodies, or homes—while beneficial influences like good angels ought to be "loosed" (more on this in the final section of this book).

Early religions and schools of mystery went into great detail about who and what were to be bound and loosed, including the advantages of how and why to do it. Beyond malevolent spirits in general, certain powerful entities that could suddenly "emerge" into man's reality were to be especially feared and avoided. These included Asmodai or Samael (the angel of death), Lilith, the mother of Ahriman and the queen of demons, Seir, a prince of hell with twenty-six legions of demons that could appear any place on earth, and thousands of others.

In Matthew 16:17–19, Jesus directly tied the binding of such supernaturalism to the work of the ministry and the enduring power of His church. To Peter, He said, "Upon this rock I will build my church; and the gates of hell shall not prevail against it. And I will give unto thee the keys of the kingdom of heaven; and whatsoever thou shalt bind on earth shall be bound in heaven: and whatsoever thou shalt loose on earth shall be loosed in heaven."

This deeply meaningful verse indicates something very important about gateways and openings, binding and loosing, who is to be bound, and the subsequent connection between this activity and the powers of heaven and earth. Note where Jesus says, "The gates of hell shall not prevail" against His church. Putting the word "hell" in context here is very important because while the Greek word transliterated "Hades" was later confused with death and the grave (*Thanatos;* also see Revelation 1:18), at the time Jesus chose to use this word, He was possibly referring to the person of Hades or Pluto, the god of the lower regions, and Orcus, the netherworld and realm of the dead. Why Jesus may have made reference to a Greek deity, combining it with the subjects of binding, loosing, gates, and spiritual warfare is important. The mythos of Hades and his connection to other deities and their ability to migrate between the spiritual and physical worlds was dominant at the time of Christ, as His disciples would have been well versed, and Jesus may have intended for His followers to immediately connect the truth behind the struggle these living enemies represent to the children of God. Both the Old and New Testaments make it clear that behind such pagan gods as Hades exists genuine, personal evil that seeks to connect with and mislead mankind.

In Greek mythology, the correlation between Hades and the references of Jesus can be illuminated in the famous metaphor of the abduction and rape of Persephone (Proserpina), and of Demeter's (Demeter is Persephone's mother) actions in searching for her daughter.

The myth claimed that Hades—the dark god of the underworld—fell in love with beautiful Persephone. One day as she plucked flowers in a grassy meadow, Hades swooped down in his chariot and dragged her down into the underworld, where he forced her to become his bride. Above ground, Demeter was distraught by her daughter's disappearance and searched the earth in vain to find her. With the help of Helios and Hecate, Demeter finally discovered the truth of what happened and in her fury demanded that Hades release her daughter. When Hades refused, Demeter sent a horrific famine upon the earth. Plants dried up, seeds refused to sprout, and the gods began to suffer from a lack of sacrifices. Finally, Zeus dispatched Hermes to intercede with the lord of the underworld, and after a great debate, Hades agreed to release Persephone if she would eat a pomegranate seed. What Persephone did not understand was that by eating the seed in the mystical location of the underworld, a sort of divine symmetry was created that bonded her with Hades. This ensured that the goddess would automatically return to the underworld for a third part of each year (in the winter), during which time the seeds of the ground would not grow. Persephone thus became the upperworld goddess of youth and happiness, and the underworld queen of the dead: a dual role that depicted her as both good and evil. On earth, she was the goddess of the young and the friend of the nymphs who appeared in the blooming of the spring flowers (symbolizing her annual return from Hades), and in the underworld she was the dreaded wife of Hades and the queen of the darkness who controlled the fates of deceased men. The reenactment of such myth—the abduction and rape of Persephone—was central to the famous rituals of the Thesmophoria, and, as such, key to interpreting the bits of information known about it.

The festival of the Thesmophoria—sometimes called the Eleusinian Mysteries—lasted between three and ten days. Each day of the festival had a different name and included specific rituals. A highlight of the festival was a procession from Athens to Eleusis led by a crowd of children known as *ephebi*. The ephebi assisted in carrying the *hiera* (sacred objects), and in pulling a statue of Dionysus as a boy (Iacchos), and finally in the ceremonial cleansing of the initiates (candidates of the mystery religion) in the sea. Upon arriving at Eleusis, the women organized the first day of the celebration *(anodos)* by building temporary shelters and electing the leaders of the camp. On the second day *(nesteia),* they initiated the "Greater Mysteries," which, according to myth, produced the cult's magical requests (a fertile harvest). Such mysteries included a parody of the abduction and rape of Persephone and the positioning of the female devotees upon the ground weeping (in the role of Demeter for her daughter) and fasting for the return of Persephone (the return of spring). The sitting upon the ground and fasting were also intended to mystically transfer the "energies" of the women into the ground, and thus into the fall seeds. Not surprisingly, the festival was held during the time of the autumn planting so as to nearly guarantee a positive response to the cult's magic. On the fifth day of the festival, the participants drank a special grain mixture called *kykeon* (a symbol of Persephone) in an attempt to assimilate the spirit of the goddess. About this same time, certain women called *antleriai* were cleansed in the sea and then sent down into the mountainside trenches to recover the sacrificial piglets and various other sacred objects that had been thrown down into the hillside canyons several days earlier. The sacred objects included dough replicas of snakes and genitalia, which were burned with the piglets, and a grain-seed mixture as an offering to Demeter. While several mystical representations can be made of the symbolism, and the dough replicas are obviously fertility representations, pigs' blood was sacred to the gods and thus the piglets are key to understanding the ritual. Greeks venerated pigs because of their uncanny ability to find and unearth underground items (roots, etc). Some scholars conclude from this that the ritual casting of the pigs "into the deep" was a form of imitative magic based on the underworld myth of Persephone and Hades. Casting the piglets into the deep canyon trenches and fetching them out again represented the descent of Persephone into the underworld and her subsequent ascension to the surface of the earth. The piglets in the trenches may have also served the practical purpose of supplying a host (body) for Persephone to hide in until the antleriai women could assist her (by retrieving the piglets) in her annual escape from the underworld. Burning the piglets later that night would, according to an ancient religious idea that fire passes the soul through a gateway from one location to another, free the spirit of Persephone into the upperworld (compare the children sacrificed to Baal who "passed through the fire" from the physical world into the spiritual in 2 Kings 23:10).

The New Testament informs us that such pagan rituals were the worship of demons. "The things which the Gentiles sacrifice," said Paul, "they sacrifice to devils" (1 Corinthians 10:20). This makes one wonder if a connection between the ritual casting of the piglets into the deep canyon trenches (representing a descent into hell) and the biblical story of the Gadarene demoniac existed.

In Luke 8, we read:

And they arrived at the country of the Gadarenes.... And when He [Jesus] went forth to land, there met Him out of the city a certain man, which had devils....When he [the demoniac] saw Jesus, he cried out, and fell down before Him, and with a loud voice said, "What have I to do with thee, Jesus, thou Son of God most high? I beseech thee, torment me not."...And Jesus asked him, saying, "What is thy name?" And he said, "Legion:" because many devils were entered into him. And they besought him that he would not command them to go out *into the deep*. And there was there an *herd of swine*

feeding on the mountain: and they besought him that
he would suffer them to enter into them. And he suf-
fered them. Then went the devils out of the man, and
entered into the swine: and the herd ran violently down
a steep place *into the sea*, and were choked. (Luke 8:26–
33, emphasis added)

The word "deep" in this text is *Abussos* (the Abyss) and
refers to the underworld "bottomless pit." Since the principal
elements of the sea, the swine, and the deep were employed;
since the Abyss (part of the underworld) was central to the narrative; and further since the cult rituals of the Thesmophoria
were well known throughout Asia Minor and considered by the
Hebrews to be activity of the devil (the inhabitants of Hades
were known as "Demeter's people," and Hecate, the goddess
of witchcraft, was Persephone's underworld guide during the
rituals), one could easily surmise that Jesus was mocking the
Thesmophoria. It's possible that Jesus was revealing to His followers and the neighboring communities that such rituals of
Dionysus and of Demeter were, in fact, the consort of devils.
It may be a stretch to suggest an interpretation of the biblical
story in this way, but clearly the similarities and historical prox-
imities are startling, especially since the demons requested entry
into the swine. Why would demons make such a plea? There
are two possible connections with the Thesmophoria: 1) The
demons believed that by entering the swine they could escape
the underworld deep (as in the magical Persephone escape ritual
described above); and 2) Jesus, by granting the request of the
devils, was illustrating that the Thesmophoria ritual of casting

the piglets into the deep was inherently demonic. Obviously, there are other possible interpretations of the narrative in Luke 8, but since this is the only record of Jesus granting the petition of demons, it seems reasonable that a powerful social commentary about spiritual warfare was made by the Master.

DEEPER TRUTH ABOUT UNDERWORLD "DEITIES"

While much is still unknown about the mysteries of Demeter, the basis of her popularity was almost certainly rooted in her divinity as a mother-earth goddess. Demeter (*de* or *da:* "earth"; *meter:* "mother") actually means "earth mother." The worship of the earth's "spirit" as a mother and the incarnation of the earth's fertility forces within specific goddesses were among the oldest and most widespread forms of paganism recorded in antiquity. Whether it was Inanna of the Sumerians, Ishtar of the Babylonians, or Fortuna of the Romans, every civilization had a sect of religion based on the embodiment of the earth's spirit as a mother goddess. The Egyptians worshipped Hathor in this way, as the Chinese worshipped Shing Moo. The Germans worshipped Hertha as the great Mother Earth, and in Greece, the queen of the Olympian goddesses and wife of Zeus was Hera, the benevolent earth mother. Before her was Gaia (*Gaea*, the Greek creator-Mother Earth), and beneath her were many other Greek earth spirits, including Demeter, Artemis, Aphrodite, Hecate, and so on.

The principal idea was, and evidently still is among New Age devotees, that the earth possesses or is a living entity. The ancient and universally accepted idea that the "living earth" was also a fertile mother was conceptualized in different ways and in various goddess myths and images throughout the ancient world. In the *Golden Asse* by second-century Roman philosopher Lucius Apuleius, evidence reveals that the spirit of the earth was perceived as a feminine *force,* and that such force incarnated itself at various times and to different people within the goddess mothers. More important, devotion to this deity would have spiritual warfare benefits for binding underworld demons in order to prevent them from passing through gateways and appearing to men. Note how Lucius prays to the earth spirit:

> O blessed Queene of Heaven, whether thou be the Dame Ceres [Demeter] which art the original and motherly source of all fruitful things in earth, who after the finding of thy daughter Proserpina [Persephone], through thy great joy which thou diddest presently conceive, madest barraine and unfruitful ground to be plowed and sowne, and now thou inhabitest in the land of Eleusie [Eleusis]; or whether thou be the celestiall Venus…[or] horrible Proserpina…*thou hast the power to stoppe and put away the invasion of the hags and ghoasts which appeare unto men, and to keep them downe in the closures [gated cells] of the earth*; thou which nourishest all the fruits of the world by thy vigor and force; with whatsoever name is or fashion it is lawful to call upon thee, I pray thee, to end my great travaile.

The earth spirit responds to Lucius:

Behold Lucius I am come, thy weeping and prayers hath mooved me to succour thee. I am she that is the natural mother of all things, mistresse and governesse of all the elements, the initial progeny of worlds, chiefe of powers divine, Queene of heaven, the principall of the Gods celestiall, the light of the goddesses: at my will the planets of the ayre [air], the wholesome winds of the Seas, and the silence of hell be disposed; my name, my divinity is adored throughout all the world in divers manners, in variable customes and in many names, for the Phrygians call me the mother of the Gods: the Athenians, Minerva: the Cyprians, Venus: the Candians, Diana: the Sicilians, Proserpina: the Eleusians, Ceres: some Juno, other Bellona, other Hecate: and principally the aethiopians…Queene Isis.[3]

One could assume, based on such texts, that a single spiritual source (or realm) energized the many goddess myths. Likewise, in the ancient hymn, *To Earth the Mother of All*, Homer illustrates how the earth spirit could migrate from its inner-world habitation to become involved in the affairs and lives of nations. Through Homer's dedication to the earth, we discover how far reaching and universal this possibility was thought to be:

I will sing of well founded Earth, mother of all, eldest of all beings. She feeds all creatures that are in the world, all that go upon the goodly land, and all that are in the paths of the seas, and all that fly: all these are fed by her store. Through you, O queen, men are blessed in their children and blessed in their harvests, and to you it belongs to give means of life to mortal men and to take it away. Happy is the man whom you delight to honour! He hath all things abundantly: his fruitful land is laden with corn, his pastures are covered with cattle, and his house is filled with good things. Such men rule orderly in their cities of fair women: great riches and wealth follow them: their sons exult with ever-fresh delight, and their daughters in flower-laden bands play and skip merrily over the soft flowers of the field. Thus it is with those whom you honour O holy goddess, bountiful spirit. Hail, mother of the gods, wife of starry Heaven; freely bestow upon me for this my song substance that cheers the heart! And now I will remember you and another song also.[4]

From these and other ancient records, it is obvious that the earth was more than an agricultural or herbaceous facility to the pagans. *She* was the "eldest of all beings" who manifested herself within the popular idols of the mother goddesses and who could loose or bind the powers held in her underworld.

Like ancient Greeks, Christian theologians affirm that the physical earth contains spiritual forces behind gateways. In Revelation 9:14, we read of "the four angels which are bound in the great river Euphrates." In Job 26:5, we find "dead things are formed from under the waters." The literal Hebrew translation says, "The Rafa [fallen angels] are made to writhe from beneath the waters." The belief by Greeks that these beings and regions were under the control of a supernatural "gatekeeper" associated with Hades is both fascinating and enlightening when compared to the previously mentioned words of Christ in Matthew 16:17–18: "Blessed art thou, Simon Barjona [son of Jonah]…thou art Peter, and upon this rock I will build my church; and the *gates of hell* shall not prevail against it" (emphasis added). In the Old Testament, Jonah 2:6 tells of Jonah going down to the bottom of the sea into a "city of gates" (Hebrew, *B@riyach:* "a fortress in the earth, a prison") from which God delivered him. There is no doubt about where Jonah was, as he prayed to God out of the belly of *hell*—the underworld prison of the dead. This unique text in Matthew connecting the rock upon which the church would be built, the name of Jonah, and the gates of hell is not coincidence. Christ made the same connection to hell's gateway, Jonah, and his mission for the church again in Matthew 12.40: "For as Jonas was three days and three nights in the whale's belly; so shall the Son of man be three days and three nights in the heart of the earth." Additional biblical references indicate the earth is a kind of holding tank or prison where God has bound certain fallen entities (2 Peter 2:4; Jude 6). That such fallen spirits seek to communicate with or participate in the affairs of humanity is defined in Scripture. The Hebrew people were aware that such spirits could seek to move from their habitation into ours (Deuteronomy 18:11), and when the woman of Endor communicated with the same, they ascended up from "out of the earth" (1 Samuel 28:13). Based on such Scriptures, the dynamic or energy behind the earth-goddess spirits is real, and according to Christian doctrine, identical with the legions of fallen spiritual forces bound within the earth and that seek association with men. Such conclusions can be made because of the obvious and physical location of the biblical demons within the body of the earth and also because of the nature of the manifestations, or attributes, of the goddesses. As previously noted, the myths and rituals behind the earth-goddess mothers Demeter, Persephone, and Hecate were openly connected with the evil spirits of the underworld.

WHEN A DEMONIC GATEKEEPER PRETENDS TO BE "MOTHER EARTH"

Hecate, the Titan earth mother of the wizards and witches who helped Demeter after Hades abducted and raped her daughter Persephone, illustrates perhaps better than any other goddess the connection between the earth goddesses, gateways, and the realm of evil supernaturalism. As the daughter of Perses and Asteria, Hecate (Hekate) was the only of the Titans to remain free under Zeus. She was the mother of the wizard Circe and of the witch Medea, and was considered to be the underworld sorceress of all that is demonic. This was because Hecate characterized the unknown night terrors that roamed the abandoned and desolate highways. She was often depicted as a young maiden with three faces, each pointing in a different direction, a role in which she was the earth spirit that haunted wherever three paths joined. As the "goddess of three forms," she was Luna (the moon) in heaven, Diana (Artemis) on earth, and Hecate in the underworld. At times of evil magic, she appeared with hideous serpents—spreading demons, encouraging criminal activity, and revealing enigmatic secrets to the crones. At other times, she roamed the night with the souls of the dead, visible only to dogs, who howled as she approached.

When the moon was covered in darkness and the hell hounds accompanied her to the path-beaten crossways, Hecate came suddenly upon the food offerings and dead bodies of murders and suicides that had been left for her by the fear-stricken common folk. Her hounds bayed, the ghost torches lit up the night, and the river nymphs shrieked as she carried away the mangled souls of the suicides into the underworld caverns of Thanatos (Death), where the shrills of such damned ones were known to occupy her presence. In our novel, *The Ahriman Gate*, we provided a fictionalized account of Hecate in this role:

> Around the would-be assassins, through the oak boughs, dark shadows began to accumulate. The demon of death, now calling itself Hecate, a black and powerful heathen goddess who enjoyed such fear in antiquity, led countless gleaming torches toward the confused, trembling souls. Horrible snakes wound about her head as hellish dogs and owl-shaped strigae emerged from the gloom and surrounded the killers. The men's eyes darted wildly as their fingers grasped frantically for a weapon. Beneath them, cold, bony fingers cracked through the ground, clasping their corrupted souls, jerking them down in a merciless earthen rend. Their senses, suddenly vivid beyond reason, filled with a burning sensation of sulfur as they burst into unquenchable fire. The mother they had so reverently obeyed during life couldn't and wouldn't help them now. What authority Gaia possessed was against these two anyway. Like Hecate, whose blood-red eyes bulged now with murderous delight, Gaia felt only satisfaction

as the doomed spirits screamed their way into the eternal torments of Thanatos and Hell.[5]

As the dark goddess of witchcraft, Hecate, like Isis, was worshipped with impure rites and magical incantations. Her name was probably derived from the ancient Egyptian word *heka* ("sorcery" or "magical"), which may explain her association with the Egyptian frog goddess of the same name. This may also explain the affiliation of frogs with witchcraft and the various potions of frogwort and *hecateis* (Hecate's hallucinogenic plant, also called aconite), which supposedly sprouted from the spittle of Cerberus (Hades' three-headed guard dog) that fell to the ground when Hercules forced him up to the surface of the earth.

Because her devotees practiced such magic wherever three paths joined, Hecate became known to the Romans as Trivia (*tri:* "three"; *via:* "roads"). Offerings were also made to her wherever evil or murderous activity occurred, as such areas were believed to be magnets of malevolent spirits, something like "haunted houses," and those who wanted to get along with the resident apparitions needed to make oblations to the ruler of their darkness—Hecate. The acceptance of the oblations was announced by Hecate's familiar (the night owl), and the spooky sound of the creature was perceived as a good omen by those who gathered on the eve of the full moon. Statues of the goddess bearing the triple face of a dog, a snake, and a horse overshadowed the dark rituals when they were performed at the crossing of three roads. At midnight, Hecate's devotees would leave the food offerings at the intersection for the goddess ("Hecate's supper"), and once deposited, quickly exit without turning around or looking back. Sometimes the offerings consisted of honey cakes and chicken hearts, while at other times, puppies, honey, and female black lambs were slaughtered for the goddess and her *strigae*—those vicious, owl-like affiliates of Hecate who flew through the night feeding on the bodies of unattended babies. During the day, the strigae appeared as simple old women, which may account for the folklore of flying witches. The same strigae hid among the leaves of the trees during the annual festival of Hecate (held on August 13), when Hecate's followers offered up the highest praise of the goddess. Hecate's devotees celebrated such festivals near Lake Averna in Campania, where the sacred willow groves of the goddess stood, and they communed with the nature spirits and summoned the souls of the dead from the mouths of nearby caves. Here Hecate was known as Hecate-Chthonia ("Hecate of the earth"), a depiction in which she most clearly embodied the earth-mother spirit that conversed through the cave stones and sacred willow trees. Elsewhere, Hecate was known as Hecate-Propolos, "the one who leads," as in the underworld guide of Persephone and of those who inhabit graveyards, and as Hecate-Phosphoros, "the light bearer," her most sacred title and one that recalls another powerful underworld spirit, Satan, whose original name was Lucifer ("the light bearer"). But it was her role as Hecate-Propylaia, "the one before the gate," where true believers most sought out (or feared) her power. In this manifestation, Hecate was believed not only to control entrances at homes and temples to nefarious evils, but spirit-traversing gateways that could be opened by her into the human mind through the use of psychoactive drugs—a practice employed throughout Greek paganism as well as by shamans of other cultures but condemned in the Scriptures (Galatians 5:20; Revelation 9:21 and 18:23) as *pharmakeia*—the administering of drugs for sorcery or magical arts in connection with demonic contact.

During our research for this book, we received an email from Dr. J. Michael Bennett pointing out that a revival of this ancient practice is back in vogue. His comments raise serious questions about the Greek "myths" mentioned above and modern spiritual warfare:

Tom and Nita:

The drug known as DMT [dimethyltryptamine], which is naturally produced in the pineal gland and is present in wild plants found in places like the Amazon basin, has been used for millennia by aboriginal shamans and medicine men to contact the spirit world and to receive information from entities there. It has recently come in "vogue" to experiment with DMT; in fact, "DMT churches" are springing up across America, which center on the ritual intake of the "theurgic" (i.e., psychoactive drug used for ritual purposes) substance to have transcendent contact with spirit intelligences. This chemical is naturally produced by the pineal gland in the brain, which is located behind the forehead. The pineal gland is called the "third eye" by biologists and spiritual teachers because it has biological elements that are common with the retina of the eye, and in fact are even used as part of parietal sensory organs in other animals. Philosopher and theologian René Descartes understood it to be the physical portal to the spirit world, and occult writer H. P. Lovecraft wrote a famous work called *From*

Beyond about a portal device that stimulated the human pineal gland in order to make contact with malevolent spirits. A *National Geographic* journalist wrote about her ingestion of DMT via the traditional ayahuasca tea delivery means within the Amazon jungle, as part of a sacred circle of fellow participants. She described falling into an abyss, being summoned by doomed souls who pleaded for release (and she was described as a nonreligious person by nature). She then encountered three sinister thrones in an infernal region, and heard threatening voices who told her she could not leave and that there was "no hope." She was "rescued" by her fellow participants, as it is common for adjoining DMT partakers to see the same apparitions, such as serpents enveloping them. Most importantly, psychologist Dr. Rick Strassman conducted a formal clinical study of DMT ingestion under the auspices of the University of New Mexico, which he detailed in his book, *DMT: The Spirit Molecule*. He found, under controlled clinical conditions, that subjects had these experiences within seconds of ingesting DMT, which almost universally mimicked what are described elsewhere as "alien abduction events" (note that these subjects were screened to be those who were not familiar with stories of UFOs or did not believe in them). The entities they encountered were typically described as traditional "grays," reptilian or insectlike. The contacts usually involved medical and reproductive experiments conducted by the entities on the subjects, described as violent rape episodes. When subjects were willing to try an additional experience, they reported that the entities acknowledged their prior disappearance with no sensation of "time loss." The episodes were so traumatic to the subjects that a support group was later formed to help them deal with the emotional trauma of the experiences.

I believe the possibility exists that the pineal gland could indeed serve as a means of interacting with the spirit world. According to ancient records, fallen angels taught early humans many things, including the use of plants and natural materials in ritual ceremonies for the practice of alchemy and sorcery, and this may include the use of certain wild plants as a source of concentrated DMT to "overload" the neutralizing effects of a chemical in our stomach that under normal circumstances nullifies the effects of DMT. It should also be noted how the Bible mentions the forehead, the region of the pineal gland, in the New Testament book of Revelation in the context of the forces of God or Satan "sealing" their followers there to protect them from the effects of the other. For example, God seals His one hundred forty-four thousand in the forehead, and subsequently they are the only ones not subject to dark angelic torment from the beings that exit the Abyss. Conversely, Satan, through the Beast, "seals" the foreheads of his followers with his "mark" and as a result they are forever doomed to his servitude and judgment. Finally, God seals the foreheads of all who enter into the New Jerusalem with His own name for eternity.

Another theurgic (or at least psychoactive) substance that was used in ancient days that has experienced a modern revival was the alcoholic-based drug "absinthe." This unique, distinctive distilled liquid of pale green color was known in the late nineteenth and early twentieth centuries as the "green fairy." Although its consumption almost became an obsession across Europe and more mystical cosmopolitan centers in America like New Orleans, it was most closely associated with the bohemian artistic culture thriving at the time. It was a favorite of eclectic artists such as the painter Salvador Dali and writer Oscar Wilde, due to its reliable propensity to facilitate their contact directly with their inspirational spirit "muses." Occult magician Aleister Crowley was so devoted to absinthe for its spiritual invocation capabilities that he wrote his famous lengthy poem, "The Green Goddess," in its honor. It was the only alcoholic beverage banned across Europe (as well as North America) because the diagnosed "absinthism" addiction and effects were deemed much worse than regular alcohol. The curious matter about absinthe is that it is distilled from the wormwood plant, which has the official name of *Artemis absinthium*. Artemis was a Greek and Roman goddess who was (a) considered a "huntress"; (b) associated with fire and keys; and (c) the sister of Apollo. She was associated with the goddess Hecate, who was known as a "luminal" god who controlled the access to portals in the spirit world.

AUGMENTED BY HUMAN BELIEF, RITUAL, AND SACRIFICE

As described above by Dr. Bennett, opening supernatural gateways that exist inside the earth, the heavens, and the mind using altered mental states induced by psychoactive drugs is but one of several "spirit-gate" mechanisms. New Age esotericists like Robert Hieronimus—one of the world's foremost authorities on the symbolism of the reverse side of the Great Seal of the United States (of which we have written extensively in *Apollyon Rising 2012*)—view the circular design and symbolism on the Great Seal to be an "initiatory mandala" that can unconsciously invoke contact with the spirit world.

Mandalas, from the Hindu term for "circle," are concentric diagrams, such as is familiar in Tantrism, Buddhism, and Hinduism, having ritual and spiritual use for "focusing" or trance-inducing aspirants and adepts who seek mystical oneness with the cosmos or deeper levels of the unconscious mind. Related to the design of the Great Seal, Hieronimus, as an occultist, views the geometric patterns as representing a type of mandala or microcosm embodying the cosmic or metaphysical divine powers at work in the secret destiny of America, including the god or universal forces represented in the diagram that herald a coming new age of gods and demigods.

Occultists often use mandalas based on the concept of a "protective circle" or variation, which they believe allow certain doorways into the supernatural to be opened or closed, and entities compelled accordingly, as in the magical, five-pointed pentagram circle. This is similar to an initiatory mandala used in Hindu and Buddhist Tantrism, in which deities are represented by specific locations in the diagram. In *Yoga: Immortality and Freedom*, scholar Mircea Eliade explains the importance of this part of the mandala design:

> At the periphery of the construction there are four cardinal doors, defended by terrifying images called "guardians of the doors." Their role is twofold. On the one hand, the guardians defend consciousness from the disintegrating forces of the unconscious; on the other, they have an offensive mission—in order to lay hold upon the fluid and mysterious world of the unconscious, consciousness must carry the struggle into the enemy's camp and hence assume the violent and terrible aspect appropriate to the forces to be combated. Indeed, even the divinities inside the *mandala* sometimes have a terrifying appearance; they are the gods whom man will encounter after death, in the state of *bardo*. The guardians of the doors and the terrible divinities emphasize the initiatory character of entrance into a *mandala*.... The typical initiatory ordeal is the "struggle with a monster"…both spiritual (against evil spirits and demons, forces of chaos) and material (against enemies)…who [attempt] to return "forms" to the amorphous state from which they originated.[6]

What makes this interesting is that the arcane symbols and mottoes of the Great Seal represent—as admitted by Masonry's greatest historians, mystics, and philosophers—gods that were known in ancient times alternatively as saviors or demons, creators and destroyers: spirits that seek entry into the conscious and unconscious world.

Even more subtle is how synergy can be created between immaterial entities and humans who wittingly or unwittingly cooperate to advance occult politics in secular or religious government. Demonologists agree that powerful, nonhuman energies can emanate from such parity and, once released, take on a mind of their own. In our best-selling book mentioned earlier, *Apollyon Rising 2012*, we documented how Gary Lachman, in writing about the Masonic involvement in the French Revolution, made an extraordinary and important observation about immaterial destructive forces—which had unseen plans of their own—released from behind their gates as a result of occult politics:

> Cazotte himself was aware of the dangerous energies unleashed by the Revolution.... Although Cazotte didn't use the term, he would no doubt have agreed that, whatever started it, the Revolution soon took on a life of its own, coming under the power of an *egregore*, Greek for "watcher," a kind of immaterial entity that is created by and presides over a human activity or collective. According to the anonymous author of the fascinating *Meditations on the Tarot*, there are no "good" *egregores*, only "negative" ones.... True or not, *egregores* can nevertheless be "engendered by the collective will and imagination of nations." As Joscelyn Godwin points out, "An *egregore* is augmented by human belief, ritual, and especially by sacrifice. If it is sufficiently nourished

by such energies, the *egregore* can take on a life of its own and appear to be an independent, personal divinity, with a limited power on behalf of its devotees and an unlimited appetite for their future devotion." If, as some esotericists believe, human conflicts are the result of spiritual forces for spiritual ends, and these forces are not all "good," then collective catastrophes like the French Revolution take on a different significance.[7]

The point that there are no "good" *egregores*, only "negative" ones, offers a disturbing challenge when attempting to determine under what conditions some people actually seek connection with evil supernaturalism. The morality play *Faust* and the adjective *Faustian* describe persons who surrender moral integrity or "sell their souls to the devil" to achieve power through access to the evil ones. History is replete with tyrants who struck Faustian deals and who seemed to know deep down that while they might gain short-term material benefits from connecting with the devil, eventually *he* would come to collect and that they would have to bear the consequences of their actions. This is especially true where occult politics generate collateral misery among blameless bystanders. It is widely held by esotericists that the Nazis were just such an example, and that their actions were the material results of the occult forces or invisible hierarchies they put themselves in league with. During the ascendancy of Nazi Germany, Hermann Rauschning, the governor of Danzig, described how Hitler "wakes up in the night screaming and in convulsions. He calls for help, and appears to be half paralyzed. He is seized with a panic that makes him tremble until the bed shakes. He utters confused and unintelligible sounds, gasping, as if on the point of suffocation." Rauschning then recited a strange episode in which Hitler (who was possessed by the devil himself, according to the Vatican's chief exorcist, Father Gabriele Amorth) was visited by an invisible being, something Hitler was utterly terrified of and seemed to know would be coming for him for what he had done to innocent victims:

> Hitler was standing up in his room, swaying and looking all around him as if he were lost. "It's he, it's he," he groaned, "he's come for me!" His lips were white; he was sweating profusely. Suddenly he uttered a string of meaningless figures, then words and scraps of sentences. It was terrifying. He used strange expressions strung together in bizarre disorder. Then he relapsed again into silence, but his lips still continued to move. He was then given a friction and something to drink. Then suddenly he screamed: "There! There! Over in the corner! He is there!"—all the time stamping with his feet and shouting. To quieten him he was assured that nothing extraordinary had happened, and finally he gradually calmed down. After that he slept for a long time and became normal again."[8]

Despite such terrifying accounts, the reader will learn in the next chapter how a growing number of individuals around the world are being drawn by curiosity to push open spiritual gates in order to make contact with this *other side*.

CHAPTER THREE

SUCH BEAUTIFUL DECEPTION

Black it stood as night, fierce as ten furies, terrible as
Hell.... Satan was now at hand; and from his seat, the
monster, moving onward, came as fast. With horrid
strides; Hell trembled as he strode.

— JOHN MILTON

O ver the past century, a generation of Christians and other
religious persons have systematically challenged and then
abandoned fundamental precepts of New Testament theology, giving birth to new forms of secularized spirituality fueled
by human potential and an amorphous mixture of Buddhism,
pantheistic Christianity, and occult traditions. Many of the
most popular doctrines celebrated today cleverly conceal this
ancient carnival of pagan mystical occultism by wrapping it
in prosperity theology, self-help messages, goddess-centered
environmental theology, and dominionism and the eleva-
tion of man. Instead of living by faith, as defined in Scriptures
centered on the person of Jesus Christ and expressed through
personal sacrifice and transformation, emergent church leaders
allure congregants with seductive messages of thrilling material

benefits that historically were shown to be keys to opening gateways to and forming pacts with Faustian forces. Nowhere is
evidence of these activities more puzzling than when manifested
in what at one time was considered mainstream evangelical
churches. A decade ago, as new necromantic channelers in the
persons of pastors and priests began rising to prominence inside
major denominations, Samantha Smith was so shocked by how
quickly orthodox theology was being surrendered to paganism
inside weekly church services that she spent an entire year investigating the phenomenon before reporting to the Eagle Forum:

> I became strongly concerned…after observing a "ser-
> vice" at a south Denver Vineyard church…[a woman]
> stood in the middle of a group of people who ran their
> hands over her body (within an inch or so of the cloth-
> ing), then kept swooshing some invisible thing toward
> her heart area. Saddened, I walked toward the door,
> where a church member said, "You should come back
> on Sunday night. That's when they levitate."…[Another
> group] in Seattle…sit[s] in circles, clucking, flapping
> their tucked arms, and visualizing themselves hatching
> the "Man Child Company," a heretical Manifested Sons
> of God concept. In Kansas City, men and women lay on
> the floor with their knees up and legs spread apart, try-
> ing to *birth* the same thing.… I tape-recorded a group of
> Episcopalians howling at the moon, like wolves—giving
> a "Howl-le-lu-ia Chorus" for Earth Day. It gets worse.
> There are reports of "holy vomiting" (seance ectoplasm?)
> and of Christians becoming demonized by being "slain
> in the spirit." How can this be?[9]

Similar to Samantha, we were taken off-guard a few years ago when speaking at a large Assemblies of God church whose pastor later became a district official. Following the morning service, the pastor asked if we would meet with the director of his intercessory prayer group to answer a question that as pastor he had been unable to determine. The staff member, who was told by the pastor that we were experts in demonology, wanted to know what we thought about him and other members of the "intercessory prayer group" experiencing temporary possession by evil spirits. Because we were taken aback by his question and thought we had misunderstood, we asked him to clarify, and he repeated that evil spirits were "hanging on the walls in the auditorium" and "coming out of people" before going into the prayer room to possess the prayer warriors in order to speak through their vocal chords during Sunday morning church services. The staff member seemed proud that this was happening, as if he and those under him were somehow "special" because of the hidden evil spirits' activity. At once confused by why the senior pastor had not already corrected this group, we explained to the director how Jews and Christians are forbidden to communicate with evil spirits, let alone allow them to speak through their vocal chords. We showed him several places where Scripture says to cease the activity, including how Michael the archangel did not discourse with the devil, but simply said, "The Lord rebuke thee" (Jude 9). Instead of receiving our instruction, the young man's countenance suddenly changed, his eyes glazed over, and a religious sneer covered his face, as if he (or something in him) considered us pathetic and unenlightened souls who could not appreciate the exceptional relationship he and his church had with supernatural entities.

Later that week, we e-mailed the pastor to share our surprise that a man in his position would be confused over how wrong this activity was and how the environment was conducive to ancient paganism, spirit channeling, and at least a dozen other heretical activities. Some years afterward, while having dinner in the home of that district's state superintendent, we told our host what was going on in one of his churches. He demanded to know where and by whom, stating that in no uncertain terms, "That pastor's credentials will be taken away immediately!" We chose not to disclose that he had already invited the man to take executive leadership inside the state office.

In addition to this kind of spiritualism sweeping most quarters of institutionalized Christianity today, expressions of neo-paganism in the larger public square now range from self-help organizations working with corporations to offer symposiums to their employees to produce positive harmony, prosperity, and overall business success to other, not-so-subtle forms of paganism such as practiced by Wicca and the women's spirituality movement, in which more than six hundred thousand women nationwide participate in the invocation of ancient earth goddesses. Retail stores in faddish malls are springing up across the United States to meet the need for replica idols of the popular female deities, and marketing occult paraphernalia used in venerating the goddesses (crystals, candles, books of spells, etc.) has become a multimillion dollar industry. Dimly lit "occult" bookstores that once inhabited shabby old buildings have been replaced with trendy New Age shops located in the most fashionable strip malls in the nicest areas of town. One such store, Necromance, resides at stylish Melrose Avenue in Los Angeles, where business is booming with sales of human fingers on a leather cord, necklaces of human teeth, bone beads, and human skulls including tiny fetal ones. While store owners are generally New Agers or practicing witches, Necromance and similar businesses are attentively supported by a growing population of churchgoers, neo-pagans, politicians, Hollywood entertainers, and teachers of the arcane rites. Not long ago, one such witch claimed to be a temple prostitute of the goddess Astarte and performed sequential gate-opening magic sex with 251 men at the University of Southern California.

Today, adherents of such mysticism boldly ask, "If God is our Father, then who is our Mother?" Then they happily answer, "Earth!" Not surprisingly, the worship of the earth's "spirit" as a goddess mother has been revived as a central feature of contemporary religious phenomena. In 2010, Earth Day was celebrated by coordinating millions of people worldwide into a universal effort aimed at saving "our endangered Mother Earth." Christian leaders signed "Green Pledges" and Wiccan witches performed arcane rituals in honor of the hoary spirit Gaia. Interest in such contraptions as the sweat lodge—a device used by several ancient religions as an apparatus whereby one reenters the womb of the Earth Mother—was emphasized as a primitive yet effective method for furrowing a womblike gateway into the surface of the earth to make contact with the underworld spirit. This method of communing with Gaia, as practiced by various religions and New Age devotees, includes sitting in a semicircle around heated stones inside the lodge and entering into a mystical state of consciousness. As with the DMT churches (mentioned by Dr. Bennett in the previous chapter) who use psychoactive drugs to open gateways into the mind, the altered mental condition in the sweat lodge is accomplished through hypnotic repetitive chanting, drumming, and breathing the fumes of stimulants such as peyote. Spirit animals, called "power animals," are invited to guide the soul through the underworld journey or "vision quest," and participants are encouraged to "dance their animal" for revelations and healing of the body and mind. Such animal dancing is accomplished by allowing the spirit of the creature to enter and take control of the participant. Dr. Leslie Gray—a noted university instructor and female shaman—employs such uses of "animal dancing" in the psychiatric (shamanic) treatment of her patients. She described the positive results of animal dancing in the case of one insecure young woman, saying, "I [laid] down on the ground next to her and put us both into an altered state of consciousness via a tape of drumming. I came back from my 'journey' and blew the spirit of a mountain lion into [her]. I then instructed her to go out into nature and dance her animal...[and when she did] she no longer felt afraid of people."[10]

Uses of animal imagery and other nature elements in the worship of the Great Earth Mother is by design. Modern pagans, drawing on Eastern philosophies and the occult, believe that, unlike the "evil human race," these elements are at one with Gaia. According to them, if it were not for male-dominated, Styrofoam-producing, beef-eating, gas-guzzling human beings, the earth would be a better place. Natural earth-centered resources such as animals, crystals, and even colors are thus the products of choice for the students of earth-centered spirituality. Light blue is the color of Mother Earth's sky, so candles of light blue are burned to acquire her magic tranquility or understanding. Red candles are burned for strength or sexual love, and green candles for financial assistance. Instruments like magic wands are also made of Mother Earth's natural supply, usually of willow, oak, or fruit tree branches. Magic potions employed during esbats (earth celebrations held during the new and full moons) also contain the earth's natural byproducts, including clover, olive oil, grape juice, garlic cloves, and rosebuds. Special ceremonies using the earth samples are conducted at the crossing of three earth paths (the triple-path haunt of Hecate) and dedicated to the Mother Earth goddesses—Gaia, Demeter, Persephone, Isis, Aphrodite, Hathor, Hera, Diana, Athene, and Hecate. The authors of this book personally witnessed officially sponsored Assemblies of God youth camps in Oregon where children were taken into the woods and taught to use tree branches, pebbles, and other natural products to outline magic prayer trails, with participants moving through the labyrinths to specific mystical areas where they would then stop and meditate to "connect with the spirit." (The occult significance of this symbolism in youth camps is dangerously meaningful, as navigating such labyrinths began in mythology with the story of Queen Pasiphae and her amorous affair with a sacrificial bull. The union resulted in the birth of the transgenic Minotaur, a creature that lived in a labyrinth where every year boys and girls were sent to be sacrificed.) While in ancient times such rituals were gender-inclusive, they were designed specifically to elevate the goddess or female divinity, which consequently also defined the "oracles" or mouthpieces and gatekeepers of even the most powerful male gods in antiquity, including Apollo, the ancient spirit the Scriptures say will rise to inhabit the Antichrist in the end times.

Located on the mainland of Greece, the *omphalos* of Delphi (the stone the Greeks believed marked the center of the earth) can still be found among the ruins of Apollo's Delphic temple. So important was Apollo's oracle at Delphi that wherever Hellenism existed, its citizens and kings—including some from as far away as Spain—ordered their lives, colonies, and wars by her sacred communications. Here the Olympian god spoke through a gateway to mortal men using a female priesthood, which interpreted the trance-induced utterances of the pythoness or pythia, a middle-aged woman who sat on a copper-and-gold tripod or, much earlier, on the "rock of the sibyl" (medium). Crouching over a fire while inhaling the smoke of burning laurel leaves, barley, marijuana, and oil, a magical intoxication *(pharmakeia)* for her prophecies opened spirit gates through which powerful hallucinogenic manifestations could emerge. Under the influence of these forces, the pythia prophesied in an unfamiliar voice thought to be that of Apollo himself. During the trance, the medium's personality often changed, becoming melancholic, defiant, or even animal-like, a psychosis that may have been the source of the werewolf myth, or lycanthropy, as the pythia became possessed by Apollo/Lykeios—the wolf god. Delphic "women of python" prophesied in this way for nearly a thousand years and were considered to be a vital part of the pagan order and local economy of every Hellenistic community. This adds to the mystery of adoption of the pythians and sibyls by certain quarters of Christianity as "vessels of truth." These women, whose lives were dedicated to channeling from frenzied lips the messages of demon gods and goddesses, turn up especially in Catholic art—from altars to illustrated books and even upon the ceiling of the Sistine Chapel, where five sibyls join the Old Testament prophets in places of sacred honor. The Cumaean Sibyl (also known as Amalthaea), whose prophecy about the return of the god Apollo is encoded on the Great Seal of the United States (discover the explosive exposé on this in *Apollyon Rising 2012* by visiting www.ApollyonRising2012. com), was the oldest of the sibyls and the seer of the underworld who, in the *Aeneid*, gave Aeneas a tour of the infernal region.

Whether by trickery or occult power, the prophecies of the sibyls were sometimes amazingly accurate. The Greek historian Herodotus (considered the father of history) recorded an interesting example of this. Croesus, the king of Lydia, had expressed doubt regarding the accuracy of Apollo's oracle at Delphi. To test the oracle, Croesus sent messengers to inquire of the pythian prophetess as to what he, the king, was doing on a certain day. The priestess surprised the king's messengers by visualizing the question and formulating the answer before they arrived. A portion of the historian's account says:

> The moment that the Lydians (the messengers of Croesus) entered the sanctuary, and before they put their questions, the Pythoness thus answered them in hexameter verse: "Lo! on my sense there striketh the smell of a shell-covered tortoise, Boiling now on a fire, with the flesh of a lamb, in a cauldron. Brass is the vessel below, and brass the cover above it."
>
> These words the Lydians wrote down at the mouth of the Pythoness as she prophesied, and then set off on their return to Sardis....

[When] Croesus undid the rolls…[he] instantly made an act of adoration…declaring that the Delphic was the only really oracular shrine.… For on the departure of his messengers he had set himself to think what was most impossible for anyone to conceive of his doing, and then, waiting till the day agreed on came, he acted as he had determined. He took a tortoise and a lamb, and cutting them in pieces with his own hands, boiled them together in a brazen cauldron, covered over with a lid which was also of brass. (*Herodotus*, Book 1:47)

Another interesting example of spiritual insight by an Apollonian sibyl is found in the New Testament book of Acts. Here the demonic resource that energized the sibyls is revealed:

And it came to pass, as we went to prayer, a certain damsel possessed with a spirit of divination [of python, a seeress of Delphi] met us, which brought her masters much gain by soothsaying: The same followed Paul and us, and cried, saying, "These men are the servants of the most high God, which shew unto us the way of salvation." And this did she many days. But Paul, being grieved, turned and said to the spirit, "I command thee in the name of Jesus Christ to come out of her." And he came out the same hour. And when her masters saw that the hope of their gains was gone, they caught Paul and Silas.… And brought them to the magistrates, saying, "These men, being Jews, do exceedingly trouble our city." (Acts 16:16–20)

The story in Acts is interesting because it illustrates the level of culture and economy that had been built around the oracle worship of Apollo. It cost the average Athenian more than two days' wages for an oracular inquiry, and the average cost to lawmakers or military officials seeking important state information was charged at ten times that rate.

But now, as the old saying goes, "everything old is new again," and across the world a staggering amount of revenue is flowing once more into oracle divining for the purpose of breaching supernatural gateways. Through *pharmakeia*, grimoires, talismans, magic diagrams, Ouija boards, sibylline channeling, and scores of other methods, adherents of new spirituality are actively seeking contact with *the powers on the other side* just as they did in days of old.

One of the most curious forms of oracular activity in use by modern soothsayers is the psychomanteum—a simple, yet eerie, idea. A chair placed in front of a large mirror in a dark room serves as the oracle. Once positioned on the chair, the occupant stares into the mirror and waits for contact with ghosts or other entities. In ancient times, a psychomanteum-like mirror system for communicating with "spirits" was employed by primitive Greeks in gloomy underground caverns called "halls of visions." Standing in front of a shining metal surface or cauldron, ancients saw and spoke with apparitions. The Sumerians, Egyptians, and Romans employed similar oracles of polished crystal, brass mirrors, and pools of water, and some argue that the apostle Paul was referring to mirror oracles when he said, "For now we see through a glass, darkly; but then face to face: now I know in part; but then shall I know even as also I am known" (1 Corinthians 13:12).

Revived as an oracle during the 1990s in the book *Reunions*, more than 50 percent of the three hundred users of the psycho-manteum in a study by Raymond Moody claimed to have been contacted by a deceased "relative" or "friend" on the first try. People interviewed by Mr. Moody included physicians, teach-ers, housewives, business owners, and law enforcement officials. One witness, an accountant who grieved over his departed mother a year after her death, testified of his experience with the psychomanteum:

> There is no doubt that the person I saw in the mirror was my mother! I don't know where she came from but I am convinced that what I saw was the real person. She was looking out at me from the mirror.... I could tell she was in her late seventies, about the same age as…when she died. However, she looked happier and healthier than she had at the end of her life. Her lips didn't move, but she spoke to me and I clearly heard what she had to say. She said, "I'm fine," and smiled.... I stayed as relaxed as I could and just looked at her.... Then I decided to talk to her. I said, "It's good to see you again." "It's good to see you too," she replied. That was it. She simply disappeared.[11]

Although the Bible warns against opening such gateways to "familiar spirits" or consulting mediums and sibyls, the revival of ancient oracles and the experiences being drawn from them are especially seductive curiosities for followers of modern religion. A quick glance through the most current popular tele-vision programs illustrates a great deal about the public's interest in this field: *Ghost Hunters, Ghost Hunters International, Ghost Hunters Academy, Ghost Whisperer, Paranormal State, Psychic Kids: Paranormal Children,* Animal Planet's *The Haunted,* and more. Sociologists understand public demand for such viewing is evidence of pop culture's preferred spirituality, an informal consensus toward a post-New Testament theological condition. As such, it is reasonable to see how modern culture may rapidly be approaching the culmination of Apollo's *novus ordo seclorum*—the prophecy on the Great Seal of the United States that forecasts the granddaddy of all spirit-gate transmigrations, an advent prophesied in 2 Thessalonians 2:3 and Revelation 17:8 in which the destroyer demon Apollo (*Apoleia:* Apollyon) rises through underworld gates in the last days to confront the world that sought it.

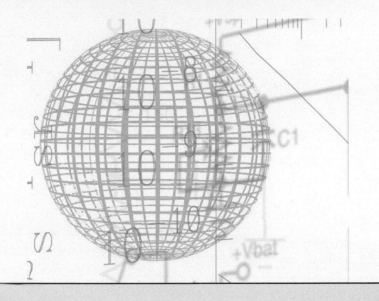

THE BATTLEFIELD UNTIL NOW

CHAPTER FOUR

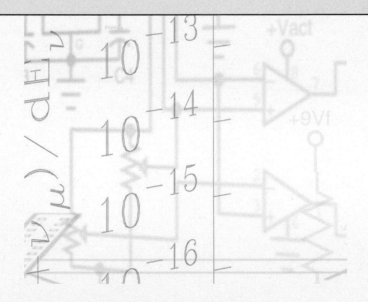

SATAN'S JURISDICTION

There is no neutral ground in the universe; every square
inch, every split second, is claimed by God and counter-
claimed by Satan.

—C. S. Lewis

During our formative years in ministry, few people
more profoundly influenced our theology and practical Christianity than pastor and theologian Dr. Robert
Cornwall. Bob—or simply "Cornwall," as his friends knew
him—had a photographic memory, and in order to pay his
way through Bible college as a young man, he had gotten a
job proofreading books for a publisher of scholarly works. As a
result of maintaining this job for years and having an uncanny
propensity for recalling facts, Cornwall retained the majority
of material he read and became one of the most well informed
and brilliant thinkers we ever had the privilege of knowing or
being mentored under. Cornwall was also a great storyteller and
could thrill audiences at churches and in conferences by weav-
ing details of true-life events with deep theological propositions.
A particular story that raised profound spiritual-warfare implications revolved around one of the first churches he pastored as

a young minister in a sleepy little town near the Oregon coast. As described by Cornwall himself at Redwood Family Camp meeting in the 1970s, he had barely settled into leadership at the church when strange things began to happen for which he had no explanation. Objects in the building seemed to move around on their own, especially overnight when the building was supposed to be unoccupied. He would hear the piano playing and go into the sanctuary to find nobody there. Doors would slam, pews would be discovered positioned backward against the wall, and his notes would disappear—then reappear. Members of the church reported similar phenomena, and Cornwall eventually learned that the activity had been going on for years.

One night, hours after he had gone home to bed, Cornwall's telephone rang and the police chief was on the other end of the line. He wanted to know what kind of party Cornwall was sponsoring at the church.

"What do you mean, a party?" Cornwall asked.

"Neighbors are calling. They say it's so loud they can't sleep. We thought maybe the youth group was having an overnight event that was getting out of hand."

Assuring the officer that nobody was supposed to be in the building, Cornwall agreed to meet him at the church. On arrival, they noticed the lights inside the auditorium were going off and on, the piano was banging loudly, and what sounded like shouting of some kind could be heard throughout the edifice. The officer drew his sidearm while Cornwall unlocked the front door. As they pushed the entrance open, all activity inside the facility abruptly ceased. The lights were still on, but the noises had suddenly gone silent. Cornwall moved through the building with the officer and found every entryway locked, with no signs of break in. This experience was documented in the police report—which, at the time, Cornwall was happy to let us confirm with the chief along with other unexplained events.

Together with his board members and ministry leaders, Cornwall began a series of special prayers over the building in what today some might call a "cleansing" ceremony to purge the house of worship of malevolent spirits mimicking trickster ghosts or poltergeists (German *poltern,* "to rumble or make a noise," and *geist,* meaning "spirit"—invisible entities that manifest by creating noises or by moving objects around). But the results of these prayers were mixed, and Cornwall could not understand why. Whenever members of the church were inside the building and prayed, the phenomenon stopped. As soon as they would leave the facility, it would start up again. This went on sporadically for some time, until one day the chief—now a member of the church—called Cornwall and asked if he could meet him downtown at the police department, saying he had found something important and wanted the pastor to see it. Arriving on schedule, Cornwall was handed an envelope that contained a copy of the original deed to the church property and other interesting documents. One of these records was very enlightening. It revealed that the structure—which was nearly one hundred years old and had been boarded up for over a decade before the organization Cornwall was a member of purchased it and turned it into a church—had originally been constructed by an occult group as a meeting place for their "order." It had been dedicated as a residence "for spirits of Lucifer as they move to and fro upon the earth."

Cornwall was shocked. Legalese existing within the building's first title and deed provided lodging for satanic spirits. Equally disturbing, the experiences at the church suggested demons were operating under some legal claim to be there.

As soon as possible, a new church was erected across the street from the old one, and subsequently the original building was torn down and an asphalt parking lot was poured over the plot of land on which it had sat for nearly a century. From that day forward, all paranormal activity on the property ceased, and a powerful and important theological proposition was born in Cornwall's mind—that under certain conditions, Satan and his spirits have legal rights to property and people.

While some may step back at this point and ask what comparable authority over earth Satan continues to hold following the redemptive work of Christ, most scholars agree that until the Second Coming of Jesus and the final judgment of men and angels, this planet remains under limited jurisdiction of Satan as "the god of this world" (2 Corinthians 4:4) and under the influence of "the rulers of the darkness of this world" (Ephesians 6:12). During this time, contracts and covenants with such spirits allowing access or entry into one's property or life do not have to be officially recorded as in the story of Cornwall's church above. They can be oral or assumed agreements, not to mention "adverse possession," or what laymen call "squatter's rights." In the physical world, this is when a person openly uses somebody else's property without permission over such a long period that eventually the "squatter" gains legal claim to the land, due to the original owner not taking legal action against him or her. These are ancient statutory principles that pertain equally to material and spiritual dynamics. They imply that wherever activity favorable to malevolent spirits occurs by consent, is tolerated, or action is not taken to force the "squatter" to cease and desist, footholds and even personal rights can be surrendered to hostile forces over people and locations.

In our 1998 book, *Spiritual Warfare: The Invisible Invasion* (download free at www.ForbiddenGate.com), we documented how, throughout history, entire geographies became strongholds of demonic activity as a result of what governments and citizens were willing to tolerate in foreign, domestic, public, and social policies. Specifically, we cited biblical examples such as the city of Pergamum, which Scripture identified as having become a seat of satanic influence (Revelation 2:12–13). More recent examples would include the history of Nazi Germany and similar cases. This phenomenon—territorial demonization—also occurs on a small scale, wherever space or property (real property including land, personal property as in possessions, commercial property, public property, and even intellectual property) is provided for purposes hostile to moral or biblical law.

As an example, many years ago as young Christians, we walked through a local mall during the Christmas season and came upon a New Age bookstore conducting a grand opening. In a derisive tone, I (Tom) said to my wife, "Can you believe the lack of intelligence of some people?" I strolled casually into the store, snatched a book from the shelf, and began offering sarcastic commentary as I read from its pages. I could tell my wife was uncomfortable with what I was doing, so I placed the book back on the shelf and proceeded out of the store. Suddenly, a dull sensation hit the pit of my stomach and shot upward through my chest into my cranium. My head started spinning, powerful nausea took hold, my hands began to shake, and I could tell I was about to collapse. It was literally as if something invisible had jumped on me and was injecting rapidly spreading poison throughout my body. Feigning interest in sales items, I moved away from the shoppers and began praying under my breath, asking for forgiveness for my smart attitude, for my lack of caution, and for my lack of concern for the lost. I prayed for deliverance from evil and for healing of my body and mind. After more than an hour of such intercession, I was finally restored. As a young preacher, I discovered a valuable lesson that day: The princes of this world are powerful and territorial, and we should enter spaces that have been dedicated to them only with the proper attitude and when guided by the Lord.

Even then, experiences with exorcism many years later taught the writers of this book that Satan's jurisdiction and legal rights to property and people are extrapolated to an entirely different level when the phenomenology involves *inner space* as opposed to external, physical territory. This is because "habitable space" and spatial occupancy—the amount of substance (or demons, in this case) that can fit into a specific area—are different between material and spiritual dimensions. A unique argument, one that has existed since the Middle Ages and highlights this concept, involves the question of how many angels can fit on the head of a pin, illustrating that even the ancients pondered advanced physics, space-time, quantum gravity densities, relativity theory, and hyperdimensional materiality (though the ancients knew nothing of these terms), allowing for different maximal density of "beings" within what otherwise appears in the physical world to be the same "space." Dr. Anders Sandberg, in the research paper, "Quantum Gravity Treatment of the Angel Density Problem" for the Royal Institute of Technology in Stockholm, Sweden, actually derived a number for the density of angels at critical mass that could fit on the head of a pin. He arrived at 8.6766*10exp49 angels (3.8807*10exp-34 kg), thus theoretically fixing through physics how an entire legion of demons (forty-two hundred to fifty-two hundred spirits, plus auxiliaries) in the fifth chapter of the New Testament book of Mark could possess the *inner space* of a single man.[12]

An important question related to this mysterious relationship between people surrendering inner and external territory to evil spirits—and the boundaries of that association—involves the difference between those who are deceived into *unwittingly* giving place to the devil and thus become "demonized," and those who *knowingly* form alliances with evil supernaturalism. The contrast between these types of persons may be defined in the most frequent New Testament expressions used to refer to demonic possession: 1) *daimonizomai*, meaning "to be demonized"; and 2) *echon daimonion*, which means "having a demon," and can actually denote a person who *possesses the demon*, not the other way around. In the Bible, this might describe persons like Saul, who sought out a woman possessed by a "familiar spirit" to summon the deceased Samuel, even though he knew God's commandment not to allow such practices in Israel (1 Samuel 28), and possibly Judas Iscariot, into whom "Satan entered" (Luke 22:3) as a result of his decision to do what his heart may have told him was betrayal of God. In *echon daimonion*, it is therefore one of the premises that territory can be surrendered to evil spirits by persons actually reaching out to and "taking hold of the demon" through willingly choosing to do what they otherwise know is satanic. That some people are not only aware of this marriage with evil, but they energetically nurture it, is difficult for most of us to understand—yet the reality exists and is growing. An example of one such person was brought to us for treatment decades ago while we were still involved with exorcism. It involved a young woman who was released from a mental institution to spend a week under the care of her family, and her family, who sought help from the church because they believed her condition was the result of diabolical possession. Having been approached by a relative of the girl, we were told how, over time, she had become withdrawn and eventually delusional. She began hearing voices and held lengthy conversations with what appeared to be empty rooms. Finally, her condition became so detached from physical reality that she had to be placed in a psychiatric facility. As time went on and her condition worsened, prayer for her by her family was met with hostility and then outright violence, and her parents were desperate for help. After consulting with our group, an agreement was reached to have the young woman brought in for evaluation. We requested privacy and asked that a limited number of family members be present. Her caregiver agreed, and the story of the girl and what happened that week remains private. What we can say is that hers was the only case ever examined by our group in which the rare determination was made that while this person was truly possessed, exorcism was not an option. The simple reason was (the reader would understand if the unthinkable facts could be published) that she actually wanted the demons. They had a right to be there.

Interestingly, some years later, the authors of this book were back in the same city and noticed that our host pastor looked tired. We asked him if it had been a busy week, and he proceeded to tell us about an exorcism he had participated in a few days earlier. As he recounted the story of a certain possessed woman and how the church had fasted and prayed for a week, followed by seventeen hours during which a select group of ministers in a private room drove multiple demons from her, we realized he was talking about the girl from the institution. We remained quiet as he repeated the exhausting story, telling of the many personalities and voices they encountered during the drawn-out ritual. He claimed that when the last spirit finally came out of her, she sat up and for the first time appeared lucid. When they asked her if she wanted to accept Jesus as Savior, she began cursing and crying, complaining that he and the others had made her friends go away. Through chest-heaving sobs, she began calling out to unknown persons by name. As she did, the pastor said he felt something move across the room into her. Her eyes rolled back, and once again she lost control of her faculties. The exorcism ended.

While the experience above is a glaring illustration of one aspect of *echon daimonion,* in which a person seeks out and "possesses the demon," over the years when on those few occasions we witnessed what was considered authentic possession (as opposed to most cases evaluated as psychological or biological issues), it was typically *daimonizomai,* wherein the individual did not want to be under the spirit's influence. Without doubt our most exceptional and public encounter with such a victim (*daimonizomai*) was recorded very early in our ministry in the book, *Spiritual Warfare: The Invisible Invasion.* The story from that work recounted how, when we were in our twenties and pastoring our first church, a supernatural event took place that was observed by dozens of eye witnesses. A portion of the chronicle reads:

> The meeting had been evangelistic in style and I [Tom] was physically exhausted. I was looking forward to my easy chair and a short nap before the evening service. I had no idea what was about to transpire. For several weeks, my sermon discussions had included thoughts on Satan's social and cultural influences, yet having no real experience with the supernatural, I was left to muster only so much doctrinal theory when it came to the subject. All of that was about to change.
>
> As I walked out the front of the church, the friendly chatter and usual handshaking by congregants was interrupted by a strange young woman who seemed to come from out of nowhere and was motioning for my attention. As she ran up to me waving her hands, muttering something about her "boyfriend" and gesturing that I follow, she moved quickly through the crowd, glancing back occasionally to make sure I was following.
>
> A moment later, she came to a standstill and pointed toward an unfamiliar vehicle sitting in the parking lot. "He told me to turn in here and park," she said. Unaware of the circumstances and surrounded by dozens of church members, I put on my best pastor's face and walked toward the automobile. As I did, what I can only describe as an ethereal uneasiness swept over me. A few more steps and I surprised myself by whispering, *Lord, the battle is yours.* I wasn't sure why I had

said it, only that somewhere deep inside, it had been prompted.

I could see a mat of tangled hair atop what was obviously a young man hunched over in the passenger seat of the car. Slowly, I approached and tapped him on the shoulder, intending to ask how I could be of help. I didn't get the chance. Without warning, his head jerked violently upward to expose a wild and beastlike snarl. The sudden action took me so off guard that I gasped and jumped backward several feet. His face, distorted and spattered in blood, looked like it had been beaten with a tire iron. He glared at me and spoke through a guttural tone; "Man of God," he said, "I'm going to kill you!" At that, he leaped over the door jackrabbit fast, shouting, "You're going to die, man of God...*I'm going to kill you!*"

My thoughts raced. I contemplated running—and probably would have—but before I could get my legs moving, a strange calm moved over me unlike anything I had experienced before. They say that when you are in the midst of an automobile accident or similar harrowing experience, time slows down. That's what happened here. Though moments earlier I had whispered, *Lord, the battle is yours*, now it was like someone else was in control of my body and mind as I observed the events unfolding around me. It was a good thing, too, because as several church members approached the commotion, the young man ran towards me—his eyes glaring and teeth snarling—and leaped through the air to tackle me.

But…and this is where it requires faith to understand what happened, he hit something invisible. I know how this sounds, and if it wasn't for the dozens of others who witnessed the phenomenon that day, I wouldn't repeat it here. Yet as surely as if he had slammed into a solid wall, something abruptly stopped the demoniac's flight. Falling straight to the ground with a look of astonishment, he began convulsing and thrashing wildly about. A second later, he jumped to his feet again, this time his jaws gritting together so hard we could hear what sounded like his teeth or bones cracking. His eyes rolled back in their sockets and his body began twisting like a contortionist, reminiscent of special effects in the film *The Exorcist*. His arms turned backward; his legs, fingers, neck, and head began bending the wrong direction, and his body writhed and trembled as blood began pouring from his mouth and nose. It was as if large invisible hands were rending him like a garment.

As more people walked out of the church and saw what was happening, the possessed youth collapsed again. Several of the biggest men took note and ran over and grabbed his arms and legs to restrain him. When they did, his eyes opened and he smiled, lifting the burly members off him as if they were small children. He grabbed a large, three-inch wide occult medallion that was hanging around his neck, pulling it with such force that he easily snapped the thick chain. He shoved the amulet and metal links into his mouth and began chewing on them, trying to swallow it all, until one of the men caught the chain and quickly pulled it out. With that, the tortured boy's hands went wild, beating and plucking at his head uncontrollably, tearing his face and eyes. The scene reminded of the young demoniac in the ninth chapter of the book of Mark, where the spirit "cast him into the fire, and into the waters, to destroy him." In the Gospels, accounts of possession reveal that some spirits upon being exorcised will attempt to destroy their hosts. In this case, like the wild man of Gadara who cried and cut himself with stones, the boy who had come to us for help was incapable of overcoming the malevolent force on his own. Thankfully, after only a few minutes, an amazing and important thing happened. In the midst of the struggle, I thought I heard a faint appeal. It was just a whisper, really. Yet I was sure I had caught the young man saying, "Please...help me." I listened closely, and between the snarling and threatening curses, I heard it again, *"Help me."* It's hard to describe my emotions at that moment, but somehow I knew the battle would soon be over. Notwithstanding an energetic, demonic last stand, accompanied by visible manifestations of super-human strength and possibly ectoplasm that moved up and spewed out from his mouth, a lasting and complete deliverance was eventually made. We glorified God and celebrated the living power and authority of Jesus Christ that day, at whose name every power in heaven, on earth, and under the earth must bow.

A final important note needs to be made about the account above. At the very moment the possessed youth convulsed and the demon came out of him, a herd of horses that had been drawn to the noise and gathered across the road watching began kicking, neighing, and running frantically the opposite direction. Throughout the neighborhood, dogs started howling an eerie, baleful wail (facts that will be important in the third section of this book), and for several weeks following, a campaign of intimidation flowed from the dark kingdom in what we can only imagine was an attempt to discourage further revelations concerning its human agenda. During that time, even our phone would ring in the middle of the night and a growling voice on the other end of the line would say, "This is principality, and I know who you are."

CHAPTER FIVE

DAIMONIONS INSIDE THE CHURCH

I saw the LORD sitting upon his throne, and all the host
of heaven standing on his right hand and on his left. And
the LORD said, "Who shall entice Ahab king of Israel, that
he may go up and fall at Ramothgilead?" And one spake
after this manner, and another saying after that manner.
Then there came out a spirit, and stood before the Lord,
and said, "I will entice him." And the LORD said unto him,
"Wherewith?" And he said, "I will go out, and be a lying
spirit in the mouth of all his prophets."

—2 CHRONICLES 18:18B–21A

W hile the pages of nearly all books on spiritual warfare
abound with examples of people becoming possessed
or demonized by entities as a result of deviant perversion, drug use, violence, occultism (as in the case of the young
man in the previous chapter), or other depravations of immoral
behavior, including infidelity and witchcraft, the most powerful instruments of satanic bondage by far witnessed during
our thirty-plus years of executive ministry were connected to
something much more dangerous than personal failings. The

superior enemies to which we refer are *demons of religion* that infest institutional Christianity.

This is not a daring statement.

Just as a lying spirit filled the mouths of the prophets in 2 Chronicles 18, and just as Jesus confronted unclean spirits inside the synagogue (Mark 1:23) and connected some of the priestly leaders of the Temple to the strongest power of Satan on earth (John 8:44; Matthew 13:38 and 23:15), robust *echon daimonion* exists today from the lowest to the highest levels of denominational establishment among institutional members who are possessed (whether they perceive it as such or not) by Luciferian ambition. This will come as no surprise to seasoned spiritual warriors, as it is the result of a common military strategy. The church represents the single establishment on earth capable of undoing Satan's plans, and is therefore the natural enemy of the kingdom of darkness and the epicenter against which all spiritual wickedness must ultimately be focused. The church, through its hierarchies and institutional constructs, is therefore the primary target for infiltration by agents of darkness wherever human weakness allows for penetration by *daimonions*. Among others, the apostle Paul recognized this specific danger, warning the church in Corinth that "false apostles" were masquerading among them as ministers of Christ. "And no marvel," he revealed, "for Satan himself is transformed into an angel of light. Therefore it is no great thing if his ministers also be transformed as the ministers of righteousness" (2 Corinthians 11:13–15).

Consistent with this phenomenon, Father Gabriele Amorth, a renowned exorcist in Rome whose book, *Memoirs of an Exorcist: My Life Fighting against Satan*, was released in 2010, admits to the existence of "satanic sects in the Vatican where participation reaches all the way to the College of Cardinals." When asked if the Pope was aware of this situation, he replied, "Of course."[13] Other Catholic priests—some deceased now, including Father John F. O'Connor, Father Alfred Kunz, and Father Malachi Martin—were likewise surprisingly outspoken in recent history on the secret satanic influences in the Vatican. In a two-hour presentation (available on DVD), Father O'Connor gave a homily titled "The Reign of the Antichrist," in which he described how sinister forces within the institution were already at work before his death to provide for the coming of Antichrist. In this sermon and elsewhere, O'Connor outlined the catalyst for this scheme unfolding as a result of "conspirators" within the church whose plan, called "Alta Vendetta," would essentially take control of the papacy and help the False Prophet deceive the world's faithful (including Catholics) into worshipping Antichrist.

O'Connor was not alone as whistleblower to the occult presence within the Vatican's ranks. Retired professor of the Pontifical Biblical Institute, eminent Catholic theologian, and former Jesuit priest, Malachi Martin was a close personal friend of Pope Paul VI. He worked within the Holy See doing research on the Dead Sea Scrolls, publishing articles in journals on Semitic paleography, and teaching Aramaic, Hebrew, and sacred Scripture. In 1965, Paul VI granted Martin a dispensation from his Jesuit and priestly duties, and Martin moved to New York, where he dedicated himself to writing about—and sometimes speaking out on—a variety of issues stemming from the Second Vatican Council to detailed insider accounts of papal history, Catholic dogma, and geopolitics. As a member of the

Vatican Advisory Council and personal secretary to renowned Jesuit Cardinal Augustin Bea, Martin had privileged information pertaining to secretive church and world issues, including the third secret of Fatima, which Martin hinted spelled out parts of the plan to formerly install the dreaded False Prophet during a "Final Conclave." On this, Martin's claim that a secret group—made up of Western plutocrats called the "Assembly" or the "Superforce"—had infiltrated the highest levels of Vatican administration and was working on an occult plot may have led to involvement by operatives of the same group concerning his untimely, some say "suspicious," death in 1999.

Ten years earlier, before "something pushed him" and Malachi Martin fell and later died, he had become increasingly candid about what he said was Satanism among certain cardinals and other clergy in league with a secret diabolicus that began following the "enthronement of the fallen Archangel Lucifer" in the Roman Catholic Citadel on June 29, 1963.

Whether Martin was killed and his death covered up for revealing the plan to use the Catholic Church as a launching pad for a Luciferic *novus ordo seclorum* may never be known. One year before he died, however, Martin's very good friend, Father Kunz, was brutally murdered in his church in Dane, Wisconsin. Kunz had been investigating the same Satanism among "priests" that Martin had warned about, and had told Martin in the weeks before his murder that he feared for his life. When Kunz was found with his throat slit, Martin went public that the "Luciferians" had killed him because he was getting ready to blow the lid off their conspiracy.

Writing about similar activity within evangelical institutions, Rev. David Wilkerson reported not long ago that:

A number of [former] witches are...warning that Satanists are infiltrating the church—especially charismatic churches. Some of these [are] telling of a diabolical plot by evil witches to enter congregations posing as super-spiritual Christians.... Many of these evil witches, they say, are already firmly established in numerous churches, controlling both the pastor and congregation and causing great confusion, wickedness, divorce—even death. We have received many letters in our office from people who say they believe their pastor must be under some kind of demonic influence—and I believe many of these letters are very legitimate.[14]

Wilkerson, who at one time was a member of the same organization we served, is correct in asserting that some of those who pose as super-spiritual Christians, department leaders, pastors, and even state office holders and denominational headquarters executives are in fact instruments of evil. Thankfully, there are other church members, pastors, and leaders who, as sincere believers, have become increasingly aware of this sinister invasion into organizations by *daimonions* and in recent years have made special efforts to teach their congregations how to identify the differences between "religious spirits" and true Christianity. Simply put, the words of Jesus that "ye shall know them by their fruits" (Matthew 7:15–16) have never been more important. These instructions of Christ should also serve as a warning to all believers to monitor their own motives, to examine their hearts, if truly they are altruistic or if in fact they are energized by selfish ambition, because the latter is the "Luciferian key" to becoming demonized.

While serving within the institutionalized church, we certainly witnessed both types of "believers" and have strong memories of the spiritual differences between the two. Recently, while searching for a particular document we had placed in an old photo album some time ago for safekeeping, we took an unexpected stroll down memory lane in this regard. We had gone through at least a dozen books of images and old newspaper clippings, seeing members of churches we had pastored and records of events frozen in time from nearly thirty years inside the organization. Finally, between dusty storage bins and spiderwebs, we found what we were looking for. We placed the coveted item among the research notes for this book, then returned everything else to the closets.

That should have been that, but for the next week, the old memories in those boxes kept calling to us about things and friends from the past—people who represented the true mission of the church and were wonderful examples of what it really means to be a Christian. Their names would not be recognized by most today—dedicated believers like O. R. Cross, Henrietta Stewart, Lorraine Morgan, Wyoming Rosebud Dollar, C. K. Barnes, Eugene and Evelyn Fuller, Annie Walton, and others of the New Testament clan.

And then there was another group hiding in plain sight among the believers, sometimes even leading them—the ones the Bible calls "clouds without water, carried about of winds; trees whose fruit withereth, without fruit, twice dead, plucked up by the roots" (Jude 1:12).

Among this second class were—and still are—some fantastic heretics we have known.

Take our old friend Carlton Pearson, for instance. When we were pastoring near Portland, Oregon, during the eighties, our church was the host for TBN's West Coast broadcasts and special events in which some of America's top evangelists—including Carlton—appeared almost nightly for a while. In those days, the church was in flux. The Great Generation with its faith of the fathers was getting older, and errant doctrines made delicious by these nasty end-time agents known as *daimonions* were finding more and more willing hearts who were having the time of their lives abandoning solid theology in exchange for such teachings as the "Doctrine of Inclusion" (in which nobody goes to hell), eventually branding such false prophets as heretics (including Carlton Pearson) among thoughtful evangelicals. We can tell you that Carlton didn't start out that way. He was a sweet man with a heart of gold who unfortunately lost his way and embraced delusion. God only knows how many he has since led astray.

MIKE MURDOCK	LAVERNE TRIPP	CARLTON PEARSON	DWIGHT THOMPSON
FEB. 13, 1988	FEB. 22nd	MARCH 7, 8, 9	APRIL 9-10

Old newspaper clipping from 1988—featuring a week of speakers at the church where Thomas and Nita Horn pastored—includes Carlton Pearson.

Then there were those who adopted things far worse than "Inclusion"—for instance, "Kingdom Age" theology (also known as Reconstructionism, Kingdom Now Theology, Theonomy, Dominion Theology, and most recently, Dominionism), which singularly has wrought some of the most far-reaching destruction within the body of Christ this century.

Dominionism is a form of hyper-Calvinism (though supported by both reconstructionists and nonreconstructionists) that ultimately seeks to establish the Kingdom of God on earth through the union of politics and religion. Though ravenously popular among most talking heads for the Religious Right, combining religious faith with politics as a legislative system of governance such as Dominionism would do, hearkens the formula upon which Antichrist will come to power. Note how in the book of Revelation, chapter 13, the *political* figure of Antichrist derives ultranational dominance from the world's *religious* faithful through the influence of an ecclesiastical leader known as the False Prophet. Similar political enthusiasm exists among Dominionists despite the fact that neither Jesus nor His disciples (who turned the world upside down through preaching the gospel of Christ, the true "power of God," according to Paul) ever imagined the goal of changing the world through supplanting secular government with an authoritarian theocracy. In fact, Jesus made it clear that His followers would not fight earthly authorities purely because His kingdom was "not of this world" (John 18:36). While every modern citizen—religious and nonreligious—has responsibility to lobby for moral good, combining the mission of the church with political aspirations is not only unprecedented in New Testament theology—including the life of Christ and the pattern of the New

Testament church—but a tragic scheme concocted by sinister forces that seek to defer the church from its true power while enriching insincere bureaucrats.

But while great heresies like Dominionism and Inclusion are, or should be, self-evident, other contenders for the most spectacular doctrines of devils in the church today would have to include the Prosperity Movement, Ecumenical Modernism, and Dual Covenant (wherein Jews do not need to accept Jesus as Messiah) espoused by some surprisingly well-known modern evangelical preachers. Yet those aged voices that called out to us recently from our fading boxes of memories also reminded that while it's easy today to get an "amen" while condemning the big lie of Dominionism, the most insidious doctrines are those "smaller lucifers" that are often harder to perceive. For instance, how easy it is (and was) to see through the glaring examples of self-serving and lavish lifestyles that some of our old televangelist friends sought support for, while overlooking or even excusing Luciferianism (selfishness) that is measured in the tiniest of portions, minute amounts so cleverly concealed within subtle and popular doctrines today that they are nearly impossible to detect.

Ask any evangelist who has tried to take the gospel outside the four doors of the local assembly what we mean by this and hear them repeat stories of how quickly certain church members arose to resist the plan and grumble over the resources that could otherwise be used to benefit *them*. This is the cancer that two decades of Prosperity preaching, inward focusing, and "me-ism" have produced. Of course, most of these anti-evangelists wrap their Luciferianism in nifty religious phrases—like Judas Iscariot did when he pretended to care for the poor but secretly wanted to steal the value of the oil that was used to anoint the feet of Jesus (John 12:1–6). These types resemble Judas in another way as well: They don't even know how they are thus being used as fleshy gloves, the earthen hands of that invisible spirit, the master of waterless clouds operating within or behind them that hates true fishers of men. But for those with eyes to see, the father of lies always gives himself away through his envy of others, seeking what he can gain from—not what he can give to—believers and religion, then pretending something is wrong with those he cannot control, those who get things done like Jesus did, disparaging them while he himself accomplishes nothing but division, diversion, and destruction.

Perhaps you have seen this spirit in the actions or heard it in the mouths of people you thought were your partners. When once you (or somebody you knew) had nothing more to give them, they turned away from you—or worse, against you—and revealed the awful truth: Their religious spirit had only ever come for what it could get, gain, take, and absorb, and then it turned "to kill and to destroy" (John 10:10a).

It was, in fact, one such incident that formed the final straw leading to the decision by these writers to leave the religious institution we had been devoted to for decades, a church organization that at least on the state level had become so criminally corrupt (an investigation regarding possible federal charges against the organization is, at the time of the writing of this book, under consideration, and we have been contacted by authorities as potential material witnesses) and infiltrated by deceptive spirits that we could no longer be part of it. But the specific situation that finally "broke the camel's back" and led to our resignation was referred to a few years ago at www. RaidersNewsNetwork.com and then by several other major news sources under the critical editorial, "New Testament Theology, According to the Vampire Lestat." A portion of that article reads:

> I [Tom] suppose when most people think of actual demonic manifestations, they recall images such as Linda Blair slithering snake-like along the floor in the movie *The Exorcist*. To be honest, during the experiences I had with exorcism, superhuman strength similar to that fictionalized in popular films and vampire lore was manifest only once. The greatest encounters I had with evil supernaturalism by far (and which I may document when the time is right), which was confronted on more than one occasion by myself, my staff, and my family, was a "spirit of religion" that wielded significant influence among church-institution leaders....
>
> Such spirits are identified in the Bible and in the actions of those who are possessed by them. They produce megalomaniacs who seek to exalt their throne while taking particular delight in enforcing private rules by which they judge the righteousness of others. They compass the world to make one disciple, "then make it twofold more a child of hell than they are themselves" (Matthew 23:15). These incredibly deceptive mummers seek institutional positions where they can nourish Christ-less attitudes among church leadership, teaching their hosts how, as actors, they must suppress their true

personality while emulating sincerity so that their victims will accept as real the "character" they portray.

Mastering dialectics thus becomes very important for the mummers to succeed. They must also develop good vocal projection for the stage, physical expressiveness, improvisation, emotional drama, and even be capable of reciting classical texts or Scripture when necessary. Well-rounded mummers will even learn singing and other performing arts, so that their false anointing will appeal to human weaknesses and convince us that they are genuine. Most of all, they need for their words to resonate as believable in order to keep their innocent victims mesmerized, at least until their life-force can be completely drained from them.

Of course, the biggest problem for such vampires is the true power of the cross, and how if they are not careful it will scorch away their cover and reveal the apathy they have for their victims.

Son-light is another problem. Vampires perish if exposed for very long to anything but synthetic illumination.

And of course there are sanctified places where vampires can never go, such as the deepest recesses of a true believer's soul. The greatest vampire killer of all time once said, "Do not fear those who kill the body but cannot kill the soul" (Matthew 10:28).

I thought of those words recently, during the passing of a dear friend. To protect her identity, I will simply call her Nettie (not her real name).

Like so many true Christians, Nettie had given her life to the ministry of others. As a result, she had very few earthly possessions and certainly nothing to compare with the wealth that is typical of Lestat-like vampires.

However, Nettie did own a home. The appraised value was a mere thirty-five thousand dollars, so it is easy to see the modesty of her lifestyle in today's United States.

Still, the place was hers.

Early last year [2006], knowing she was getting too old to live alone anymore and that ultimately she would need to be cared for by her daughter, Nettie made a deal to sell her house to the religious institution we both had worked for. Nettie had served tirelessly and without pay for the organization for several decades. As executive director of a particular board, I was familiar with the district office's interest in acquiring land, and I was there when several properties, including Nettie's, were approved for purchase. Though Nettie's was the least expensive, the other properties were owned by younger, healthier persons, not nearly as easy to victimize as Nettie, and so these were paid off immediately and closed escrow posthaste. Nettie, on the other hand waited, and deteriorated, until her body and mind slowly began giving in to the last enemy she faced—death. As the end drew near and she needed money for medical expenses, she asked my wife to check in with the Christian organization's state office to see when she would be paid.

"Well, since Nettie is going to die before long," the secretary for the coven's head vampire stammered, "We've decided just to wait, since we'll inherit the property anyway once she's gone."

My wife was in shock. Yet unlike her, I'd been inside the vaults and among the vampires long enough to understand how mummers think. We both cried a few months later when Nettie, still hoping for some crumbs to fall from the rich man's table, had a stroke and died not very long afterward.

For me, it was the last straw. After almost thirty years in the theatre I decided I would be better off not treading the rafters anymore. I had made some great friends and there are still some vampire hunters in the organization I respect, but the glory days are gone and the theatre's headquarters have become too infested with spiderwebs, moths, bats, and other creepy things.

Yet I would leave a warning behind for vampires everywhere. For those who would sell their soul to the devil for thirty-five thousand dollars worth of real estate, you've done all that you can do to hurt the old woman who will rise up in judgment against you in the day that matters most.

Of course, I suppose until then, you could wring the blood out of the money and use it to purchase some really cool new capes or a row of dazzling lights to keep your audience spellbound.[15]

If the reader picks up on a bit of righteous indignation in the excerpt above, you have perceptively discerned why we came to believe that we had to break away from the institution, if for no other reason than to preserve our own spiritual health. If it also sounds like we were being judgmental, correct again. In 1 Peter 4:17, we read that "judgment must begin at the house of God." People who care about modern Christianity should consider that a time for such introspection and judgment is long overdue. We are in a battle—a spiritual war for the minds and souls of a generation—and frankly, the time has come for new Martin Luthers to nail their theses on some institution doors where *echon daimonion* may have become so deeply entrenched as to have literally forged the latter-day "habitation of devils, and the hold of every foul spirit, and a cage of every unclean and hateful bird" (Revelation 18:2).

CHAPTER SIX

TEMPTATION, INFLUENCE, OBSESSION, DEMONIZATION, POSSESSION

Wherever God erects a house of prayer, The Devil
always builds a chapel there; And 't will be found, upon
examination, The latter has the largest congregation.

—DANIEL DEFOE

And he called them unto him, and said unto them in
parables, "How can Satan cast out Satan? And if a kingdom
be divided against itself, that kingdom cannot stand."

—MARK 3:23–24

Given the content of the previous chapter and the inevitability during the study of spiritual warfare that the thorny (if not polarizing) question will arise concerning whether true Christians can become demon possessed, we need to state unequivocally at this juncture that although *daimonizomai* ("to be demonized") and *echon daimonion* ("having a demon") are manifested within institutionalized Christianity, it is our belief that those who are truly born again can never actually be *possessed*—as in *inhabited*—by demons. There are numerous reasons for this conclusion, not the least of which is that there are no instances of "possession" of believers anywhere in the Bible. Not a single verse in the Scripture even warns of the possibility, and there are zero examples in the life of Jesus Christ and the early church of demons being cast out of Christians.

What we do find in Scripture regarding the inner space of believers is that our body "is the temple of the Holy Ghost, which is in you, which ye have of God, and ye are not your own" (1 Corinthians 6:19). In fact, John writes that "he that is begotten of God, keepeth himself, and that wicked one toucheth him not" (1 John 5:18). Therefore, "What communion hath light with darkness? And what concord hath Christ with Belial…. And what agreement hath the temple of God with idols? for ye are the temple of the living God; as God hath said, 'I will dwell in them; and I will be their God, and they shall be my people'" (2 Corinthians 6:14b–16). These and similar Scriptures verify for those who have the Holy Spirit residing within them that they are positively redeemed and sealed from the torment of diabolical possession. As John also certified, "If the Son therefore shall make you free, ye shall be free indeed" (John 8:36).

Though in recent years, burgeoning "Christian deliverance ministries" have suggested otherwise, claiming that *daimonizomai* and *echon daimonion* infer the Lord's body can actually be inhabited by demons, it is usually a matter of semantics. Confusion over the meaning of the terms "possession" and "demonization" is somewhat understandable from an exegetical standpoint, especially given how *daimonizomai* is used in Scripture to refer to a variety of problems and demonic manifestations. But because it is dangerous to promote precise definitions where none exist in Scripture, it should be noted that the actual phrase "demon possession" does not even appear in the Bible (Josephus coined this phrase near the end of the first century), and what some teachers classify as "possession" is actually demonization—a spirit from an external posture gains control or influence over a person. As such, literal possession is different than demonization, and ample evidence exists in the New Testament to conclude that whereas believers may never be "possessed," they most certainly can be tempted, influenced, oppressed, and even demonized by evil supernaturalism. To this end, the apostle Paul warned the Christians at Ephesus (Ephesians 4:25–31) not to give "place" (Greek: *topos*) to the devil, meaning a foothold, opportunity, power, occasion for acting, or doorway into one's personal space through which demonic strongholds can be established. Paul even listed particular behaviors that could lead to this fiend-ish union—lying, anger, wrath, stealing, bitterness, clamor, evil speaking (Greek *blasphemia:* "to blaspheme, gossip, slander others"), and malice. Elsewhere in the Bible, we learn that door-ways for agents of Satan to enter a believer's life can also include encumbrances like fear, such as the fear that led Peter to deny Christ in Luke chapter 22 and that Jesus made clear was an effort by Satan to cause Peter to stumble (v. 31), and greed—as illustrated in the story of Ananias and Sapphira in Acts chapter 5, where "Satan" (v. 3) filled the couple's hearts to lie and to hold back a portion of money. Demonization of a Christian through these and similar weaknesses is usually gradual, where small decisions are made over an extended period of time dur-ing which the individual gives in to temptation, followed by ongoing and progressive surrender of territory within the mind and finally the flesh. Such steps to demonization may be sum-marized accordingly:

Temptation: The enemy discovers a weakness and appeals to it.

Influence: The individual entertains the idea and finally gives in to temptation. A foothold is established in the person's life, making it harder to resist the same or related activity in the future.

Obsession: The activity eventually becomes an unhealthy pre-occupation and irresistible impulse leading to critical degrees of control over the individual. The power to resist is practically gone.

Demonization: Control over the individual by external power becomes substantial. What at one time was considered sinful and to be avoided is now an addiction. The person may no longer even recognize the tendency as immoral, and little or no fortitude to cease participating in the activity remains.

Possession: This can occur if the individual turns his or her back on God so as to fully embrace carnality, surrendering the body and mind to Satan's control. The desire to resist invasion by discarnate supernaturalism is vacated.

What immediately stands out in these steps and doorways to demonization is how central the mind of man is to the functioning battleground where spiritual warfare takes place. Whether it is lying, anger, wrath, stealing, bitterness, clamor, evil speaking, malice, fear, greed, or another human frailty, the battle begins in our thought life where we are tempted to give in to sin. "That's where Satan can manipulate people toward his ends discreetly and invisibly," writes Chip Ingram in *The Invisible War.* "If he can distort our thoughts, our emotions, and our knowledge, then our behaviors and relationships will fall the way he wants them to. And even if he doesn't manage to turn us to overt evil, a little bit of distorted thinking can neutralize us and render us practically ineffective."[16] In other words, if Satan cannot possess or demonize an individual, he will settle for what he can get, influencing the mind and spirit to whatever extent he can, keeping people ineffective or causing them to become a problem for their families, their communities, or their churches.

The emphasis on the human mind as the primary battleground upon which the forces of good and evil struggle to dominate the will of men not only fills the pages of Scripture but was recognized by many ancient cultures, including the Greeks, who were so intrigued by the concept that they literally built a large part of the fables of their thirteenth god, Dionysus, around it. Often depicted by modern writers as the inventor of wine, abandon, and revelry, these descriptions are inadequate in that they refer only to the basic elements of intoxication and enthusiasm that were used as tools by the Bacchae (the female participants of the Dionystic mysteries, also known as Maenads and Bacchantes) in their rituals to experience the intoxicating god of unbridled human desire. Followers of Dionysus believed that he was actually the *presence* that is otherwise defined as the craving within man that longs to "let itself go" and to "give itself over" to base earthly desires. What a Christian might resist as the lustful wants of the carnal man, the followers of Dionysus embraced as the incarnate power that would, in the next life, liberate the souls of men from the constraints of the present world and from the customs that sought to define respectability through a person's obedience to moral law. Until that "liberating" day arrived, the worshippers of Dionysus attempted to bring themselves into union with the god through a ritual casting off of the bonds of sexual denial and primal constraint by seeking to attain the higher state of *ecstasy*. The uninhibited rituals of *ecstasy* (Greek for "outside the body") were thought to bring followers of Dionysus into a supernatural condition that enabled them to escape the temporary limitations of the body and mind and to achieve a state of *enthousiasmos*, or "outside the body and inside the god." In this sense, Dionysus represented a dichotomy within the Greek religion, as the primary maxim of the Greek culture was one of moderation, or "nothing too extreme." But Dionysus embodied the absolute extreme in that he sought to inflame the forbidden passions of human desire within the mind.

Interestingly, as most students of psychology will understand, this gave Dionysus a stronger allure among the Greeks who otherwise tried in so many ways to suppress and control the wild and secret lusts of the human heart. But Dionysus resisted every such effort and, according to myth, visited a terrible madness upon those who would deny him free expression. The Dionystic idea of mental disease resulting from the suppression of secret inner desires, especially aberrant sexual desires, was later reflected in the teachings of Sigmund Freud. Freudianism might therefore be thought of as the grandchild of the cult of Dionysus. Conversely, the person who gave himself over to the will of Dionysus was rewarded with unlimited psychological and physical delights. Such mythical systems of mental punishments and physical rewards based on resistance and/or submission to Dionysus were both symbolically and literally illustrated in the cult rituals of the Bacchae, as the Bacchae women (married and unmarried Greek women had the "right" to participate in the mysteries of Dionysus) migrated in frenzied hillside groups, dressed transvestite in fawn skins and accompanied by screaming, music, dancing, and licentious behavior.

When, for instance, a baby animal was too young and lacking in instinct to sense the danger and run away from the revelers, it was picked up and suckled by nursing mothers who participated in the hillside rituals. But when older animals sought to escape the marauding Bacchae, they were considered "resistant" to the will of Dionysus and were torn apart and eaten alive as a part of the fevered ritual. Human participants were sometimes subjected to the same orgiastic cruelty, as the rule of the cult was "anything goes," including lesbianism and bestiality. Later versions of the ritual (bacchanalia) expanded to include pedophilia and male revelers, and perversions of sexual behavior were often worse between men than they were between men and women. Any creature that dared to resist such perversion of Dionysus could be subjected to *sparagmos* ("torn apart") and *omophagia* ("consumed raw").

In 410 BC, Euripides wrote of the bloody rituals of the Bacchae in his famous play, *The Bacchantes*:

The Bacchantes…with hands that bore no weapon of steel, attacked our cattle as they browsed. Then wouldst thou have seen Agave mastering some sleek lowing calf, while others rent the heifers limb from limb. Before thy eyes there would have been hurling of ribs and hoofs this way and that, and strips of flesh, all blood be-dabbled, dripped as they hung from the pine branches. Wild bulls, that glared but now with rage along their horns, found themselves tripped up, dragged down to earth by countless maidens hands.

Euripedes went on to describe how Pentheus, the King of Thebes, was torn apart and eaten alive by his own mother as, according to the play, she fell under the spell of Dionysus. The tearing apart and eating alive of a sacrificial victim may refer to the earliest history of the cult of Dionysus. An ancient and violent cult ritual existing since the dawn of paganism stipulated that by eating alive (or by drinking the blood of) an enemy or an animal, a person might somehow capture the essence, or "soul strength," of the victim. The earliest Norwegian huntsmen believed in this idea, and they drank the blood of bears in an effort to capture their physical strength. East African Masai warriors also practiced omophagia, and they sought to gain the strength of the wild by drinking the blood of lions. Human victims were treated in this way by Arabs before Mohammed, and headhunters of the East Indies practiced omophagia in an effort to capture the essence of their enemies.

Today, omophagia is practiced by certain voodoo sects as well as by cult satanists, and it should be pointed out that in some cases it is a demonization of the Eucharist, or Holy Communion. But sparagmos and omophagia, as practiced by the followers of Dionysus, were not an attempt of transubstantiation (as in the Catholic Eucharist) or of consubstantiation (as in the Lutheran communion), or yet of a symbolic ordinance (as in the fundamentalist denomination)—all of which have as a common goal the elevating of the worshipper into a sacramental communion with God. The goal of the Bacchae was the opposite. The frenzied dance, the thunderous song, the licentious behavior, the tearing apart and eating alive—all were efforts on the part of the Bacchae to capture the essence of the god (Dionysus) and bring him down into an incarnated rage within man. The idea was not one of Holy Communion, but of *possession* by the spirit of Dionysus. When one recalls the horrific rituals of the followers of Dionysus, it's easy to believe that such demonic possession actually occurred.

SO WHO'S IN CONTROL OF YOUR MIND?

Unfortunately in Christendom, it is within this same mind-domain battleground where vulnerable people can be controlled by satanic forces to cripple the effectiveness of the ministry. God only knows how many resources of time, energy, and money have been exhausted over the centuries as a result of "churchgoers" like those Jesus warned of when He said, "Many will say to me in that day, 'Lord, Lord, have we not prophesied in thy name? and in thy name have cast out devils? and in thy name done many wonderful works?' And then will I profess unto them, 'I never knew you: depart from me, ye that work iniquity'" (Matthew 7:22–23). In the parable of the tares and wheat, Jesus compared these types to weeds that germinate among devout believers (the wheat), choking their outgrowth until the day that He returns to judge them, while in the metaphor of the sheep and the goats, He described how, during this judgment, these "cursed" ones will be separated from the true believers and "shall go away into everlasting punishment." Matthew records this future event, saying:

> When the Son of man shall come in His glory, and all the holy angels with Him, then shall He sit upon the throne of His glory: And before Him shall be gathered all nations: and He shall separate them one from another, as a shepherd divideth his sheep from the goats: And He shall set the sheep on His right hand, but the goats on the left. Then shall the King say unto them on His right hand, "Come, ye blessed of my Father, inherit the kingdom prepared for you from the foundation of the world:" For I was an hungred, and ye gave me meat: I was thirsty, and ye gave me drink: I was a stranger, and ye took me in: Naked, and ye clothed me: I was sick, and ye visited me: I was in prison, and ye came unto me. Then shall the righteous answer him, saying, "Lord, when saw we thee an hungred, and fed thee? or thirsty, and gave thee drink? When saw we thee a stranger, and took thee in? or naked, and clothed thee? Or when saw we thee sick, or in prison, and came unto thee?" And the King shall answer and say unto them, "Verily I say unto you, Inasmuch as ye have done it unto one of the least of these my brethren, ye have done it unto me." Then shall He say also unto them on the left hand, "Depart from me, ye cursed, into everlasting fire, prepared for the devil and his angels: For I was an hungred, and ye gave me no meat: I was thirsty, and ye gave me no drink: I was a stranger, and ye took me not in: naked, and ye

clothed me not: sick, and in prison, and ye visited me not." Then shall they also answer him, saying, "Lord, when saw we thee an hungred, or athirst, or a stranger, or naked, or sick, or in prison, and did not minister unto thee?" Then shall He answer them, saying, "Verily I say unto you, 'Inasmuch as ye did it not to one of the least of these, ye did it not to me.' And these shall go away into everlasting punishment: but the righteous into life eternal. (Matthew 25:31–46)

When considering the verses above, it becomes frighteningly clear that those who lack discipline in their thought life and who drift into "playing church" are actually playing with fire. We cannot help but shudder at some of the congregants we have known through the years who surrendered their minds to malevolent religious spirits and afterward left a trail of questions, division, and destruction in their wake. As the reader, perhaps you at one time also observed such damage to a congregation before the responsible party moved down the road to repeat the mayhem elsewhere. Concerning these kind of troublesome individuals, Christians are often confused over what role, if any, spiritual warfare should play with respect to them—especially given that Ephesians 6:12 says "we wrestle not against flesh and blood." Yet hermeneutically speaking, it is often impossible to discern exactly how "principalities and powers" engage the church in warfare without taking the human element into account—that sometimes *people*, because of the choices they make, *are* the problem, or least a part of it. Second Timothy 4:14–15 illustrates that this is not a contradiction of Ephesians 6:12, as the writer of Ephesians himself refers to a man named

Alexander the coppersmith, saying that he "did me much evil: the Lord reward him according to his works: Of whom be thou ware also; for he hath greatly withstood our words [the Gospel]." The great commentator Matthew Henry says this text illustrates that "there is as much danger from false brethren, as from open enemies." Though Paul wrote the book on spiritual warfare, including the phrase, "we wrestle not against flesh and blood," he did not blame immaterial spirits that may have been operating behind Alexander the coppersmith. He named the man himself as the culprit and warned Timothy to beware of the damage he could do to the work of the ministry. The point to be made from this is not one of personal revenge toward a wrongdoer, but that wisdom is needed during spiritual warfare because prayer is most profitable when it is directed with specificity—in this case, recognizing the source of the problem, the conduit, even when it is made of flesh.

Jesus likewise verbalized the difference between people who attend religious services and become tools for evil as opposed to good, and we note with particular interest His genius in using the small yet powerful word "of" to contrast the two for His followers. In John 8:44, He said of the Pharisees, "Ye are *of* your father the devil, and the lusts of your father ye will do" (emphasis added), while in Luke 9:51–56, when James and John wanted to call fire down from heaven upon Samaritan villagers, He rebuked them and said, "Ye know not what manner of spirit ye are *of.* For the Son of man is not come to destroy men's lives; but to save them" (emphasis added).

This amazing yet insightful little term "of" probes beyond temporal human activity to identify whose dominion one belongs to and what spirit holds one's allegiance and offers one motivation. The Pharisees were "of" their father the devil, while the disciples James and John were still learning the nature of the spirit they were "of." The Word of God was therefore used by the Pharisees as a tool for destruction, illustrating what spirit they were "of," while Jesus and His followers used the same tool to give life to others.

Some years ago, one of the writers of this book (Nita) worked in a state department beneath a woman who was driven by similar thirst for Pharisee-like church authority and who not only made a habit of demeaning those under her but actually seemed to delight in being as hurtful as possible to people she viewed as not having the same level of political influence she did (though later she was disciplined for conspiring against state leaders). Her spirit seemed to especially enjoy using the Bible as a weapon to denigrate and control others. Nita did her best to simply stay out of the woman's way, but wasn't always successful. One day, with the woman's department department informational packet scheduled to be mailed and a distressed-looking secretary whose job it was to get them collated looking for assistance, Nita jumped in to help. A few moments later, the woman who could wield the Word like an unholy sword came in and began reciting a finely tuned sermon from memory. She was good with words and practiced at sermonizing, and this three-pointer was especially designed to illustrate this fact and to demean anybody not as eloquently instructed as she. When finished, she looked at Nita and said, "So, Nita, where are *you* in God's Word, hmm?" The sermon had its intended effect, and for a few moments Nita felt as unworthy to be in that office as the supervisor had probably hoped she would. *Who am I, really, to serve in this capacity as state director for a girl's ministry?* she thought to herself. *I don't preach, don't prophesy, and don't do miracles. I didn't even have time for devotions this morning.*

As the swordswoman cocked her head, somehow knowing she had found important organs, Nita answered, "Well, I usually have devotions each day. Right now, I'm using *My Utmost for His Highest* as an outline with my Bible reading." Then, for some reason, she added, "But, I didn't have devotions this morning. Time got away from me, and I had to hurry and hit the road to get here on time." It was a two-hour drive to the office one way.

"Well, Nita," the swordswoman replied caustically, turning aristocratically to walk away, "We *must* make sure that we are in God's Word so that we can be *good* examples to those under our leadership."

After helping the secretary finish her work, Nita returned to her office and placed her head in her hands. "Lord, why did you bring me here?" she prayed. "There are so many other women who are much more qualified than I am to lead this department. Women who somehow manage to read the Bible every day, quote Scriptures at the drop of a hat, and rattle off a perfect homiletic." Nita brooded and cried over the slight for nearly two weeks. Just to think that she had displeased her supervisor, set a poor example for the secretary…such shame. Then, a few days later, still feeling the pain, still asking God if she should resign so that a more worthy person like the supervisor could fill her spot, a profound but still quiet voice whispered to her, "Nita, your qualification to do what I have called you to do is not measured by where you are in my Word. The question is not 'Where are *you* in my Word, but where is *my Word* in you?' Satan knows my Word and can quote it *ad nauseam*, but it is not within him to do my will." In that moment, Nita bowed her head and asked forgiveness for doubting her placement in the state office.

Nita learned a valuable lesson that day. Knowing what spirit one is *of* and employing the Word of God accordingly is important. But how these basic facts will soon be elevated to historic, even preternatural, levels is revealed in the following chapters as we turn now in this study. This century, emerging technology will radically alter what it means to be human, and, in so doing, frighteningly—*even tangibly*—alter what is meant by "whom one is *of.*"

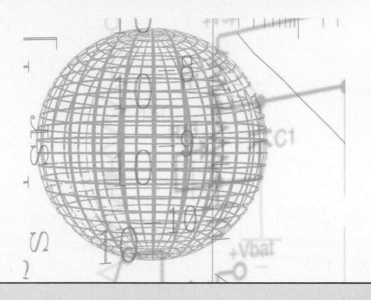

SECTION THREE

THE EMERGING BATTLEFIELD— READY OR NOT

CHAPTER SEVEN

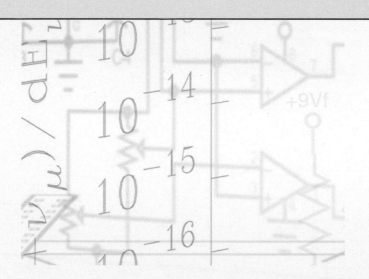

THE COMING BATTLE...WILL BE MORE THAN COSMISTS vs. TERRANS

The ability to tinker with our genes offers the astounding promise—and peril—of immortality, which mythically has been the defining difference between gods and mortals. It also offers the possibility of an even greater variety of breeds of humans than there is of dogs.

—JOEL GARREAU, *Radical Evolution*

The prospect of building godlike creatures fills me with a sense of religious awe that goes to the very depth of my soul and motivates me powerfully to continue, despite the possible horrible negative consequences.

—PROF. HUGO DE GARIS,
artificial brain designer

I n recent years, astonishing technological developments have pushed the frontiers of humanity toward far-reaching morphological transformation that promises in the very near future to redefine what it means to be human. An international, intellectual, and fast-growing cultural movement known as *transhumanism,* whose vision is supported by a growing list of

U.S. military advisors, bioethicists, law professors, and academics, intends the use of genetics, robotics, artificial intelligence and nanotechnology (GRIN technologies) as tools that will radically redesign our minds, our memories, our physiology, our offspring, and even perhaps—as Joel Garreau, in his bestselling book *Radical Evolution,* claims—our very souls.

Unfortunately for mankind, the technological and cultural shift now underway not only unapologetically forecasts a future dominated by a new species of unrecognizably superior humans, but an unfathomable war—both physical and spiritual—that the world is not prepared for. It will be fought on land, within the air and sea, and in dimensions as yet incomprehensible. Even now, the synthetic forces that will plot man's wholesale annihilation are quietly under design in leading laboratories, public and private, funded by the most advanced nations on earth, including the official governments of the United States, France, Britain, Australia, and China, to name a few. As a result of progressive deduction, reasoning, and problem solving in fields of neurotechnology and cybernetics, strong artificial intelligence or "artilects" will emerge from this research, godlike, massively intelligent machines that are "trillions of trillions of times smarter than humans" and whose rise will prove profoundly disruptive to human culture, leading to a stark division between philosophical, ideological, and political groups who either support the newly evolved life forms as the next step in human and technological evolution or who view this vastly superior intellect as an incalculable risk and deadly threat to the future of humanity. These diametrically opposed worldviews will ultimately result in a preemptive new world war—what is already being described as *gigadeath,* the bloodiest battle in history with billions of deaths before the end of the twenty-first century.

For those who find the fantastic elements in the statements above implicative of science fiction or even future Armageddon as forecast in the ancient apocalyptic and prophetic books of the Bible, the catastrophic vision is actually derived from near-future scenarios, which leading scientists like Prof. Hugo de Garis, director of the Artificial Brain Lab at Xiamen University in China, outlines in his book, *The Artilect War: Cosmists vs. Terrans: A Bitter Controversy Concerning Whether Humanity Should Build Godlike Massively Intelligent Machines,* as unfolding due to exponential growth and development this century in GRIN technologies.

"I believe that the twenty-first century will be dominated by the question as to whether humanity should or should not build artilects, i.e., machines of godlike intelligence," de Garis says. "I see humanity splitting into two major political groups, which in time will become increasingly bitterly opposed, as the artilect issue becomes more real."

Professor de Garis continues:

The human group in favor of building artilects, I label the "Cosmists" [to whom] building artilects will be like a religion…something truly magnificent and worthy of worship….

The second human group, opposed to the building of artilects, I label the "Terrans"…who will argue that allowing the Cosmists to build [artilects] implies accepting the *risk*, that one day, the artilects might decide…that the human species is a pest. Since the artilects would be so vastly superior to human beings in intelligence, it would be easy for [them] to exterminate the human species....

Thus to the Terrans, the Cosmists are...far worse than the regimes of Hitler, Stalin, Mao...or any other regime that murdered tens of millions of people in the twentieth century, because [this] time...we are talking about the potential annihilation of the whole human species, billions of people.[17]

Professor de Garis continues in his book to describe how the work to build artilects is proceeding nonetheless with anticipation of its realization potentially close at hand. As a result, he falls asleep at night thinking about the godlike synthetic intelligence he and others are constructing. Sometimes his mind becomes enraptured of his creations with a sense of intellectual and spiritual awe. Then, waking up a few hours later in a cold sweat, he is jolted from bed by a horrific dream in which vivid scenes depict the slaughter of his descendents at the hands of the artificial deities.

Dr. de Garis is not alone in this fear, that what he and other research scientists are feverishly working toward could soon become a nightmarish predicament mankind will not survive. Because it is difficult, if not impossible, to accurately predict how strong artificial intelligence will actually affect the world, it is unclear whether humans will be viewed by the unnatural life-forms as serving a purpose in a world dominated by super-intelligent machines or whether they will be weighed as lacking any practical function and therefore be considered expendable. It could be that we won't even see the question coming. In other words, we may already be in the process of being lulled into subservience toward the rise of the machines. As the brilliantly insane Theodore Kaczynski, in his thirty-five-thousand-word paper, "Industrial Society and Its Future" (also called the "Unabomber Manifesto"), wrote:

> As society and the problems that face it become more and more complex and machines become more and more intelligent, people will let machines make more of their decisions for them, simply because machine-made decisions will bring better result than man-made ones. Eventually a stage may be reached at which the decisions necessary to keep the system running will be so complex that human beings will be incapable of making them intelligently. At that stage, the machines will be in effective control. People won't be able to just turn the machines off, because they will be so dependent on them that turning them off would amount to suicide.[18]

Crazy or not, Kaczynski may be right in that man's demise at the hands of machines will happen gradually, during which time we humans will become the proverbial frogs in the kettle set to boil. On the other hand, we are more likely to be reduced any day now in the blink of an enhanced eye to the status of domestic animals in the minds of artificial intelligence, as *Technological Singularity*—that magical future moment that many futurists and tech experts believe could be imminent—gives birth overnight to some version of the artilects, who suddenly come online as conscious, living super-minds, immensely more powerful than human beings.

"As a metaphor for mind-boggling social change, the Singularity has been borrowed from math and physics," writes Joel Garreau in *Radical Evolution*. "In those realms, singularities are the point where everything stops making sense. In math it is a point where you are dividing through by zero [and in physics it is] black holes—points in space so dense that even light cannot escape their horrible gravity. If you were to approach one in a spaceship, you would find that even the laws of physics no longer seemed to function. That's what a Singularity is like."[19] Ray Kurzweil, who is credited with groundbreaking work in artificial intelligence and is, among other things, the co-founder of an interdisciplinary graduate studies program backed by NASA known as the Singularity University, appreciates the comparison between the coming Technological Singularity and the physics of black holes:

> Just as a black hole in space dramatically alters the patterns of matter and energy accelerating toward its event horizon, the impending Singularity in our future is [a] period during which the pace of technological change will be so rapid, its impact so deep, that human life will be irreversibly transformed.... The key idea underlying the impending Singularity is that the rate of change of our human-created technology is accelerating and its powers are expanding at an exponential pace. Exponential growth is deceptive. It starts out almost imperceptibly and then explodes with unexpected fury.[20]

In plain language, Abou Farman says Kurzweil's work on the Singularity:

...analyzes the curve of technological development from humble flint-knapping to the zippy microchip. The curve he draws rises exponentially, and we are sitting right on the elbow, which means very suddenly this trend toward smaller and smarter technologies will yield greater-than-human machine intelligence. That sort of superintelligence will proliferate not by self-replication, but by building other agents with even greater intelligence than itself, which will in turn build more superior agents. The result will be an "intelligence explosion" so fast and so vast that the laws and certainties with which we are familiar will no longer apply. That event-horizon is called the Singularity.[21]

Kurzweil elaborates on what the Singularity will mean to human biology.

Our version 1.0 biological bodies are...frail and subject to a myriad of failure modes.... The Singularity will allow us to transcend these limitations.... We will gain power over our fates. Our mortality will be in our own hands [and] the nonbiological portion of our intelligence will be trillions of trillions of times more powerful than unaided human intelligence.

We are now in the early stages of this transition. The acceleration of paradigm shift...as well as the exponential growth of the capacity of information technology are both beginning to reach the "knee of the curve," which is the stage at which an exponential trend becomes noticeable. Shortly after this stage, the trend becomes explosive. [Soon] the growth rates of our technology—which will be indistinguishable from ourselves—will be so steep as to appear essentially vertical.... That, at least, will be the perspective of unenhanced biological humanity.

The Singularity will represent the culmination of the merger of our biological thinking and existence with our technology, resulting in a world that...transcends our biological roots. There will be no distinction, post-Singularity, between human and machine.[22]

In 1993, critical thinking about the timing of the Singularity concerning the emergence of strong artificial intelligence led retired San Diego State University professor and computer scientist Vernor Vinge, in his often-quoted and now-famous lecture, "The Coming Technological Singularity," (delivered at VISION-21 Symposium sponsored by NASA Lewis Research Center and the Ohio Aerospace Institute), to add that when science achieves "the technological means to create superhuman intelligence[,] shortly after, the human era will be ended."[23] In contrast to Vinge, cyborgists like Kevin Warwick, professor of cybernetics at Reading University in England who endorsed de Garis' book, believe Singularity will not so much represent the end of the human era as it will the assimilation of man with machine intelligence, like the Borg of *Star Trek* fame. This is because, according to Warwick, Technological Singularity will not occur as a result of freestanding independent machines, but inside human cyborgs where human-machine integration is realized and enhanced biology is recombined to include living brains that are cybernetic, machine readable, and interfaced with artificial neural networks where transhumans with amplified intelligence become so completely superior to their biological counterparts (normal humans) as to be incomprehensible—ultimately "posthuman." The technology to accomplish this task is already well underway and is considered by researchers like Warwick to be one of the most important scientific utilities currently under employment toward man's posthuman future. As a result of this bridge between technology and human biology being attained this century, nothing less than the wholesale redesign of humans, including genetic integration with other life-forms—plants, animals, and synthetic creations—will be realized. This vision—the borgification (marriage between biology and machine) of man—is supported in the latest "State of the Future" report (2010) by the global think tank, the Millennium Project, founded after a three-year feasibility study with the United Nations University, Smithsonian Institution, and the Futures Group International, where synthetic biologists affirm that "as computer code is written to create software to augment human capabilities, so too *genetic code will be written to create life forms to augment civilization.*"[24] Furthermore, as biotech, infotech, nanotech, and cognotech breakthroughs quickly migrate with appropriate synergies to create widespread man-machine adaptation within society, a "global collective intelligence system [hive supermind] will be needed to track all these science and technology advances," the report goes on to say.

I (Tom) have personally debated leading transhumanist, Dr. James Hughes, concerning this inevitable techno-sapien future on his weekly syndicated talk show, *Changesurfer*

Radio. Hughes is executive director of the Institute for Ethics and Emerging Technologies and teaches at Trinity College in Hartford, Connecticut. He is the author of *Citizen Cyborg: Why Democratic Societies Must Respond to the Redesigned Human of the Future*, a sort of bible for transhumanist values. Dr. Hughes joins a growing body of academics, bioethicists, and sociologists who support:

> Large-scale genetic and neurological engineering of our-selves…[a] new chapter in evolution [as] the result of accelerating developments in the fields of genomics, stem-cell research, genetic enhancement, germ-line engineering, neuro-pharmacology, artificial intelligence, robotics, pattern recognition technologies, and nanotechnology…at the intersection of science and religion [which has begun to question] what it means to be human.[25]

Though the transformation of man to this posthuman condition is in its fledgling state, complete integration of the technology necessary to replace existing Homo sapiens as the dominant life-form on earth is approaching Kurzweil's exponential curve. A Reuters article dated November 9, 2009, titled "Scientists Want Debate on Animals with Human Genes," hinted at just how far scientists have come and how far they intend to go. The news piece started out, "A mouse that can speak? A monkey with Down's Syndrome? Dogs with human hands or feet? British scientists want to know if such experiments are acceptable," and it continued with revelations that scientists inside Britain are comfortable now with up to 50/50 animal-human integration. The article implied that not all the research currently under design is kept at the embryonic level, and that fully mature monstrosities (like the creature in the 2010 movie *Splice*) may be under study as "some scientists in some places want to push boundaries." *National Geographic* magazine speculated in 2007 that within ten years, the first of such human-animals would walk the earth, and Vernor Vinge agreed recently that we are entering that period in history when questions like "What is the meaning of life?" will be nothing more than an engineering question.

2010 movie *Splice* depicts fully grown human-animal chimera.

Most readers may be surprised to learn that in preparation for this posthuman revolution, the United States government, through the National Institute of Health, recently granted Case Law School in Cleveland $773,000 of American taxpayers' money to begin developing the actual guidelines that will be used for setting government policy on the next step in human evolution–"genetic enhancement." Maxwell Mehlman, Arthur E. Petersilge Professor of Law, director of the Law-Medicine Center at the Case Western Reserve University School of Law, and professor of bioethics in the Case School of Medicine, led the team of law professors, physicians, and bioethicists over the two-year project "to develop standards for tests on human subjects in research that involves the use of genetic technologies to enhance 'normal' individuals."[26] Following the initial study, Mehlman began offering two university lectures: "Directed Evolution: Public Policy and Human Enhancement" and "Transhumanism and the Future of Democracy," addressing the need for society to comprehend how emerging fields of science will, in approaching years, alter what it means to be human, and what this means to democracy, individual rights, free will, eugenics, and equality. Other law schools, including Stanford and Oxford, are now hosting similar annual "Human Enhancement and Technology" conferences, where transhumanists, futurists, bioethicists, and legal scholars are busying themselves with the ethical, legal, and inevitable ramifications of posthumanity.

As the director of the Future of Humanity Institute and a professor of philosophy at Oxford University, Nick Bostrom (www.NickBostrom.com) is a leading advocate of transhumanism who, as a young man, was heavily influenced by the works of Friedrich Nietzsche (from whom the phrase "God is dead" derives) and Goethe, the author of *Faust*. Nietzsche was the originator of the *Übermensch* or "Overman" that Adolf Hitler dreamed of engineering, and the "entity" that man—who is nothing more than a rope "tied between beast and Overman, a rope over an abyss"—according to Nietzsche, will eventually evolve into. Like the ancient Watchers before him, Bostrom envisions giving life to Nietzsche's Overman (posthumans) by remanufacturing men with animals, plants, and other synthetic life-forms through the use of modern sciences including recombinant DNA technology, germ-line engineering, and transgenics (in which the genetic structure of one species is altered by the transfer of genes from another). Given that molecular biologists classify the functions of genes within native species yet remain unsure in most cases how a gene's coding might react from one species to another, one should expect the genetic structure of the modified animal/humans to be changed in physical appearance, sensory modalities, disease propensity, personality, behavior traits, and more as a result of these modifications.

Despite these unknowns, such genetic tinkering as depicted in the movie *Splice* is already taking place in thousands of research laboratories around the world, including the United States, Britain, and Australia, where animal eggs are being used to create hybrid human embryos from which stem-cell lines can be produced for medical research. Not counting synthetic biology, where entirely new forms of life are being brewed, there is no limit to the number of human-animal concoctions currently under development within openly contracted as well as top-secret science facilities. A team at Newcastle and Durham universities in the United Kingdom recently illustrated this when they announced plans to create "hybrid rabbit and human embryos, as well as other 'chimera' embryos mixing human and cow genes." The same researchers more alarmingly have already managed to reanimate tissue "from dead human cells in another breakthrough which was heralded as a way of overcoming ethical dilemmas over using living embryos for medical research."[27]

In the United States, similar studies led Irv Weissman, director of Stanford University's Institute of Cancer/Stem Cell Biology and Medicine in California, to create mice with partly human brains, causing some ethicists to raise the issue of "humanized animals" in the future that could become "self aware" as a result of genetic modification. Even former president of the United States, George W. Bush, in his January 31, 2006, State of the Union address, called for legislation to "prohibit...creating human-animal hybrids, and buying, selling, or patenting human embryos." His words mostly fell on deaf ears, and now "the chimera, or combination of species, is a subject of serious discussion in certain scientific circles," writes senior counsel for the Alliance Defense Fund, Joseph Infranco. "We are well beyond the science fiction of H. G. Wells' tormented hybrids in the *Island of Doctor Moreau;* we are in a time where scientists are seriously contemplating the creation of human-animal hybrids."[28] When describing the benefits of man-with-beast combinations in his online thesis, "Transhumanist Values," Bostrom cites how animals have "sonar, magnetic orientation, or sensors for electricity and vibration," among other extrahuman abilities. He goes on to include how the range of sensory modalities for transhumans would not be limited to those among animals, and that there is "no fundamental block to adding, say, a capacity to see infrared radiation or to perceive radio signals and perhaps to add some kind of telepathic sense by augmenting our brains,"[29] a position verified by the U.S. National Science Foundation and Department of Commerce in the report, *Converging Technologies for Improving Human Performance.*

Bostrom and the U.S. government are correct in that the animal kingdom has levels of perception beyond human. Some animals can "sense" earthquakes and "smell" tumors. Others, like dogs, can hear sounds as high as 40,000 Hz—and dolphins can hear even higher. It is also known that at least some animals see wavelengths beyond normal human capacity. This is where things start getting interesting, perhaps even supernatural, as Bostrom may understand and anticipate. According to the biblical story of Balaam's donkey, certain animals see into the *spirit world.* Contemporary and secular studies likewise indicate animals may at times be reacting to intelligence beyond normal human perception. Will this have peculiar consequences for enhanced humans with animal DNA? Earlier in this book, we described how opening supernatural gateways that exist within the mind can be achieved through altered mental states induced by psychoactive drugs such as DMT and absinthe. Do transhumanists and/or military scientists imagine a more stable pathway or connection with the beyond—the ability to see into other dimensions or the spirit world—as a result of brain enhancement through integrating men with beasts? Do they envision reopening the portions of the mind that some scholars believe were closed off following the fall of man? Late philosopher and scientist Terrance McKenna, originator of "Novelty Theory," speculated that brain enhancement following Technological Singularity might accomplish this very thing—contact with other-dimensional beings. More recently, at Arizona State University (ASU), where the Templeton Foundation has been funding a long series of pro-transhumanist lectures titled "Facing the Challenges of Transhumanism: Religion, Science, Technology,"[30] some of the instructors agree that radical alteration of Homo sapiens could open a door to *unseen intelligence*. Consequently, in 2009, ASU launched another study, this time to explore discovery of—and communication with—"entities." Called the SOPHIA project (after the Greek goddess), the express purpose of this university study is to verify communication "with deceased people, spirit guides, angels, otherworldly entities/extraterrestrials, and/or a Universal Intelligence/God."[31] Imagine what this could mean if government laboratories with unlimited budgets working beyond congressional review were to decode the gene functions that lead animals to have preternatural capabilities of sense, smell, and sight, and then blended them with Homo sapiens. Among other things, something that perhaps DARPA (Defense Advanced Research Projects Agency) has envisioned for years could be created for use against entire populations—genetically engineered "Nephilim agents" that appear to be human but that hypothetically see and even interact with invisible forces. Overnight, the rules for spiritual warfare as well as regular warfare would take on an unprecedented (at least in modern times) dimension.

ENHANCED HUMANS:
THE NEW (NEPHILIM) ARMS RACE

While the former chairman of the President's Council on Bioethics, Leon Kass, does not elaborate on issues of spiritual warfare, he provided a status report on how real and how imminent the dangers of GRIN technologies could be in the hands of transhumanists. In the introduction to his book, *Life, Liberty and the Defense of Dignity: The Challenges of Bioethics,* Kass warned:

> Human nature itself lies on the operating table, ready for alteration, for eugenic and psychic "enhancement," for wholesale redesign. In leading laboratories, academic and industrial, new creators are confidently amassing their powers and quietly honing their skills, while on the street their evangelists [transhumanists] are zealously prophesying a posthuman future. For anyone who cares about preserving our humanity, the time has come for paying attention.[32]

The warning by Kass of the potential hazards of emerging technologies coupled with transhumanist aspirations is not an overreaction. One law school in the United Kingdom where students are taught crime-scene investigation is already discussing the need to add classes in the future devoted to analyzing crime scenes committed by posthumans. The requirement for such specially trained law enforcement personnel will arise due to part-human, part-animal beings possessing behavior patterns not consistent with present-day profiling or forensics understanding. Add to this other unknowns such as "memory transference" (an entirely new field of study suggesting that complex behavior patterns and even memories can be transferred from donors of large human organs to their recipients), and the potential for tomorrow's human-animal chimera issues multiplies. How would the memories, behavior patterns, and instincts, for instance, of a wolf affect the mind of a human? That such unprecedented questions will have to be dealt with sooner than later has already been illustrated in animal-to-animal experiments, including those conducted by Evan Balaban at McGill University in Montreal, where sections of brain from embryonic quails were transplanted into the brains of chickens, and the resultant chickens exhibited head bobs and vocal trills unique to quail.[33] The implication from this field of study alone proves that complex behavior patterns can be transferred from one species to another, strongly suggesting that transhumans will likely bear unintended behavior and appetite disorders that could literally produce lycanthropes (werewolves) and other nightmarish Nephilim traits.

As troubling as those thoughts are, some in government and science communities believe these dangers could be just the tip of the iceberg. One-on-one, interpersonal malevolence by human-animals might quickly be overshadowed by global acts of swarm violence. The seriousness of this for the conceivable future is significant enough that a recent House Foreign Affairs (HFA) committee chaired by California Democrat Brad Sherman, best known for his expertise on the spread of nuclear weapons and terrorism, is among a number of government panels currently studying the implications of genetic modification and human-transforming technologies related to future terrorism. *Congressional Quarterly* columnist Mark Stencel listened to the HFA committee hearings and wrote in his March 15, 2009, article, "Futurist: Genes without Borders," that the conference "sounded more like a Hollywood pitch for a sci-fi thriller than a sober discussion of scientific reality…with talk of biotech's potential for creating supersoldiers, superintelligence, and superanimals [that could become] agents of unprecedented lethal force."[34] George Annas, Lori Andrews, and Rosario Isasi were even more apocalyptic in their *American Journal of Law and Medicine* article, "Protecting the Endangered Human: Toward an International Treaty Prohibiting Cloning and Inheritable Alterations," when they wrote:

> The new species, or "posthuman," will likely view the old "normal" humans as inferior, even savages, and fit for slavery or slaughter. The normals, on the other hand, may see the posthumans as a threat and if they can, may engage in a preemptive strike by killing the posthumans before they themselves are killed or enslaved by them. It is ultimately this predictable potential for genocide that makes species-altering experiments potential weapons of mass destruction, and makes the unaccountable genetic engineer a potential bioterrorist.[35]

Observations like those of Annas, Andrews, and Isasi support Prof. Hugo de Garis' nightmarish vision of a near future wherein artilects and posthumans join against "normals" in an incomprehensible war leading to gigadeath. Notwithstanding such warnings, the problem could be unavoidable, as Prof.

Gregory Stock, in his well-researched and convincing book, *Redesigning Humans: Our Inevitable Genetic Future,* argues that stopping what we have already started (planned genetic enhancement of humans) is impossible. "We simply cannot find the brakes."[36] Verner Vinge agrees, adding, "Even if all the governments of the world were to understand the 'threat' and be in deadly fear of it, progress toward the goal would continue. In fact, the competitive advantage—economic, military, even artistic—of every advance in automation is so compelling that passing laws, or having customs, that forbid such things merely assures that someone else will get them first."[37] In what the writers of this book found to be a bit unnerving, academic scientists and technical consultants to the U.S. Pentagon have advised the agency that the principal argument by Vinge is correct. As such, the United States could be forced into large-scale species-altering output, including human enhancement for military purposes. This is based on solid military intelligence, which suggests that America's competitors (and potential enemies) are privately seeking to develop the same this century and use it to dominate the U.S. if they can. This worrisome "government think tank" scenario is even shared by the JASONS—the celebrated scientists on the Pentagon's most prestigious scientific advisory panel who now perceive "Mankind 2.0" as the next arms race. Just as the old Soviet Union and the United States with their respective allies competed for supremacy in nuclear arms following the Second World War through the 1980s (what is now commonly known as "the nuclear arms race during the cold war"), the JASONS "are worried about adversaries' ability to exploit advances in Human Performance Modification, and thus create a threat to national security," wrote military analyst

Noah Shachtman in "Top Pentagon Scientists Fear Brain-Modified Foes." This recent special for *Wired* magazine was based on a leaked military report in which the JASONS admitted concern over "neuro-pharmaceutical performance enhancement and brain-computer interfaces" technology being developed by other countries ahead of the United States. "The JASONS are recommending that the American military push ahead with its own performance-enhancement research—and monitor foreign studies—to make sure that the U.S.' enemies don't suddenly become smarter, faster, or better able to endure the harsh realities of war than American troops," the article continued. "The JASONS are particularly concerned about [new technologies] that promote 'brain plasticity'—rewiring the mind, essentially, by helping to 'permanently establish new neural pathways, and thus new cognitive capabilities.'"[38] Though it might be tempting to disregard the conclusions by the JASONS as a rush to judgment on the emerging threat of techno-sapiens, it would be a serious mistake to do so. As GRIN technologies continue to race toward an exponential curve, parallel to these advances will be the increasingly sophisticated argument that societies must take control of human biological limitations and move the species—or at least some of its members—into new forms of existence. Prof. Nigel M. de S. Cameron, director for the Council for Biotechnology Policy in Washington DC, documents this move, concluding that the genie is out of the bottle and that "the federal government's National Nanotechnology Initiative's Web site already gives evidence of this kind of future vision, in which human dignity is undermined by [being transformed into posthumans]."[39] Dr. C. Christopher Hook, a member of the government committee on human genetics who has given testimony before the U.S. Congress, offered similar insight on the state of the situation:

> [The goal of posthumanism] is most evident in the degree to which the U.S. government has formally embraced transhumanist ideals and is actively supporting the development of transhumanist technologies. The U.S. National Science Foundation, together with the U.S. Department of Commerce, has initiated a major program (NBIC) for converging several technologies (including those from which the acronym is derived—nanotechnology, biotechnologies, information technologies and cognitive technologies, e.g., cybernetics and neurotechnologies) for the express purpose of *enhancing human performance.* The NBIC program director, Mihail Roco, declared at the second public meeting of the project... that the expenditure of financial and human capital to pursue the needs of *reengineering humanity* by the U.S. government will be second in equivalent value only to the moon landing program.[40]

The presentation by Mihail Roco to which Dr. Hook refers is contained in the 482-page report, *Converging Technologies for Improving Human Performance,* commissioned by the U.S. National Science Foundation and Department of Commerce. Among other things, the report discusses planned applications of human enhancement technologies in the military (and in rationalization of the human-machine interface in industrial settings) wherein DARPA is devising "Nano, Bio, Info, and Cogno" scenarios "focused on enhancing human performance." The plan echoes a Mephistophelian bargain (a deal with the devil) in which "a golden age" merges technological and human cognition into "a single, distributed and interconnected brain."[41] Just visiting the U.S. Army Research Laboratory's Web site is dizzying in this regard, with its cascading pages of super-soldier technology categories including molecular genetics and genomics; biochemistry, microbiology and biodegradation; and neurophysiology and cognitive neurosciences. If writers like us can so easily discover these facts on the Web, just imagine what is happening in Special Access Programs (SAPs) where, according to the Senate's own Commission on Protecting and Reducing Government Secrecy, there are hundreds of "waived SAPs"—the blackest of black programs—functioning at any given time beyond congressional oversight. Because of this and given the seriousness of weaponized biology and human enhancement technology blossoming so quickly, on May 24, 2010, a wide range of experts from the military, the private sector, and academia gathered in Washington DC for an important conference titled "Warring Futures: A Future Tense Event: How Biotech and Robotics are Transforming Today's Military—and How That Will Change the Rest of Us." Participants explored how human enhancement and related technologies are unfolding as an emerging battlefield strategy that will inevitably migrate to the broader culture, and what that means for the future of humanity. As the conference Web site noted:

New technologies are changing warfare as profoundly as did gunpowder. How are everything from flying robots as small as birds to "peak warrior performance" biology [human enhancement] altering the nature of the military as an institution, as well as the ethics and strategy of combat? How will the adoption of emerging technologies by our forces or others affect our understanding of asymmetrical conflict? New technologies are always embraced wherever there is the greatest competition for advantage, but quickly move out to the rest of us not engaged in sport or warfare.[42]

The impressive list of speakers at the DC conference included Vice Admiral Joseph W. Dyer (U.S. Navy, retired), president of the Government and Industrial Robots Division at iRobot; Major General Robert E. Schmidle Jr., United States Marine Corps lead for the 2010 Quadrennial Defense Review; Robert Wright, author of *The Evolution of God* and a Global Governance Fellow; P. W. Singer, Senior Fellow and director of the Twenty-First Century Defense Initiative at the Brookings Institution; Stephen Tillery from the Harrington Department of Bioengineering at Arizona State University; and Jon Mogford, acting deputy director of the Defense Sciences Office at DARPA.

Having taken the lead in human-enhancement studies as a U.S. military objective decades ago, DARPA saw the writing on the wall and in scenes reminiscent of Saruman the wizard creating monstrous Uruk-Hai to wage unending, merciless war (from J. R. R. Tolkein's *Lord of the Rings*), began investing billions of American tax dollars into the Pentagon's Frankensteinian dream of "super-soldiers" and "extended performance war fighter" programs. Not only has this research led to diagrams of soldiers "with hormonal, neurological, and genetic concoctions; implanting microchips and electrodes in their bodies to control their internal organs and brain functions; and plying them with drugs that deaden some of their normal human tendencies: the need for sleep, the fear of death, [and] the reluctance to kill their fellow human beings," but as Chris Floyd, in an article for *CounterPunch* a while back, continued, "some of the research now underway involves actually altering the genetic code of soldiers, modifying bits of DNA to fashion a new type of human specimen, one that functions like a machine, killing tirelessly for days and nights on end...mutations [that] will 'revolutionize the contemporary order of battle' and guarantee 'operational dominance across the whole range of potential U.S. military employments.'"[43]

Related to these developments and unknown to most Americans was a series of hushed events following the sacking of Admiral John Poindexter (who served as the director of the DARPA Information Awareness Office from 2002 to 2003) during a series of flaps, which resulted in public interest into the goings-on at the agency and brief discovery of DARPA's advanced human enhancement research. When the ensuing political pressure led the Senate Appropriations Committee to take a deeper look into just how money was flowing through DARPA, the staffers were shocked to find "time-reversal methods" in the special focus area, and unstoppable super-soldiers—enhanced warriors with extra-human physical, physiological, and cognitive abilities that even allowed for "communication by thought alone" on the drawing board. Prof. Joel Garreau, investigative journalist, provides a summary of what happened next:

The staffers went down the list of DARPA's projects, found the ones with titles that sounded frighteningly as though they involved the creation of a master race of superhumans, and zeroed out their budgets from the defense appropriations bill. There is scant evidence they knew much, if anything, about these projects. But we will probably never know the details, because significant people are determined that the whole affair be forever shrouded in mystery. The levels of secrecy were remarkable even for DARPA; they were astounding by the standards of the notoriously leaky Senate. Even insiders said it was hard to get a feel for what the facts really were. It took months of reporting and questioning, poking, and prodding even to get a formal "no comment" either from the leadership of the Senate Appropriations Committee or from Anthony J. Tether, the director of DARPA.

A careful study of DARPA's programs a year later, however, showed little change. Considerable creative budgetary maneuvering ensued. The peas of quite a few programs now reside under new, and much better camouflaged, shells. "They're saying, 'Okay, this is the second strike. Do we have to go three strikes?'" one manager said. "It doesn't stop anything. We'll be smarter about how we position things." Meanwhile, he said, new human enhancement programs are in the pipeline, "as bold or bolder" than the ones that preceded them.[44]

Recent hints at DARPA's "bold or bolder" investment in human enhancement as part of an emerging arms race is reflected in two of its newest projects (launched July 2010), titled "Biochronicity and Temporal Mechanisms Arising in

Nature" and "Robustness of Biologically-Inspired Networks," in which the express intention of transforming "biology from a descriptive to a predictive field of science" in order to boost "biological design principles" in troop performance is made.[45] DARPA's Department of Defense Fiscal Year 2011 President's Budget also includes funding for science that will lead to "editing a soldier's DNA"[46] while more exotically providing millions of dollars for the creation of "BioDesign," a mysterious artificial life project with military applications in which DARPA plans to eliminate the randomness of natural evolution "by advanced genetic engineering and molecular biology technologies," the budget report states. The language in this section of the document actually speaks of eliminating "cell death" through creation of "a new generation of regenerative cells that could ultimately be programmed to live indefinitely." In other words, whatever this synthetic life application is (*Wired* magazine described it as "living, breathing creatures"), the plan is to make *it* immortal.[47] To this end, the authors of this book believe the "it" that man may soon uncover through its species-barrier-crossing technologies dates back to ancient times, and that the science of human enhancement and transhumanism is unwittingly playing into the hands of powerful supernaturalism toward a Luciferian endgame—something "it" tried once before, and which "it" was prophesied to attempt again just before the end of time.

UNCLASSIFIED

Exhibit R-2A, RDT&E Project Justification: PB 2011 Defense Advanced Research Projects Agency			DATE: February 2010
APPROPRIATION/BUDGET ACTIVITY 0400: Research, Development, Test & Evaluation, Defense-Wide BA 1: Basic Research	R-1 ITEM NOMENCLATURE PE 06011101E: DEFENSE RESEARCH SCIENCES	PROJECT ES-01: ELECTRONIC SCIENCES	

B. Accomplishments/Planned Program ($ in Millions)

	FY 2009	FY 2010	FY 2011 Base	FY 2011 OCO	FY 2011 Total
On the cell-level of the scale, the aim is to be able to increase by several decades the speed with which we sequence, analyze and functionally edit cellular genomes. With microsystem approaches, a prime goal is to be able to address large populations of cells, select as few as one, capture it, make specific edits to its DNA, and examine or replicate the cell as needed. Such capability will be applicable to a wide variety of problems including biological weapons countermeasures and understanding the underpinnings of human cancers. At an intermediate scale, new insights into the interactions of photons with the nervous system tissues of mammals will allow the development of mm-scale microphotonic implants that have the potential to restore sensory and motor function to individuals with traumatic spinal injury, for example. On the other end of the size scale, a primary goal is to apply microsystem techniques to soldier-protective biomedical systems. One example is an in-canal hearing protection device that will provide enhanced hearing capabilities in some settings, but be able to instantly muffle loud sounds of weapons fire. This one example will improve inter-personnel communications and at the same time drastically reduce the incidence of hearing loss in combat situations. For these examples and many more, the goal is to bring exceptionally potent technical approaches to bear on biological and biomedical applications where their capabilities will be significant force multipliers for the DoD. *FY 2011 Base Plans:* - Demonstrate isolation and manipulation of primitive pluripotent stem cells. - Investigate problem statements that can be addressed using quantum information science and technology. - Develop roadmap to algorithm to compute protein folding using quantum computing, as example of speed-up enabled by quantum simulations. - Demonstrate microsystems elements such as inductors and microactuators using high permeability as proof of feasibility to integrate magnetic micro/nanomaterials in wafer-scale processes. - Investigate physical mechanism of cross grain boundary transport in nanocrystalline materials. - Simulate RF performance limits of nanocrystalline channel transistors including current density limits.					

UNCLASSIFIED
R-1 Line Item #2

Defense Advanced Research Projects Agency   Page 39 of 57

Volume 1 - 39

UNCLASSIFIED

Exhibit R-2A, RDT&E Project Justification: PB 2011 Defense Advanced Research Projects Agency			DATE: February 2010
APPROPRIATION/BUDGET ACTIVITY 0400: Research, Development, Test & Evaluation, Defense-Wide BA 2: Applied Research	R-1 ITEM NOMENCLATURE PE 0602715E: MATERIALS AND BIOLOGICAL TECHNOLOGY	PROJECT MBT-02: BIOLOGICALLY BASED MATERIALS AND DEVICES	

B. Accomplishments/Planned Program ($ in Millions)

	FY 2009	FY 2010	FY 2011 Base	FY 2011 OCO	FY 2011 Total
(U) BioDesign is a new intellectual approach to biological functionality. The intrinsic concept is that by using gained knowledge of biological processes in combination with biotechnology and synthetic chemical technology, humans can employ system engineering methods to originate novel beneficial processes. BioDesign eliminates the randomness of natural evolutionary advancement primarily by advanced genetic engineering and molecular biology technologies to produce the intended biological effect. This thrust area includes designed molecular responses that increase resistance to cellular death signals and improved computational methods for prediction of function based solely on sequence and structure of proteins produced by synthetic biological systems. Development of technologies to genetically tag and/or lock synthesized molecules would provide methods for identifying the origin and source of synthetic biologicals (e.g., genes or proteins) allowing for traceability and prevention of manipulation ("tamper proof" synthetic biological). *FY 2011 Base Plans:* - Demonstrate computation protein conformation algorithms that model one residue per minute with 99.5% accuracy for every one kilodalton of mass regardless of protein class. - Develop conformation prediction algorithms for biomimetic polymers and biological-nonbiological hybrids involving unnatural amino acids or inorganic materials. - Demonstrate a robust understanding of the collective mechanisms that contribute to cell death. - Identify and initiate strategies that would enable a new generation of regenerative cells that could ultimately be programmed to live indefinitely until needed for an injury repair or therapeutic application. - Develop genetically encoded locks to create "tamper proof" DNA and protect commercial applications. - Develop strategies to create a synthetic organism "self-destruct" option to be implemented upon nefarious removal of organism. - Permanently append a synthetic organism's genome and prevent foul play by tracking organism use and history, similar to a traceable serial number on a handgun.					
Pathogen Defeat	0.000	0.000	4.000	0.000	4.000

UNCLASSIFIED
R-1 Line Item #19

Defense Advanced Research Projects Agency   Page 47 of 49

Volume 1 - 247

Department of Defense Fiscal Year (FY) 2011 President's Budget includes funding for DNA editing and BioDesign

CHAPTER EIGHT

THE HELL SCENARIO WILL BE NOTHING TO *GRIN* ABOUT

Synthetic biologists forecast that as computer code is
written to create software to augment human capabilities,
so too genetic code will be written to create life forms to
augment civilization.

—JEROME C. GLENN

Homo sapiens, the first truly free species, is about to
decommission natural selection, the force that made us....
Soon we must look deep within ourselves and decide what
we wish to become.

—EDWARD OSBORNE WILSON

Resistance is futile! You will be assimilated!

—THE BORG

N ot long ago, a writer for *Wired* magazine named Elizabeth
Svoboda contacted me (Tom) to let me know she was
writing an article about "research advances using transgenic animals to produce pharmaceutical compounds." She
had come across an editorial by me raising caution about this

kind of experimentation and wondered if I might be willing to provide points for her article, elaborating in areas where I saw producing transgenic human-animals as potentially harmful. She stated that most of the scientists she planned to quote were "pretty gung-ho about the practice," and said she thought it would be important to provide some balance. I thanked her for the invitation and sent a short summary of some, though not all, of the areas where concerns about this science could be raised.

When the article was finally published by *Wired*, I was surprised that none of my notes had made it into the story. I contacted Elizabeth and asked why, and she replied that they had originally been included in her article, "Pharm Animals Crank Out Drugs," but in order to create a positive spin on the story, the editors had censored my cautionary notes during the editing process. Elizabeth apologized and said she hoped the experience had not soured me on dealing with the magazine.

"It doesn't sour me," I assured her. "I just think the reporting by most agencies is lopsided and missing the opportunity to thoroughly engage such an important issue." The fact was, *Wired* magazine deprived the public of balanced treatment on an important subject and concluded instead with a scientist by the name of Marie Cecile Van de Lavoir saying that potential human health benefits from transgenic research "justify tinkering" with nature's plan. "If a transgenic animal produces a great cancer therapy," she said, "I won't hear anyone saying, 'You shouldn't do that.'" Van de Lavoir's comments were undoubtedly in response to some of my observations before they were pulled, because in offering caution, I had specifically used the phrase "tinkering with nature's plan." Van de Lavoir's short-sighted approach, like too many bioethicists engaged in the current debate, is as scary as the science, in our opinion. We wanted to contact her to suggest that she watch the film *I Am Legend* starring Will Smith, which opens appropriately enough with a scientist announcing the cure to cancer using a genetically engineered vaccine that blends animal and human genetics. If you've seen the film, you know the "cure" results in a human form of rabies that wipes out most life on earth—a real possibility, given the scenario.

Because any attempt at covering each potential GRIN-tech, catastrophic, *I-Am-Legend* possibility in this book would be impractical, we summarize below a few of the most important areas in which conservatives, bioethicists, regulators, and especially Christians could become informed and involved in the public dialogue over the potential benefits and threats represented by these emerging fields of science:

GENETICALLY MODIFIED FOOD

Besides potential problems with transgenic animals, we have cited laboratory results in the past that were first reported by Dr. Árpád Pusztai, repeat verified by scientist Irina Ermakova, and later substantiated by the *International Journal of Biological Sciences* that showed genetically modified (GM) food had surprisingly ill effects on the health of test rats, including the deterioration of every animal organ, atrophied livers, altered cells, testicular damage, altered sperm counts, shortened life spans, and cancer development. The laboratory findings led to the biotech industry suppressing the data and an eight-year court battle with monster corporations that did not want these results made public. Over the last year, the silenced information has been in the news again as Greenpeace activists published evidence from the Russian trials verifying the ramifications of the negative health issues related to genetically modified foods. The wider ramifications from these and similar controlled experiments suggest that as current technology inserts pesticides, insect genes, animal DNA, and other modified organisms directly into crops, the threat of hybrid viruses, prion contamination and new disease strains—which man can neither anticipate or prepare for—may arise. The prospects of this having an impact on mammalian health is almost certain to be a "when," not "if," concern, because, as Momma always said, "you are what you eat," and the fact that the food you consumed this week most likely contained genetically modified ingredients is a current reality. For example, a large portion of the soybean, corn, cottonseed, and canola in today's human food supply and sold in most developed countries including the United States now has genes spliced in from foreign species—including bacteria and viruses—in its genetic makeup. These genetically modified organisms (GMOs) have not only been linked to sickness, sterility, allergies, and even death among animals, but the Institute for Responsible Technology (IRT) documents how the functioning genetically modified genes from these foods linger inside the human body, which could be future-catastrophic. "The only published human feeding experiment verified that genetic material inserted into GM soy transfers into the DNA of intestinal bacteria and continues to function," IRT published. "This means that long after we stop eating GM foods, we may still have their GM proteins produced continuously inside us."[48]

Among other things, IRT says this means that: 1) If the antibiotic gene inserted into most GM crops were to transfer, it could create super diseases resistant to antibiotics; 2) If the gene that creates Bt toxin in GM corn were to transfer, it might turn our intestinal flora into living pesticide factories; and 3) Animal studies show that DNA in food can travel into organs throughout the body, even into the fetus. Add to this the growing secrecy over the use of nanoparticles (eighty-four food-related uses are already on the market and in numerous consumer products such as sunscreens and cosmetics), which as a result of their size behave fundamentally different than other particles, and the possibility of health-related complications increases exponentially. Due to the large corporations (that stand to make billions of dollars from these products) having co-opted the FDA into not requiring food labeling or package warnings on GMO foods and health products, you and I are now the biggest lab rats of all time in a "wait-and-see" experiment that will, feasibly within the decade, illustrate whether Pusztai and Ermakova's rodent findings apply to us and our children.

SYNTHETIC BIOLOGY

Synthetic biology is one of the newest areas of biological research that seeks to design new forms of life and biological functions not found in nature. The concept began emerging in 1974, when Polish geneticist Waclaw Szybalski speculated about how scientists and engineers would soon enter "the synthetic biology phase of research in our field. We will then devise new control elements and add these new modules to the existing genomes or build up wholly new genomes. This would be a field with the unlimited expansion [of] building new…'synthetic' organisms, like a 'new better mouse.'"[49] Following Szybalski's speculation, the field of synthetic biology reached its first major milestone in 2010 with the announcement that researchers at the J. Craig Venter Institute (JCVI) had created an entirely new form of life nicknamed "Synthia" by inserting artificial genetic material, which had been chemically synthesized, into cells that were then able to grow. The JCVI Web site explains:

> Genomic science has greatly enhanced our understanding of the biological world. It is enabling researchers to "read" the genetic code of organisms from all branches of life by sequencing the four letters that make up DNA. Sequencing genomes has now become routine, giving rise to thousands of genomes in the public databases. In essence, scientists are digitizing biology by converting the A, C, T, and G's of the chemical makeup of DNA into 1's and 0's in a computer. But can one reverse the process and start with 1's and 0's in a computer to define the characteristics of a living cell? We set out to answer this question [and] now, this scientific team headed by Drs. Craig Venter, Hamilton Smith, and Clyde Hutchison have achieved the final step in their quest to create the first…synthetic genome [which] has been "booted up" in a cell to create the first cell controlled completely by a synthetic genome.[50]

The JCVI site goes on to explain how the ability to routinely write the software of life will usher in a new era in science, and with it, unnatural "living" products like Szybalski's "new better mouse." Better mice, dogs, horses, cows, or humans that grow from this science will be unlike any of the versions God made. In fact, researchers at the University of Copenhagen may look at what Venter has accomplished as amateur hour compared to their posthuman plans. They're working on a third Peptide Nucleic Acid (PNA) strand—a synthetic hybrid of protein and DNA—to upgrade humanity's two existing DNA strands from double helix to triple. In so doing, these scientists "dream of synthesizing life that is utterly alien to this world—both to better understand the minimum components required for life (as part of the quest to uncover the essence of life and how life originated on earth) and, frankly, to see if they can do it. That is, they hope to put together a novel combination of molecules that can self-organize, metabolize (make use of an energy source), grow, reproduce and evolve."[51] Our good friend Gary Stearman of *Prophecy in the News* and other biblical scholars are raising red flags over Synthia technology, warning that any biotech life application leading to modification of the human genotype for "improved" humans will be an inconceivable affront to God and could result in divine repercussions.

PATENTING NEW LIFE-FORMS

Questions are evolving now over "patenting" of transgenic seeds, animals, plants, and synthetic life-forms by large corporations, which at a minimum has already begun to impact the economy of rural workers and farmers through such products as Monsanto's "terminator" seeds. Patenting of human genes will escalate these issues, as best-selling author Michael Crichton pointed out a while back in a piece for the *New York Times* titled, "Gene Patents Aren't Benign and Never Will Be," in which he claimed that people could die in the future from not being able to afford medical treatment as a result of medicines owned by patent holders of specific genes related to the genetic makeup of those persons. Former special counsel for President Richard Nixon, Charles Colson, added, "The patenting of genes and other human tissue has already begun to turn human nature into property. The misuse of genetic information will enable insurers and employers to exercise the ultimate form of discrimination. Meanwhile, advances in nanotechnology and cybernetics threaten to 'enhance' and one day perhaps rival or replace human nature itself—in what some thinkers are already calling 'transhumanism.'"[52]

ANIMAL RIGHTS

Animal-rights activists have raised similar questions having to do with the ethics of altering animals in ways that could be demeaning to them—for instance, creating zombielike creatures that grow in feeder labs and gaze off into space from birth until death. Militarized animals that behave in unnatural, unpredictable ways. Humanized animals that become "self-aware," or animals that produce human sperm and eggs, which then are used for in vitro fertilization to produce a human child. Who would the parents be? A pair of mice?

HUMAN CLONING

The prospect of human cloning was raised in the nineties immediately after the creation of the much-celebrated "Dolly," a female domestic sheep clone. Dolly was the first mammal to be cloned using "somatic cell nuclear transfer," which involves removing the DNA from an unfertilized egg and replacing the nucleus of it with the DNA that is to be cloned. Today, a version of this science is common practice in genetics engineering labs worldwide, where "therapeutic cloning" of human and human-animal embryos is employed for stem-cell harvesting (the stem cells, in turn, are used to generate virtually any type of specialized cell in the human body). This type of cloning was in the news during the writing of this book when it emerged from William J. Clinton Presidential Center documents that the newest member of the Supreme Court, Elena Kagan, had opposed during the Clinton White House any effort by Congress to prevent humans from being cloned specifically for experimental purposes, then killed. A second form of human cloning is called "reproductive cloning" and is the technology that could be used to create a person who is genetically identical with a current or previously existing human. While Dolly was created by this type of cloning technology, the American Medical Association and the American Association for the Advancement of Science have raised caution on using this approach to create human clones, at least at this stage. Government bodies including the U.S. Congress have considered legislation to ban mature human cloning, and though a few states have implemented restrictions, contrary to public perception and except where institutions receive federal funding, no federal laws exist at this time in the United States to prohibit the cloning of humans. The United Nations, the European Union, and Australia likewise considered and failed to approve a comprehensive ban on human cloning technology, leaving the door open to perfect the science should society, government, or the military come to believe that duplicate or replacement humans hold intrinsic value.

REDEFINING HUMANS AND HUMAN RIGHTS

Where biotechnology is ultimately headed includes not only redefining what it means to be human, but redefining subsequent human rights as well. For instance, Dr. James Hughes wants transgenic chimps and great apes uplifted genetically so that they achieve "personhood." The underlying goal behind this theory would be to establish that basic cognitive aptitude should equal "personhood" and that this "cognitive standard" and not "human-ness" should be the key to constitutional protections and privileges. Among other things, this would lead to nonhuman "persons" and "nonperson" humans, unhinging the existing argument behind intrinsic sanctity of human life and paving the way for such things as harvesting organs from people like Terry Schiavo whenever the loss of cognitive ability equals the dispossession of "personhood." These would be the first victims of transhumanism, according to Prof. Francis Fukuyama, concerning who does or does not qualify as fully human and is thus represented by the founding concept that "all men are created equal." Most would argue that *any* human fits this bill, but women and blacks were not included in these rights in 1776 when Thomas Jefferson wrote the Declaration of Independence. So who is to say what protections can be automatically assumed in an age when human biology is altered and when personhood theory challenges what bioethicists like Wesley J. Smith champion as "human exceptionalism": the idea that human beings carry special moral status in nature and special rights, such as the right to life, plus unique responsibilities, such as stewardship of the environment. Some, but not all, believers in human exceptionalism arrive at this concept from a biblical worldview based on Genesis 1:26, which says, "And God said, 'Let us make man in our image, after our likeness: and let them have dominion over the fish of the sea, and over the fowl of the air, and over the cattle, and over all the earth, and over every creeping thing that creepeth upon the earth.'"

NANOTECHNOLOGY AND CYBERNETICS

As discussed in the previous chapter, technology to merge human brains with machines is progressing at a fantastic rate. Nanotechnology—the science of engineering materials or devices on an atomic and molecular scale between 1 to 100 nanometers (a nanometer is one billionth of a meter) in size— is poised to take the development between brain-machine interfaces and cybernetic devices to a whole new adaptive level for human modification. This will happen because, as Dr. C. Christopher Hook points out:

> Engineering or manipulating matter and life at nanometer scale [foresees] that the structures of our bodies and

our current tools could be significantly altered. In recent years, many governments around the world, including the United States with its National Nanotechnology Initiative, and scores of academic centers and corporations have committed increasing support for developing nanotechnology programs. The military, which has a significant interest in nanotechnology, has created the Center for Soldier Nanotechnologies (CSN) [which is] interested in the use of such technology to help create the seamless interface of electronic devices with the human nervous system, engineering the cyborg soldier.[53]

TRANSHUMAN EUGENICS

In the early part of the twentieth century, the study and practice of selective human breeding known as *eugenics* sought to counter dysgenic aspects within the human gene pool and to improve overall human "genetic qualities." Researchers in the United States, Britain, Canada, and Germany (where, under Adolf Hitler, eugenics operated under the banner of "racial hygiene" and allowed Josef Mengele, Otmar von Verschuer, and others to perform horrific experiments on live human beings in concentration camps to test their genetic theories) were interested in weeding out "inferior" human bloodlines and used studies to insinuate heritability between certain families and illnesses such as schizophrenia, blindness, deafness, dwarfism, bipolar disorder, and depression. Their published reports fueled the eugenics movement to develop state laws in the 1800s and 1900s that forcefully sterilized persons considered unhealthy or mentally ill in order to prevent them from "passing on" their genetic inferiority to future generations. Such laws were not abolished in the U.S. until the mid-twentieth century, leading to more than sixty thousand sterilized Americans in the meantime. Between 1934 and 1937, the Nazis likewise sterilized an estimated four hundred thousand people they deemed of inferior genetic stock while also setting forth to selectively exterminate the Jews as "genetic aberrations" under the same program. Transhumanist goals of using biotechnology, nanotechnology, mind-interfacing, and related sciences to create a superior man and thus classifications of persons—the enhanced and the unenhanced—opens the door for a new form of eugenics and social Darwinism.

GERM-LINE GENETIC ENGINEERING

Germ-line genetic engineering has the potential to actually achieve the goals of the early eugenics movement (which sought to create superior humans via improving genetics through selective breeding) through genetically modifying human genes in very early embryos, sperm, and eggs. As a result, germ-line engineering is considered by some conservative bioethicists to be the most dangerous of human-enhancement technology, as it has the power to truly reassemble the very nature of humanity into posthuman, altering an embryo's every cell and leading to inheritable modifications extending to all succeeding generations. Debate over germ-line engineering is therefore most critical, because as changes to "downline" genetic offspring are set in motion, the nature and physical makeup of mankind will be altered with no hope of reversal, thereby permanently reshaping humanity's future. A respected proponent of germ-line technology is Dr. Gregory Stock, who, like cyborgist Kevin Warwick, departs from Kurzweil's version of Humans 2.0 first arriving as a result of computer Singularity. Stock believes man can choose to transcend existing biological limitations in the nearer future (at or before computers reach strong artificial intelligence) through germ-line engineering. If we can make better humans by adding new genes to their DNA, he asks, why shouldn't we? "We have spent billions to unravel our biology, not out of idle curiosity, but in the hope of bettering our lives. We are not about to turn away from this," he says, before admitting elsewhere that this could lead to "clusters of genetically enhanced superhumans who will dominate if not enslave us."[54] The titles to Stock's books speak for themselves concerning what germ-line engineering would do to the human race. The name of one is *Redesigning Humans: Our Inevitable Genetic Future* and another is *Metaman: The Merging of Humans and Machines into a Global Superorganism.*

Besides the short list above, additional areas of concern where readers may wish to become well advised on the pros and cons of enhancement technology include immortalism, postgenderism, augmented reality, cryonics, designer babies, neurohacking, mind uploading, neural implants, xenotransplantation, reprogenetics, rejuvenation, radical life extension, and more.

HEAVEN AND HELL SCENARIOS

While positive advances either already have been or will come from some of the science and technology fields we have discussed, learned men like Prof. Francis Fukuyama, in his book, *Our Posthuman Future: Consequences of the Biotechnology Revolution,* warn that unintended consequences resulting from what mankind has now set in motion represents the most dangerous time in earth's history, a period when exotic technology in the hands of transhumanist ambitions could forever alter what it means to be human. To those who would engineer a transhuman future, Fukuyama warns of a dehumanized "hell scenario" in which we "no longer struggle, aspire, love, feel pain, make difficult moral choices, have families, or do any of the things that we traditionally associate with being human." In this ultimate identity crisis, we would "no longer have the characteristics that give us human dignity" because, for one thing, "people dehumanized à la *Brave New World*...don't know that they are dehumanized, and, what is worse, would not care if they knew. They are, indeed, happy slaves with a slavish happiness."[55] The "hell scenario" envisioned by Fukuyama is but a beginning to what other intelligent thinkers believe could go wrong.

On the other end of the spectrum and diametrically opposed to Fukuyama's conclusions is an equally energetic crowd that subscribes to a form of technological utopianism called the "heaven scenario." Among this group, a "who's who" of transhumansist evangelists such as Ray Kurzweil, James Hughes, Nick Bostrom, and Gregory Stock see the dawn of a new Age of Enlightenment arriving as a result of the accelerating pace of GRIN technologies. As with the eighteenth-century Enlightenment in which intellectual and scientific reason elevated the authority of scientists over priests, techno-utopians believe they will triumph over prophets of doom by "stealing fire from the gods, breathing life into inert matter, and gaining immortality. Our efforts to become something more than human have a long and distinguished genealogy. Tracing the history of those efforts illuminates human nature. In every civilization, in every era, we have given the gods no peace."[56] Such men are joined in their quest for godlike constitutions by a growing list of official U.S. departments that dole out hundreds of millions of dollars each year for science and technology research. The National Science Foundation and the United States Department of Commerce anticipated this development over a decade ago, publishing the government report *Converging Technologies for Improving Human Performance*—complete with diagrams and bullet points—to lay out the blueprint for the radical evolution of man and machine. Their vision imagined that, starting around the year 2012, the "heaven scenario" would begin to be manifested and quickly result in (among other things):

- The transhuman body being "more durable, healthy, energetic, easier to repair, and resistant to many kinds of stress, biological threats, and aging processes."
- Brain-machine interfacing that will "transform work in factories, control automobiles, ensure military superiority, and enable new sports, art forms and modes of interaction between people."

- "Engineers, artists, architects, and designers will experience tremendously expanded creative abilities," in part through "improved understanding of the wellspring of human creativity."
- "Average persons, as well as policymakers, will have a vastly improved awareness of the cognitive, social, and biological forces operating their lives, enabling far better adjustment, creativity, and daily decision…making."
- "Factories of tomorrow will be organized" around "increased human-machine capabilities."[57]

Beyond how human augmentation and biological reinvention would spread into the wider culture following 2012 (the same date former counter-terrorism czar, Richard Clark, in his book, *Breakpoint*, predicted serious GRIN rollout), the government report detailed the *especially* important global and economic aspects of genetically superior humans acting in superior ways, offering how, as a result of GRIN leading to techno-sapien DNA upgrading, brain-to-brain interaction, human-machine interfaces, personal sensory device interfaces, and biological war fighting systems, "The twenty-first century could end in world peace, universal prosperity, and evolution to a higher level [as] humanity become[s] like a single, transcendent nervous system, an interconnected 'brain' based in new core pathways of society." The first version of the government's report asserted that the only real roadblock to this "heaven scenario" would be the "catastrophe" that would be unleashed if society fails to employ the technological opportunities available to us now. "We may not have the luxury of delay, because the remarkable economic, political and even violent turmoil of recent years implies that the world system is unstable. If we fail to chart the direction of change boldly, we may become the victims of unpredictable catastrophe."[58] This argument parallels what is currently echoed in military corridors, where sentiments hold that failure to commit resources to develop GRIN as the next step in human and technological evolution will only lead to others doing so ahead of us and using it for global domination.

Not everybody likes the "heaven scenario" imperative, and from the dreamy fantasies of Star Trek to the dismal vision of Aldous Huxley's Brave New World, some have come to believe there are demons hiding inside transhumanism's mystical (or mythical?) "Shangri-la."

"Many of the writers [of the government report cited above] share a faith in technology which borders on religiosity, boasting of miracles once thought to be the province of the Almighty," write the editors of *The New Atlantis: A Journal of Technology and Society.* "[But] without any serious reflection about the hazards of technically manipulating our brains and our consciousness…a different sort of catastrophe is nearer at hand. Without honestly and seriously assessing the consequences associated with these powerful new [GRIN] technologies, we are certain, in our enthusiasm and fantasy and pride, to rush headlong into disaster."[59]

Few people would be more qualified than computer scientist Bill Joy to annunciate these dangers, or to outline the "hell scenario" that could unfold as a result of GRIN. Yet it must have come as a real surprise to some of those who remembered him as the level-headed Silicon Valley scientist and co-founder of

Sun Microsystems (SM) when, as chief scientist for the corporation, he released a vast and now-famous essay, "Why the Future Doesn't Need Us," arguing how GRIN would threaten in the very near future to obliterate mankind. What was extraordinary about Joy's prophecy was how he saw himself—and people like him—as responsible for building the very machines that "will enable the construction of the technology that may replace our species."

"From the very moment I became involved in the creation of new technologies, their ethical dimensions have concerned me," he begins. But it was not until the autumn of 1998 that he became "anxiously aware of how great are the dangers facing us in the twenty-first century." Joy dates his "awakening" to a chance meeting with Ray Kurzweil, whom he talked with in a hotel bar during a conference at which they both spoke. Kurzweil was finishing his manuscript for *The Age of Spiritual Machines* and the powerful descriptions of sentient robots and near-term enhanced humans left Joy taken aback, "especially given Ray's proven ability to imagine and create the future," Joy wrote. "I already knew that new technologies like genetic engineering and nanotechnology were giving us the power to remake the world, but a realistic and imminent scenario for intelligent robots surprised me."

Over the weeks and months following the hotel conversation, Joy puzzled over Kurzweil's vision of the future until finally it dawned on him that genetic engineering, robotics, artificial intelligence, and nanotechnology posed "a different threat than the technologies that have come before. Specifically, robots, engineered organisms, and nanobots share a dangerous amplifying factor: They can self-replicate. A bomb is blown up only once—but one bot can become many, and quickly get out of control." The unprecedented threat of self-replication particularly burdened Joy because, as a computer scientist, he thoroughly understood the concept of out-of-control replication or viruses leading to machine systems or computer networks being disabled. Uncontrolled self-replication of nanobots or engineered organisms would run "a much greater risk of substantial damage in the physical world," Joy concluded before adding his deeper fear:

> What was different in the twentieth century? Certainly, the technologies underlying the weapons of mass destruction (WMD)—nuclear, biological, and chemical (NBC)—were powerful, and the weapons an enormous threat. But building nuclear weapons required...highly protected information; biological and chemical weapons programs also tended to require large-scale activities.
>
> The twenty-first-century technologies—genetics, nanotechnology, and robotics...are so powerful that they can spawn whole new classes of accidents and abuses. Most dangerously, for the first time, these accidents and abuses are widely within the reach of individuals or small groups. They will not require large facilities or rare raw materials. Knowledge alone will enable the use of them.
>
> Thus we have the possibility not just of weapons of mass destruction but of knowledge-enabled mass destruction (KMD), this destructiveness hugely amplified by the power of self-replication.

I think it is no exaggeration to say we are on the cusp of *the further perfection of extreme evil, an evil whose possibility spreads well beyond that which weapons of mass destruction bequeathed to the nation states, on to a surprising and terrible empowerment.*[60] (emphasis added)

Joy's prophecy about self-replicating "extreme evil" as an imminent and enormous transformative power that threatens to rewrite the laws of nature and permanently alter the course of life as we know it was frighteningly revived this year in the creation of Venter's "self-replicating" Synthia species (Venter's description). Parasites such as the mycoplasma mycoides that Venter modified to create Synthia can be resistant to antibiotics and acquire and smuggle DNA from one species to another, causing a variety of diseases. The dangers represented by Synthia's self-replicating parasitism has thus refueled Joy's opus and given experts in the field of counter-terrorism sleepless nights over how extremists could use open-source information to create a Frankenstein version of Synthia in fulfillment of Carl Sagan's *Pale Blue Dot*, which Joy quoted as, "the first moment in the history of our planet when any species, by its own voluntary actions, has become a danger to itself." As a dire example of the possibilities this represents, a genetically modified version of mouse pox was created not long ago that immediately reached 100 percent lethality. If such pathogens were unleashed into population centers, the results would be catastrophic. This is why Joy and others were hoping a few years ago that a universal moratorium or voluntary relinquishment of GRIN developments would be initiated by national laboratories and governments.

But the genie is so far out of the bottle today that even college students are attending annual synthetic biology contests (such as the International Genetically Engineered Machine Competition, or iGEM) where nature-altering witches' brews are being concocted by the scores, splicing and dicing DNA into task-fulfilling living entities. For instance, the iGEM 2009 winners built "E. chromi"—a programmable version of the bacteria that often leads to food poisoning, *Escherichia coli* (commonly abbreviated *E. coli*). A growing list of similar DNA sequences are readily available over the Internet, exasperating security experts who see the absence of universal rules for controlling what is increasingly available through information networks as threatening to unleash a "runaway sorcerer's apprentice" with unavoidable biological fallout. Venter and his collaborators say they recognize this danger—that self-replicating biological systems like the ones they are building—hold peril as well as hope, and they have joined in calling on Congress to enact laws to attempt to control the flow of information and synthetic "recipes" that could provide lethal new pathogens for terrorists. The problem, as always, is getting all of the governments in the world to voluntarily follow a firm set of ethics or rules. This is wishful thinking at best. It is far more likely the world is racing toward what Joel Garreau was first to call the "hell scenario"—a moment in which human-driven GRIN technologies place earth and all its inhabitants on course to self-eradication.

Ironically, some advocates of posthumanity are now using the same threat scenario to advocate *for* transhumanism as the best way to deal with the inevitable extinction of mankind via GRIN. At the global interdisciplinary institute Metanexus (www.metanexus.net/), Mark Walker, assistant professor at New Mexico State University (who holds the Richard L. Hedden of Advanced Philosophical Studies Chair) concludes like Bill Joy that "technological advances mean that there is a high probability that a human-only future will end in extinction." From this he makes a paradoxical argument:

> In a nutshell, the argument is that even though creating posthumans may be a very dangerous social experiment, it is even more dangerous not to attempt it....
>
> I suspect that those who think the transhumanist future is risky often have something like the following reasoning in mind: (1) If we alter human nature then we will be conducting an experiment whose outcome we cannot be sure of. (2) We should not conduct experiments of great magnitude if we do not know the outcome. (3) We do not know the outcome of the transhumanist experiment. (4) So, we ought not to alter human nature.
>
> The problem with the argument is.... Because genetic engineering is already with us, and it has the potential to destroy civilization and create posthumans, we are already entering uncharted waters, so we must experiment. The question is not whether to experiment, but only the residual question of which social experiment will we conduct. Will we try relinquishment? This would be an unparalleled social experiment to eradicate knowledge and technology. Will it be the steady-as-she-goes experiment where for the first time

governments, organizations and private citizens will have access to knowledge and technology that (accidently or intentionally) could be turned to civilization ending purposes? Or finally, will it be the transhumanist social experiment where we attempt to make beings brighter and more virtuous to deal with these powerful technologies?

I have tried to make at least a *prima facie* case that transhumanism promises the safest passage through twenty-first century technologies.[61]

The authors of this book believe the "brighter and more virtuous beings" Professor Walker and others are arguing for possess supernatural elements and that the *spirit* behind the transhumanist nightmare will put the "hell" in the "hell scenario" sooner than most comprehend.

CHAPTER NINE

THE SPIRIT BEHIND TRANSHUMANISM

It would be nice to be an artilect, a god, a supremely powerful omnipotent being. I could be such a creature [soon.] It's possible. It's not an unattainable dream.... All I can do here is attempt to convey some measure of the strength of "religious" feeling that I and other[s] will make public this century.

—PROF. HUGO DE GARIS,
artificial brain designer

All of the boundaries are up for grabs. All of the boundaries that have defined us as human beings, boundaries between a human being and an animal and between a human being and a super human being or a god.

—LEON R. KASS, former chairman,
President's Council on Bioethics

A non-human race once lived upon earth. They came to be called the Rephaim [Nephilim]. They were genetic monsters, mutants whose end is darkness, just as was their society upon earth. Will JCVI's [J. Craig Venter Institute, which created the entirely new life form nicknamed "Synthia"] work result in another such atrocity?

—GARY STEARMAN, Bible scholar

English theologian George Hawkins Pember, in his 1876 masterpiece, *Earth's Earliest Ages*, analyzed the prophecy of Jesus Christ that says the end times would be a repeat of "the days of Noah." Pember outlined the seven great causes of the antediluvian destruction and documented their developmental beginnings in his lifetime. The seventh and most fearful sign, Pember wrote, would be the return of the spirits of Nephilim, "the appearance upon earth of beings from the Principality of the Air, and their unlawful intercourse with the human race."

Jesus Himself, in answering His disciples concerning the signs of His coming and of the end of the world, said it would be "as the days of [Noah] were" (Matthew 24:37). The implication is, just as it was before the Flood when the spirits of Nephilim were powerful upon earth (Genesis 6:4), mankind would experience an end-times renaissance of the influence of these entities. From Scripture we are made to understand the purpose of this latter-day wave of supernaturalism includes deception (2 Timothy 3:13), and the effect upon mankind would be so successful that heresy and delusion would become firmly entrenched—even within institutionalized Christianity. In writing of this scenario, Paul prophesied to Timothy that "in the latter times, some shall depart from the faith, giving heed to seducing spirits, and doctrines of devils" (1 Timothy 4:1).

Based on contemporary developments, the foretold increase in demonism and its influence within secular and religious society is rapidly unfolding this century—abruptly, dramatically, and suspiciously. In a recent edition of *Prophecy in the News* magazine, biblical scholar Gary Stearman agreed, stating in disturbing language how the manifestation of these powers is quickening now because the world is under conditions "in which the influence of God's Holy Spirit is diminishing."[62] This is apparent not only in metaphysics, but within science and technology, where genetic engineering and transhumanist aspirations seem literally hell-bent on repeating what the Watchers did in giving birth to the spirits of Nephilim as in the days of Noah.

THE FIRST TIME NEPHILIM APPEARED ON EARTH

As far back as the beginning of time and within every major culture of the ancient world, the astonishingly consistent story is told of "gods" who descended from heaven and materialized in bodies of flesh. From Rome to Greece—and before that, to Egypt, Persia, Assyria, Babylonia, and Sumer—the earliest records of civilization tell of the era when powerful beings known to the Hebrews as "Watchers" and in the book of Genesis as the *b'nai ha Elohim* ("sons of God") mingled themselves with humans, giving birth to part-celestial, part-terrestrial hybrids known as "Nephilim." The Bible says this happened when men began to increase on earth and daughters were born to them. When the sons of God saw the women's beauty, they took wives from among them to sire their unusual offspring. In Genesis 6:4, we read the following account: "There were giants [Nephilim] in the earth in those days; and also after that, when the sons of God came in unto the daughters of men, and they bare children to them, the same became mighty men which were of old, men of renown."

When this Scripture is compared with other ancient texts,

including Enoch, Jubilees, Baruch, Genesis Apocryphon, Philo, Josephus, Jasher, and others, it unfolds to some that the giants of the Old Testament such as Goliath were the part-human, part-animal, part-angelic offspring of a supernatural interruption into the divine order and natural development of the species. The apocryphal Book of Enoch gives a name to the angels involved in this cosmic conspiracy, calling them "Watchers." We read:

> And I Enoch was blessing the Lord of majesty and the King of the ages, and lo! the Watchers called me—Enoch the scribe—and said to me: "Enoch, thou scribe of righteousness, go, declare to the Watchers of the heaven who have left the high heaven, the holy eternal place, and have defiled themselves with women, and have done as the children of earth do, and have taken unto themselves wives: Ye have wrought great destruction on the earth: And ye shall have no peace nor forgiveness of sin: and inasmuch as they delight themselves in their children [the Nephilim], The murder of their beloved ones shall they see, and over the destruction of their children shall they lament, and shall make supplication unto eternity, but mercy and peace shall ye not attain."
> (1 Enoch 10:3–8)

According to Enoch, two hundred of these powerful angels departed "high heaven" and used women (among other DNA providers) to extend their progeny into mankind's plane of existence. The Interlinear Hebrew Bible (IHN) offers an interesting interpretation of Genesis 6:2 in this regard. Where the

King James Version of the Bible says, "The sons of God saw the daughters of men that they [were] fair," the IHN interprets this as, "The *[b'nai ha Elohim]* saw the daughters of Adam, that they were *fit extensions*" (emphasis added). The term "fit extensions" seems applicable when the whole of the ancient record is understood to mean that the Watchers wanted to leave their proper sphere of existence in order to enter earth's three-dimensional reality. They viewed women—or at least their genetic material—as part of the formula for accomplishing this task. Departing the proper habitation that God had assigned them was grievous to the Lord and led to divine penalization. Jude described it this way: The "angels which kept not their first estate, but left their own habitation, He hath reserved in everlasting chains under darkness unto the judgment of the great day" (Jude 6).

Besides apocryphal, pseudepigraphic, and Jewish traditions related to the legend of the Watchers and the "mighty men" born of their union with humans, mythologized accounts tell the stories of "gods" using humans and animals to produce heroes or demigods (half-gods). When the ancient Greek version of the Hebrew Old Testament (the LXX or Septuagint) was made, the word "Nephilim"—referring to the part-human offspring of the Watchers—was translated *gegenes*, a word implying "earth born." This same terminology was used to describe the Greek Titans and other legendary heroes of part-celestial and part-terrestrial origin, such as Hercules (born of Zeus and the mortal Alcmena), Achilles (the Trojan hero son of Thetis and Peleus), and Gilgamesh (the two-thirds god and one-third human child of Lugalbanda and Ninsun). These demigods were likewise accompanied in texts and idol representation by half-animal and half-human creatures like centaurs (the part-human, part-horse offspring of Apollo's son, Centaurus), chimeras, furies, satyrs, gorgons, nymphs, Minotaurs, and other genetic aberrations. All of this seems to indicate that the Watchers not only modified human DNA during the construction of Nephilim, but that of animals as well, a point the Book of Enoch supports, saying in the seventh chapter that the fallen angels "sinned" against animals as well as humans. Other books such as Jubilees add that this interspecies mingling eventually resulted in mutations among normal humans and animals whose "flesh" (genetic makeup) was "corrupted" by the activity, presumably through crossbreeding (see 5:1–5; 7:21–25). Even the Old Testament contains reference to the genetic mutations that developed among humans following this time frame, including "men" of unusual size, physical strength, six fingers, six toes, animal appetite for blood, and even lion-like features (2 Samuel 21:20, 23:20). But of all the ancient records, the most telling extrabiblical script is from the Book of Jasher, a mostly forgotten text referred to in the Bible in Joshua 10:13 and 2 Samuel 1:18. Jasher records the familiar story of the fall of the Watchers, then adds an exceptional detail that none of the other texts is as unequivocal about, something that can only be understood in modern language to mean advanced biotechnology, genetic engineering, or "transgenic modification" of species. After the Watchers had instructed humans "in the secrets of heaven," note what Jasher says occurred: "[Then] the sons of men [began teaching] the mixture of animals of one species with the other, in order therewith to provoke the Lord" (4:18).

The phrase "the mixture of animals of one species with the other" does not mean Watchers had taught men hybridization, as this would not have "provoked the Lord." God made like animals of different breeds capable of reproducing. For example, horses can propagate with other mammals of the equidae classification (the taxonomic "horse family"), including donkeys and zebras. It would not have "provoked the Lord" for this type of animal breeding to have taken place, as God Himself made the animals able to do this.

If, on the other hand, the Watchers were crossing species boundaries by mixing incompatible animals *of one species with the other,* such as pig DNA with humans like science is doing today, this would have been a different matter and may cast light on the numerous ancient stories of mythical beings of variant-species manufacturing that fit perfectly within the records of what the Watchers were accomplishing. Understandably, this kind of chimera-making would have "provoked the Lord," and raises the serious question of why the Watchers would have risked eternal damnation by tinkering with God's creation in this way. Yahweh had placed boundaries between the species and strictly ordered that "each kind" reproduce only after its "own kind." Was the motive of the Watchers to break these rules simply the desire to rebel, to assault God's creative genius through biologically altering what He had made? Or was something of deeper significance behind the activity?

Some believe the corruption of antediluvian DNA by Watchers was an effort to cut off the birth line of the Messiah. This theory posits that Satan understood the protoevangelium—the promise in Genesis 3:15 that a Savior would be born, the seed of the woman, and that He would destroy the fallen angel's power. Satan's followers therefore intermingled with the human race in a conspiracy to stop the birth of Christ.

If human DNA could be universally corrupted or "demonized," they reasoned, no Savior would be born and mankind would be lost forever. Those who support this theory believe this is why God ordered His people to maintain a pure bloodline and not to intermarry with the other nations. When men breached this command and the mutated DNA began rapidly spreading among humans and animals, God instructed Noah to build an ark and prepare for a flood that would destroy every living thing. That God had to send such a universal fiat illustrates how widespread the altered DNA eventually became. In fact, the Bible says in Genesis 6:9 that only Noah—and by extension, his children—were found "perfect" in their generation. The Hebrew word for "perfect" in this case is *tamiym*, which means "without blemish" or "healthy," the same word used in Leviticus to describe an unblemished sacrificial lamb. The meaning was not that Noah was morally perfect, but that his physical makeup—his DNA—had not been contaminated with Nephilim descent, as apparently the rest of the world had become. In order to preserve mankind as He had made them, God destroyed all but Noah's family in the Flood. The ancient records including those of the Bible appear to agree with this theology, consistently describing the cause of the Flood as happening in response to "all flesh" having become "corrupted, both man and beast."

While we believe the theory of DNA corruption as an intended method for halting the coming of Christ has merit, an alternative or additional reason the Watchers may have blended living organisms exists in a theory we postulated in our book, *Apollyon Rising 2012: The Lost Symbol Found and the Final Mystery of the Great Seal Revealed.* In that book, we speculated that the manipulation of DNA may have had a deeper purpose—namely, to create a hybrid form that neither the spirit of man nor God would inhabit because it was neither man nor beast, and thus provided an unusual body made up of human, animal, and plant genetics known as Nephilim, an earth-born facsimile or "fit extension" into which the Watchers could extend themselves.

Given advances in GRIN technology, transhumanist aspirations, and the admitted new arms race of human enhancement discussed in the previous chapter, imagine the staggering spiritual warfare implications of such science if dead Nephilim tissue were discovered with intact DNA and a government somewhere was willing to clone or mingle the extracted organisms for use in (re)creating the ultimate super soldier—Homo-Nephilim. If one accepts the biblical story of Nephilim as real, such discovery could actually be made someday—or perhaps already has been and was covered up. As an example of this possibility, in 2009, blood was extracted from the bone of a dinosaur that scientists insist is eighty million years old. Nephilim would have existed in relatively recent times comparably, making clonable material from dead biblical giants feasible. The technology to resurrect extinct species already exists. The Pyrenean ibex, an extinct form of wild mountain goat, was brought back to life in 2009 through cloning of DNA taken from skin samples. This was followed in June of 2010 by researchers at Jeju National University in Korea cloning a bull that had been dead for two years. Cloning methods are also being studied for use in bringing back Tasmanian tigers, woolly mammoths, and other extinct creatures, and in the March/April 2010 edition of the respected *Archaeology* magazine, a feature article by Zah Zorich ("Should

We Clone Neanderthals?") called for the resurrection via cloning of what some consider to be man's closest extinct relative, the Neanderthals. *National Geographic* confirmed this possibility in its May 2009 special report, "Recipe for a Resurrection," quoting Hendrik Poinar of McMaster University, an authority on ancient DNA who served as a scientific consultant for the movie *Jurassic Park*, saying: "I laughed when Steven Spielberg said that cloning extinct animals was inevitable. But I'm not laughing anymore.... This is going to happen. It's just a matter of working out the details."[63]

The ramifications of using science to revive extinct animals or Nephilim could extend beyond cloning to include a mysterious germ-line connection with the armies of Armageddon and the kingdom of Antichrist. This is because as interbreeding begins between transgenic animals, genetically modified humans, and species as God made them, the altered DNA will quickly migrate into the natural environment. When that happens (as is already occurring among genetically modified plants and animals), "alien" and/or animal characteristics will be introduced to the human gene pool and spread through intermarriage, altering the human genetic code and eventually eliminating humanity as we know it. According to many theologians, this is what happened before the Great Flood, allowing for Nephilim incarnation and perhaps has been the whole idea for the end times as well—to create a generation of genetically altered "fit extensions" for the resurrection of underworld Nephilim hordes in preparation of Armageddon.

If, as we believe, the Antichrist is the reincarnation of the ancient demon deity Apollo (the Old Testament Nimrod) as prophesied by the apostles Paul in 2 Thessalonians 2:3 and

John in Revelation 17:8, not only will he be the exact opposite of Jesus (Son of God), but he will be the forerunner of the return of the Nephilim. The prophet Isaiah (chapters 13 and 14) spoke of the return of these beings, and tied the advent to the destruction of the city of Babylon in the final age (which should give us pause in light of the ongoing presence of U.S. armed forces in Iraq/Babylon and the powder keg surrounding it). From the Septuagint, we read:

> The vision which Esaias son of Amos saw against Babylon. Lift up a standard on the mountain of the plain, exalt the voice to them, beckon with the hand, open the gates, ye ruler. I give command and I bring them: *giants are coming to fulfill my wrath.…* For behold! The day of the LORD is coming which cannot be escaped, a day of wrath and anger, to make the world desolate.… And Babylon…shall be as when God overthrew Sodom and Gomorrah.… It shall never be inhabited…and monsters shall rest there, and devils shall dance there and satyrs shall dwell there. (Isaiah 13:1–3, 9, 19–22, emphasis added)

One can only speculate if something more than is casually perceived is meant by Isaiah when he says, "open the gates, ye ruler," but whoever this ruler is, he opens "gates" in Iraq/Babylon through which end-times giants (gibborim) return to the surface of earth as agents of God's wrath. Noting that Isaiah ties the destruction of Iraq/Babylon with the reappearance of gibborim in this way, we recall how thousands of U.S. troops, on invading Iraq during the Bush administration, admittedly filled U.S. containers with archaeological materials, including what some have speculated to be cuneiform tablets pointing to the location of pure-blooded Nephilim buried in underground caves. This is exactly where Enoch said the dead antediluvian Nephilim are, and raises fascinating questions: Would agencies like DARPA have interest in studying or cloning the extinct beings if they were, or have been, found? Could man in his arrogance revive ancient DNA, revitalizing or blending it with other living organisms in a way similar to what the Watchers did in making the first Nephilim? Is the factual reappearance on earth of such legendary beings verified by Isaiah, who also foresaw transhuman creatures such as *satyrs* (transgenic half-men, half-goats) accompanying the return of giants in the end times, or why other apocryphal books like 2 Esdras 5:8 prophesy the birth of "monsters" for the same period of time? Some may be shocked to learn that in addition to the citations above, the Bible actually describes an ultimate end-times spiritual warfare between the "mythological gods" and Christ. "The LORD will be terrible unto them: for he will famish all the gods of the earth" says Zephaniah 2:11. "The LORD of hosts, the God of Israel, saith; 'Behold, I will punish the…gods'" (Jeremiah 46:25). Human followers of the pagan deities will join the conflict, calling upon their idols (Revelation 9:20) to convene their powers against the Christian God, uniting with "the spirits of devils working miracles, which go forth unto the kings of the earth…to gather them to the battle of that great day…[to] a place called in the Hebrew tongue Armageddon [Megiddo]" (Revelation 16:13–14, 16). The ancient Book of Jubilees—another apocryphal text—considers the same time frame and verifies contemporaneous Nephilim resurrection. The familiar word "corruption" turns up again in association with these beings, insinuating an end-times repeat of what the Watchers did by corrupting human DNA and blending it with animals to retrofit human bodies for Nephilim incarnation. Note that this happens just before Satan is judged:

> The malignant evil ones [spirits of Nephilim destroyed in the Flood] were bound in the place of condemnation, but a tenth part of them were left that they might be subject before Satan on the earth. These are for corruption [corruption of DNA as in days of old?] and leading astray men before Satan's judgment. (Jubilees 10:7–12)

The well-known prophecy in the second chapter of the book of Joel also includes reference to returning gibborim (giants, Nephilim offspring). Though expositors tend to view Joel describing an army of locusts, he includes gibborim in his descriptions in the phrase "they shall run like *mighty men* [gibborim]." Does this mean something besides the fact that grasshoppers will be involved in Joel's end-times army?

> [They are] a great people and a strong; there hath not been ever the like, neither shall be any more after it... and nothing shall escape them. The appearance of them is as the appearance of horses; and as horsemen, so shall they run.... They shall run like mighty men *[gibbowr, gibborim]*; they shall climb the wall like men of war.... They shall run to and fro in the city; they shall run upon the wall, they shall climb up upon the houses;

they shall enter in at the windows like a thief. The earth shall quake before them.... And the LORD shall utter His voice before His army: for His camp is very great: for He is strong that executeth His word: for the day of the LORD is great and very terrible; and who can abide it? (Joel 2:2–11)

Another expression Joel uses—"the appearance of them is as the appearance of horses; and as horsemen, so shall they run"—sounds like the last-days locusts and transgenic horse-men mutations in Revelation 9:7–19. When all such texts are added up, there is persuasive evidence that the massive gib-borim army that runs upon the wall from which nobody can escape could be the result of man's willingness to play "god" in reviving forbidden science and opening "gates" to gibborim lurking in the beyond.

Does a curious verse in the book of Daniel also hint at this? Speaking of the last days of human government, Daniel said: "They shall mingle themselves with the seed of men: but they shall not cleave one to another, even as iron is not mixed with clay" (Daniel 2:43).

While Daniel does not explain who "they" that "mingle themselves with the seed of men" are, the personal pronoun "they" caused Chuck Missler and Mark Eastman, in their book, *Alien Encounters,* to ask: "Just what (or who) are 'mingling with the seed of men?' Who are these non-seed? It staggers the mind to contemplate the potential significance of Daniel's pas-sage and its implications for the future global governance."[64] Daniel's verse also troubled Missler and Eastman because it seemed to indicate that the same phenomenon that occurred in Genesis chapter 6, where nonhuman species or "nonseed" mingled with human seed and produced Nephilim would happen again in the end times. When this verse from Daniel is coupled with Genesis 3:15, which says, "And I will put enmity between thee and the woman, and between thy *seed* [*zera*, meaning "offspring," "descendents," or "children"] and her *seed*," an incredible tenet emerges—that Satan has seed, and that it is at enmity with Christ.

To "mingle" nonhuman seed with Homo sapiens through altering human DNA while simultaneously returning Nephilim to earth has been the inspiration of the spirit of Antichrist ever since God halted the practice during the Great Flood. According to Louis Pauwells and Jacques Bergier in *The Dawn of Magic* (first published in France in 1960 under the title *Le Matin des Magiciens*), this was certainly the goal of the antichrist Adolf Hitler:

> Hitler's aim was neither the founding of a race of supermen, nor the conquest of the world; these were only means towards the realization of the great work he dreamed of. His real aim was to perform an act of creation, a divine operation, the goal of a biological mutation which would result in an unprecedented exaltation of the human race and the "apparition of a new race of heroes and demigods and god-men."[65]

One cannot read the conclusion by Pauwells and Bergier regarding Hitler's antichrist ambition without seeing how it corresponds perfectly with the goals of transhumanism, even to the connection of creating posthuman bodies fit for deity incarnation through genetic engineering.

BIBLICAL EXAMPLE OF NEPHILIM RESURRECTION?

We believe an example of such Nephilim "resurrection" may exist in the Bible, which evolved as a result of human genetic alteration. The story is doubly important to our book because it centers around Nimrod, the original character who later was mythologized as the god Apollo prophesied by the apostle Paul in the New Testament (and by the occult elite on the Great Seal of the United States as detailed in *Apollyon Rising 2012*) as the ancient spirit that will return to earth to rule the *novus ordo seclorum.* The story of Nimrod in the book of Genesis may illustrate how this could happen through genetic engineering or a retrovirus of demonic design that integrates with a host's genome and rewrites the living specimen's DNA, thus making it a "fit extension" or host for infection by the entity. Note what Genesis 10:8 says about Nimrod: "And Cush begat Nimrod: he began to be a mighty one in the earth."

Three sections in this unprecedented verse indicate something very peculiar happened to Nimrod. First, note where the text says, "he *began* to be." In Hebrew, this is *chalal,* which means "to become profaned, defiled, polluted, or desecrated ritually, sexually or genetically." Second, this verse tells us exactly *what* Nimrod began to be as he changed genetically—"a mighty one" *(gibbowr, gibborim),* one of the offspring of Nephilim.

As Annette Yoshiko Reed says in the Cambridge University book, *Fallen Angels and the History of Judaism and Christianity*, "The Nephilim of Genesis 6:4 are always…grouped together with the gibborim as the progeny of the Watchers and human women."[66] And the third part of this text says the change to Nimrod started while he was on "earth." Therefore, in modern language, this text could accurately be translated to say: "And Nimrod began to change genetically, becoming a gibborim, the offspring of watchers on earth."

To understand how as a mature, living specimen Nimrod could have "begun to be a gibborim," it is helpful to imagine this in terms of biology as we know it. For instance, not long ago, I (Tom) "began to be" a diabetic. Because of poor choices of food, diet, and exercise, my doctor tells me that I triggered a genetic inherent and that it began changing me genetically. Yet just because I had the heritable, disease-related genotype that can lead to diabetes, this did not mean necessarily that I would develop the medical condition. It is entirely possible to be a carrier of a genetic mutation that increases the risk of developing a particular disease without ever actually becoming afflicted with the disorder in the course of a lifetime. Due to my earlier lifestyle, or maybe even certain environmental conditions I was unaware of, the gene mutation involved in the action of insulin "turned on" and I "began to be" a diabetic.

We've often wondered if the record of Nimrod that says he "began to be" a "gibborim" indicated something similar about his genetics, DNA, or bloodline that "turned on" as a result of his decisions, triggering a change in him from one type of being to another. It is also a possibility, we suppose, that Nimrod became afflicted with a retrovirus that integrated with his genome and, in essence, "rewrote" his genetic makeup, fashioning him into a transhuman or posthuman "fit extension" for an underworldly spirit. When we asked Sharon Gilbert, author of *The Armageddon Strain* whose formal education includes theology, molecular biology, and genetics, if she thought this was possible, she said:

> Absolutely! Retroviruses essentially inject single-stranded RNA strands into somatic (body) cells during "infection." These ssRNA strands access nucleotide pools in the host cell and form a double-stranded DNA copy. This dsDNA can then incorporate itself into the host chromosome using a viral enzyme called "integrase." The new "fake gene" then orders the cell to make more mRNA copies of the original virus RNA. These then travel out of the cell and infect the next cell, and so on.

Perhaps this type of genetic rewriting is implied in Genesis 10:8, which says, "And Cush begat Nimrod: he began to be a mighty one *[gibborim]* in the earth."

In addition to such scientific deduction, another reason we believe this story is suspicious is because of what Nimrod did immediately following Genesis chapter 10. As soon as he "began to be a mighty one," he set out to build a tower whose top would "reach unto heaven" (Genesis 11:4). This was the infamous Tower of Babel, and Nimrod was designing it so that the top of it would extend into *Shamayim* ("heaven"), the abode of God. The *Jewish Encyclopedia* confirms several historical records that Nimrod, whom it establishes was also identified by various ancient cultures alternatively as the god Apollo, built the Tower of Babel in an attempt to defiantly ascend into the presence of God. Jehovah Himself came down and said of the Tower's design: "Nothing will be restrained from them, which they have imagined to do" (Genesis 11:6). In other words, according to the Lord, Nimrod would have accomplished what he "imagined" to do—to build a tower whose top would reach into the abode of God.

Tower of Babel

That this section of Scripture could be viewed as a secondary support for the concept of Nimrod having become "revived Watcher offspring" is supported by Nimrod seeming to be abruptly aware of *where* and *how tall* to build a tower so that the top of it would penetrate the dwelling place of God. Were his eyes suddenly opened to realities that are outside man's normal mode of perception? Did he become Prof. Nick Bostrom and the Arizona State University's SOPHIA Project dream come true, capable of seeing into the spirit world as a result of trans-human or posthuman alteration? If Nimrod was genetically modified according to the original Watcher formula, he would have inherited animal characteristics (Bostrom's method) within his new material makeup, and according to the bibli-cal story of Balaam's donkey, animals can, like angels, perceive "domains" that humans cannot. This includes obvious things, such as wavelengths of the electromagnetic spectrum, but evi-dently something even more substantial, like the spirit realm. Additionally, as Nimrod/Apollo became *gibborim*, he would have taken on Watchers' propensities, which, as angels, could see into the supernatural realm including where heaven is located and possibly where to enter it. Even the name "Babylon" implies this, meaning the "gate of God" or "gateway *to* God." Sacred locations where beings that can see into the supernatu-ral realm could literally walk up onto a high place and enter heaven is not as farfetched as it sounds. Numerous examples from the Bible may substantiate the idea that heaven could be attained on high towers or mountainous locations. Consider Moses meeting with God on Sinai, Jesus returning atop the Mount of Olives, the two hundred Watchers that "descended in the days of Jared on the summit of Mount Hermon" (from the Apocryphal Book of Enoch 6:6) and other examples, including Jacob's ladder. This could also explain why, in the deep recesses of our psyche, people tend to believe that they can draw closer to God when going up onto mountains.

The big question is this: Could a modern form of a geneti-cally altered Nimrod/Apollo returning as the Antichrist with an army of revived Nephilim reopen these gateways (Isaiah 13:2–3) and fulfill the sign of "the days of Noah," which Jesus said would mark the time just prior to His return? A growing body of theologians believes so, and we make no argument against it, but we are happy in the next and final section of this book to share "other" signs of the days of Noah, ones we believe could be manifested in these troubling times as well—signs wherein true believers become the only power on earth against which this *spirit of transhumansim* cannot prevail.

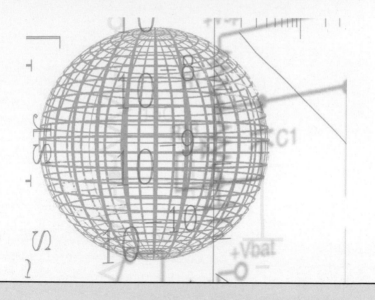

THE "OTHER" SIGNS OF
THE DAYS OF NOAH

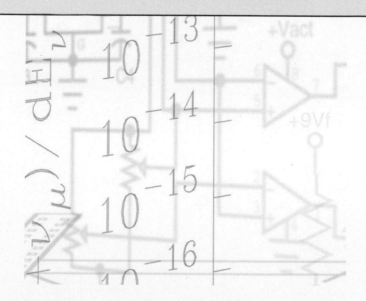

CHAPTER TEN

THE TRANSHUMAN NEW FACE OF SPIRITUAL WARFARE

If the U.S. [today] has a national religion, the closest thing to it is faith in technology.

—SCOTT KEETER, director of survey research for the Pew Research Center

Yet again humankind seems ready to plunge headlong into another human, or demonic, contrivance promising salvation and eternal happiness for all. This time the Faustian bargain is being struck with technology, what John McDermott referred to as the "opiate of the intellectuals."

—C. CHRISTOPHER HOOK, MD

When the stars align, Cthulhu will rise again to resume His dominion over the Earth, ushering in an age of frenzied abandon. Humankind will be "free and wild and beyond good and evil, with laws and morals thrown aside and all men shouting and killing and reveling in joy."

—MARK DERY, celebrating the rise of H. P. Lovecraft's cosmic monster

On July 20, 2010, the *New York Times* ran a feature article introducing a new nonprofit organization called the Lifeboat Foundation.[67] The concept behind the group is simple yet disturbing. Protecting people from threats posed by potentially catastrophic technology—ranging from artificial intelligence running amok to self-replicating nanobots—represents an emerging opportunity for designing high-tech "shields," and lots of them, to protect mankind this century.

"For example," the article says, "there's talk of a Neuroethics Shield to prevent abuse in the areas of neuropharmaceuticals, neurodevices, and neurodiagnostics. Worse cases include enslaving the world's population or causing everyone to commit suicide.

"And then there's a Personality Preserver that would help people keep their personalities intact and a Nano Shield to protect against overly aggressive nanocreatures."

If the Lifeboat Foundation sounds like a storehouse for overreacting geeks or even outright nut jobs, consider that their donors involve Google, Hewlett-Packard, Sun Microsystems, and an impressive list of industry and technology executives, including names on their advisory boards like Nobel laureate and Princeton University Prof. Eric Maskin.

What the development of such enterprising research groups illustrates is that even if one does not believe speculation from the previous chapters suggesting mind-bending concepts like Nephilim being resurrected into posthuman bodies via GRIN technology, all of society—regardless of religious or secular worldviews—should consider that what we are doing now through genetic modification of living organisms and the wholesale creation of new synthetic life-forms is either a violation of the divine order (biblical creation, such as the authors of this book believe) or chaos upon natural evolution, or both. The road we have started down is thus wrought with unknown perils, and the Lifeboat Foundation is correct to discern how the transhuman era may abruptly result in the need for "shields" to protect earth species from designer viruses, nanobugs, prion contamination, and a host of other clear and present dangers. Part of the obvious reasons behind this is, in addition to the known shortcomings of biotechnology corporations and research facilities to remain impartial in their safety reviews (they have a vested interest in protecting approval and distribution of their products), futurist think tanks such as the Lifeboat Foundation understand that the phrase, "those who fail to learn from history are doomed to repeat it" is axiomatic for a reason. Human nature has a clear track record of developing defense mechanisms only after natural or manufactured threats have led to catastrophe. We humans seem doomed to learn from our mistakes far more often than from prevention. Consider how nuclear reactors were forced to become safer only after the Chernobyl disaster, or how a tsunami warning system was developed by the United Nations following 230,000 people being killed by a titanic wave in the Indian Ocean. This fact of human nature portends an especially ill wind for mankind when viewed against the existential threats of biological creations, artificial intelligence systems, or geo-engineering of nature, which carry the potential not only of backfiring but of permanently altering the course of humanity. "Our attitude throughout human history has been to experience events like these and then to put safeguards in place," writes Prof. Nick Bostrom. "That strategy is completely futile

with existential risks [as represented in GRIN tech]. By definition, you don't get to learn from experience. You only have one
chance to get it right."[68] Because of the truly catastrophic threat
thus posed by mostly unregulated GRIN advances this century,
Richard Posner, a U.S. appeals court judge and author of the
book *Catastrophe: Risk and Response*, wants "an Office of Risk
and Catastrophe set up in the White House. The office would
be charged with identifying potentially dangerous technologies
and calling in experts to inform its own risk assessment." The
problem right now, Posner adds, "is that no single government
department takes responsibility for these kinds of situations."[69]
Not surprisingly, many transhumanists contest Posner's idea,
saying it represents just another unnecessary bureaucracy that
would stand in the way of scientific progress.

Yet of greater significance and repeatedly missing from
such secular considerations is what the authors of this book
believe to be the more important element: supernaturalism and
spirituality. Beyond the material ramifications of those threats
posed by the genetics revolution is something most scientists,
engineers, and bioethicists fail to comprehend—that man is
not just a series of biological functions. We are spirit and soul
and vulnerable to spiritual, not just environmental, dangers.
Thus the "shields" that the Lifeboat Foundation is working on
will only protect us so far. We will need *spiritual shields* too
as GRIN raises those bigger issues of how human-transforming
enhancements may alter our very souls (says Joel Garreau) as
well as hundreds of immediate new challenges that Christians,
families, and ministries will be facing.

It is an understatement to say that technology often works
hand in hand with unseen forces to challenge our faith or open

new channels for spiritual warfare. This has been illustrated in thousands of ways down through time—from the creation of Ouija boards for contacting the spirit world to online pornography gateways. But the current course upon which GRIN technology and transhumanist philosophy is taking mankind threatens to elevate the reality of these dangers to quantitatively higher levels. Some of the spiritual hazards already surfacing as a result of modern technology include unfamiliar terms like "i-Dosing," in which teens get "digitally high" by playing specific Internet videos through headphones that use repetitive tones to create binaural beats, which have been shown in clinical studies to induce particular brain-wave states that make the sounds appear to come from the center of the head. Shamans have used variations of such repetitive tones and drumming to stimulate and focus the "center mind" for centuries to make contact with the spirit world and to achieve altered states of consciousness.

More broadly, the Internet itself, together with increasing forms of electronic information-driven technology, is creating a new kind of addiction by "rewiring our brains," says Nora Volkow, world-renowned brain scientist and director of the National Institute of Drug Abuse. The lure of "digital stimulation" can actually produce dopamine releases in the brain that affect the heart rate and blood pressure and lead to drug-like highs and lows. As bad, the addictive craving for digital stimulation is leading to the electronic equivalent of Attention Deficit Disorder (ADD) among a growing population in which constant bursts of information and digital stimulation undermine one's ability to focus—especially in children, whose brains are still developing and who naturally struggle to resist impulses or to neglect priorities. A growing body of literature is verifying this e-connection to personality fragmentation, cyberrelationships over personal ones, and other psychosocial issues. Volkow and other researchers see these antisocial trends leading to widespread diminished empathy between people—which is essential to the human condition—as a result of humans paying more and more attention to iPads, cell phones, and computer screens than to each other, even when sitting in the same room. New research shows this situation becoming an electronic pandemic as people escalate their detachment from traditional family relationships while consuming three times as much digital information today as they did in 2008, checking e-mails, texting thirty-seven times per hour, and spending twelve hours per day on average taking in other e-media.

How brain-machine interfacing will multiply this divide between human-to-human relationships versus human-machine integration should be of substantial concern to readers for several reasons, including how 1) the Borgification of man will naturally exasperate the decline of the family unit and interpersonal relationships upon which society has historically depended; 2) the increase of euphoric cybernetic addiction will multiply as cerebral stimulation of the brain's pleasure centers is added to existing natural senses—sight, hearing, taste, smell, and touch; and 3) the threat of computer viruses or hijackers disrupting enhanced human neural or cognitive pathways will develop as cyber-enhanced individuals evolve. To illustrate the latter, Dr. Mark Gasson, from the School of Systems Engineering at the University of Reading in the United Kingdom, intentionally contaminated an implanted microchip in his hand that allows him biometric entry through security doors and that also communicates with his cell phone and other external devices. In the experiment, Dr. Gasson (who agrees that the next step in human evolution is the transhuman vision of altered human biology integrated with machines) was able to show how the computer virus he infected himself with spread to external computer systems in communication with his microchip. He told BBC News, "With the benefits of this type of technology come risks. We [will] improve ourselves...but much like the improvements with other technologies, mobile phones for example, they become vulnerable to risks, such as security problems and computer viruses."[70]

Such threats—computer viruses passing from enhanced humans to enhanced humans via future cybernetic systems—is the tip of the iceberg. The real danger, though it may be entirely unavoidable for some, will be the loss of individuality, anonymity, privacy, and even free will as a result of cybernetic integration. Dr. Christopher Hook contends, "If implanted devices allow the exchange of information between the biological substrate and the cybernetic device," such a device in the hippocampus (the part of the brain involved in forming, storing, and processing memory) for augmenting memory, for instance, "would be intimately associated with the creation and recall of memories as well as with all the emotions inherent in that process. If this device were...to allow the importation of information from the Internet, could the device also allow the memories and thoughts of the individual to be downloaded or read by others? In essence, what is to prevent the brain itself from being hacked [or externally monitored]? The last bastion of human privacy, the brain, will have been breached."[71]

Despite these significant ethical and social dangers, industry and government interest in the technological dream of posthumanism, as documented earlier in this book, is more than *laissez-faire*. The steady migration toward the fulfillment of biologically and cybernetically modified humans combined with corporate and national investments will predictably fuse this century, ultimately leading to strong cultural forces compelling all individuals to get "plugged in" to the grid. Whoever resists will be left behind as inferior Luddites (those who oppose new technology), or worse, considered enemies of the collectives' progress, as in de Garis' nightmarish vision in the *Artilect War* or former counter-terrorism czar Richard Clark's *Breakpoint,* which depicts those who refuse technological enhancement as "terrorists."

According to the work *Human Dignity in the Biotech Century,* this pressure to become enhanced will be dramatic upon people in all social strata, including those in the middle class, law, engineering, finance, professional fields, and the military, regardless of personal or religious views:

> Consider…whether the military, after investing billions in the development of technologies to create the cyborg soldier…would allow individual soldiers to decline the enhancements because of religious or personal qualms. It is not likely. Individuals may indeed dissent and decline technological augmentation, but such dissenters will find job options increasingly scarce.

> Because the network of cyborgs will require increasing levels of cooperation and harmonious coordination to further improve efficiency, the prostheses will continue to introduce means of controlling or modulating emotion to promote these values. Meanwhile, the net-

work is increasingly controlled by central planning structures to facilitate harmony and efficiency. While everyone still considers themselves fully autonomous, in reality behavior is more and more tightly controlled. Each step moves those who are cybernetically augmented toward becoming like the Borg, the race of cybernetic organisms that inhabit the twenty-sixth century of the *Star Trek* mythology. The Borg, once fully human, become "assimilated" by the greater collective mind, losing individuality for the good of the whole.[72]

Lest anyone think the writers of *Human Dignity in the Biotech Century* are overly paranoid, consider that NBIC (Nanotechnology, Biotechnology, Information Technology, and Cognitive Science) director Mihail Roco, in the U.S. government report, *Converging Technologies for Improving Human Performance*, wrote:

Humanity would become like a single, distributed and interconnected "brain" based in new core pathways in society.... A networked society of billions of human beings could be as complex compared to an individual being as a human being is to a single nerve cell. From local groups of linked enhanced individuals to a global collective intelligence, key new capacities would arise from relationships arising from NBIC technologies.... Far from unnatural, such a collective social system may be compared to a larger form of biological organism.... We envision the bond of humanity driven by an *interconnected virtual brain* of the Earth's communities searching for intellectual comprehension and conquest of nature."[73]

Nowhere will the struggle to resist this human biological alteration and machine integration be more immediate than in those religious homes where transhumanism is seen as an assault on God's creative genius, and where, as a result, people of faith seek to maintain their humanity. Yet the war against such believers is poised to emerge over the next decade as much from inside these homes and families as it will from external social influences.

As a simple example, flash forward to the near future when much of the technology previously discussed—factually based on emerging technologies and anticipated time frames—is common. Your tenth-grade daughter, Michelle, walks in from a first day at a new school.

"Well, how did it go, Honey?" you ask with a smile.

"It was okay," she says, "though the kids here are even smarter than at the last school." But then she pauses. She knows begging to be enhanced like most of her classmates will only lead to more arguing—common between you two on this subject. How can she make you understand what it's like even trying to compete with the transhumans? The fact that most of the student body, students who are half her age, will graduate from college *summa cum laude* with IQs higher than Einstein's by the time she even enters is a ridiculous and unnecessary impediment, she feels. She can't understand it. You've seen the news, the advertising, the *H+* magazines articles and television specials outlining the advantages of enhancement. Even the family doctor tried to convince you.

But it will probably take a visit from Child Welfare Services, which in the U.S. is soon to follow the European model where, starting in 2019, parents whose children went without basic modifications were charged with neglect and had their kids put in foster homes. She just wishes it wouldn't come to that. If only you could be like those Emergent Christians 2.0 whose techno-theology arose during the early enhancement craze of 2016–2018, based on a universalist imperative for "perfectionist morality" and the Christian duty to be "healers and perfecters" as opposed to the "bio-Luddite theology" of your outdated religious "divine order" concept, which only serves to keep people like her at disadvantage. That's why she gave you the school report compiled by Prof. Joel Garreau describing the average high school pupil today, so you could understand how her classmates:

- Have amazing thinking abilities. They're not only faster and more creative than anybody she's ever met, but faster and more creative than anybody she's ever imagined.
- They have photographic memories and total recall. They can devour books in minutes.
- They're beautiful, physically. Although they don't put much of a premium on exercise, their bodies are remarkably ripped.
- They talk casually about living a long time, perhaps being immortal. They're always discussing their "next lives." One fellow mentions how, after he makes his pile as a lawyer, he plans to be a glassblower, after which he wants to become a nanosurgeon.

- One of her new friends fell while jogging, opening up a nasty gash on her knee. Your daughter freaked, ready to rush her to the hospital. But her friend just stared at the gaping wound, focusing her mind on it. Within minutes, it simply stopped bleeding.

- This same friend has been vaccinated against pain. She never feels acute pain for long.

- These new friends are always connected to each other, sharing their thoughts no matter how far apart, with no apparent gear. They call it "silent messaging." It seems like telepathy.

- They have this odd habit of cocking their head in a certain way whenever they want to access information they don't yet have in their own skulls—as if waiting for a delivery to arrive wirelessly…which it does.

- For a week or more at a time, they don't sleep. They joke about getting rid of their beds, since they use them so rarely.[74]

Even though these enhanced students treat her with compassion and know that she is biologically and mentally handicapped by no fault of her own, she hates it when they call her a "Natural." It feels so condescending. And then, at the last school, there was that boy she wanted to date, only to discover it was against the informed-consent regulations passed by the Department of Education two years ago restricting romantic relationships between "Naturals" and the "Enhanced." She could have crawled into a hole, she was so embarrassed. But she's decided not to fight you anymore about it. Next year she will be eighteen years old and has been saving her money. With the federal Unenhanced Student Aid programs administered by the U.S. Department of Education and the United Naturals Student Fund (UNSF) that provides financial assistance and support for "Disaugmented American Students," grades pre-kindergarten to twelve, whose motto is "An augmented mind is a terrible thing to waste," she'll have enough for Level 1 Genetic Improvement plus a couple of toys like Bluetooth's new extra-cranial cybernetic communicator. It's not much, but it's a start, and though you will tell her that her brain-machine interface, and especially her genetic upgrade, makes her—as well as any kids she has in the future—inhuman, according to the school's genetic guidance counselor, there will be nothing you can do to legally stop her.

THE DEVIL IS IN THE DETAILS

As transhumanist philosophy and GRIN technology become integrated within society and national and private laboratories with their corporate allies provide increasingly sophisticated arguments for its widest adoption, those of us who treasure the meaning of life and human nature as defined by Judeo-Christian values will progressively find ourselves engaged in deepening spiritual conflicts over maintaining our humanity in the midst of what the authors believe is fundamentally a supernatural conflict.

Just as the fictional exercise with the seventeen-year-old "Michelle" above illustrates, intensifying techno-spiritual issues, which Christian families will face this century, will escalate simultaneously at both spiritual and scientific levels. This material/immaterial struggle, which philosopher and theologian Francis Schaeffer once described as always at war "in the thought-world," is difficult for some to grasp. The idea that human-transforming technology that mingles the DNA of natural and synthetic beings and merges man with machines could somehow be used or even inspired by *evil supernaturalism* to foment destruction within the material world is for some people so exotic as to be inconceivable. Yet nothing should be more fundamentally clear, as students of spiritual warfare will understand. We are body (physical form), mind (soul, will, emotions), and spirit, thus everything in the material and immaterial world has potential to influence our psychosomatic existence and decisions. "There is no conflict in our lives that is strictly a spiritual issue," writes Robert Jeffress in his book, *The Divine Defense.* This is because "there is never a time when the spirit is divorced from the body. Likewise, there is no turmoil in our lives that is solely psychological or physical, because our spirit, along with God's Spirit within us and demonic spirits around us, is always present as well."[75] Jeffress' point that material stimulus cannot be divorced from spiritual conditions conveys why the Bible is so concerned with the antitheses of transhumanism; the integrity of our bodies and minds. The goal is to bring both into obedience to Christ (2 Chronicles 10:5) because this is where the battle is first fought and won. No marriage breakup ever transpired that did not start there—no murder, no theft, no idolatry—but that the contest was staged in the imagination, then married to the senses, and the decision to act given to the victor.

How technology is now poised to raise this mind-body-spirit game is hidden in the shadows of the National Institute of Health and DARPA, which for more than three decades have invested hundreds of millions of dollars not only designing new DNA constructs but crafting arrays of microelectrodes, super-computers, and algorithms to analyze and decipher the brain's neural code, the complex "syntax" and communication rules that transform electrical neuron pulses in the brain into specific digital and analog information that we ultimately perceive as decisions, memories, and emotions. Understanding how this secret brain language functions, then parsing it down into digital computer code (strings of ones and zeros) where it can be reassembled into words and commands and then manipulated is at the center of military neurobiology, artificial intelligence research, and cybernetics.

While significant studies in neurosciences have been conducted with "neuro-prostheses" in mind to help the handicapped—for instance, the artificial cochlear implant that approximately 188,000 people worldwide have received thus far—DARPA "is less interested in treating the disabled than in enhancing the cognitive capacities of soldiers," says former senior writer at *Scientific American*, John Horgan. "DARPA officials have breached the prospect of cyborg warriors downloading complex fighting procedures directly into their brains, like the heroes of the Matrix," and has "interest in the development of techniques that can survey and possibly manipulate the mental processes of potential enemies [by] recording signals from the brains of enemy personnel at a distance, in order to 'read their minds and to control them.'"[76] Because what develops within military technology eventually migrates into the broader culture, where it is quickly embraced for competitive or mutual advantages, the ramifications of neurobiology has not escaped international interests in both public and private agencies. Entire fields of research are now under development worldwide based on the notion that breakthroughs will provide unprecedented opportunities for reading, influencing, and even controlling human minds this century. The implications from this field are so staggering that France, in 2010, became the first nation to establish a behavioral research unit specifically designed to study and set "neuropolicy" to govern how such things as "neuromarketing" (a new field of marketing that analyzes consumers' sensorimotor and cognitive responses to stimuli in order to decode what part of the brain is telling consumers to make certain buying decisions) may be used in the future to access unconscious decision-making elements of the brain to produce desired responses. This precedent for government neuropolicy comes not a second too soon, as the world's largest semiconductor chip maker, Intel Corp., wants brain communicators on the market and "in its customers' heads" before the year 2020. In what can only be described as *Matrix* creep, researchers at Intel Labs Pittsburgh are designing what it bets will be "the next big thing"—brain chips that allow consumers to control a host of new electronic and communication gadgets by way of neural commands. Developers at Toyota and the University of Utah are also working on brain transmitters, which they hope will contribute to building a global "hive mind."

From these developments comes the distant groaning of a "fearful unknown" in which the architecture of the human brain—as transformed by current and future cybernetic inventions—begins to act in ways that borderline the supernatural.

Consider experimental telepathy, which involves mind-to-mind thought transference that allows people to communicate without the use of speaking audibly. Most do not know that Hans Berger, the inventor of electroencephalography (EEG, the recording of electrical activity along the scalp produced by the firing of neurons within the brain) was a strong believer in psychic phenomena and wanted to decode brain signals in order to establish nonverbal transmission between people. GRIN technology proposes to fulfill his dream.

Another example is telekinesis (psychokinesis), which involves the movement or manipulation of physical matter via direct influence of the mind. As incredible as it may seem, both this idea and the one above are under research by DARPA and other national laboratories as no pipe dream. Such brain-to-brain transmission between distant persons as well as mind-to-computer communication was demonstrated last year at the University of Southampton's Institute of Sound and Vibration Research using electrodes and an Internet connection. The experiment at the institute went farther than most brain-to-machine interfacing (BMI) technology thus far, actually demonstrating brain-to-brain (B2B) communication between persons at a distance. Dr. Christopher James, who oversaw the experiment, commented: "Whilst BCI [brain-computer interface] is no longer a new thing and person-to-person communication via the nervous system was shown previously in work by Prof. Kevin Warwick from the University of Reading, here we show, for the first time, true brain to brain interfacing. We have yet to grasp the full implications of this." The experiment allowed one person using BCI to transmit thoughts, translated as a series of binary digits, over the Internet to another person whose computer received the digits and transmitted them to the second user's brain.[77]

The real danger is how these accomplishments within human-mind-to-synthetic intelligence may take the proverbial "ghost in the machine" where no *modern man* has gone before, bridging a gap between unknown entities (both virtual and real), perhaps even inviting takeover of our species by malevolent intelligence. Note that the experiments above are being conducted at Southampton's Institute of Sound and Vibration Research. Some years ago, scientist Vic Tandy's research into sound, vibration frequencies, and eyeball resonation led to a thesis (actually titled "Ghosts in the Machine") that was published in the *Journal of the Society for Psychical Research*. Tandy's findings outlined what he thought were "natural causes" for particular cases of specter materialization. Tandy found that 19-Hz standing air waves could, under some circumstances, create sensory phenomena in an open environment suggestive of a ghost. He actually produced a frightening manifested entity resembling contemporary descriptions of "alien grays." A similar phenomenon was discovered in 2006 by neurologist Olaf Blanke of the Brain Mind Institute in Lausanne, Switzerland, while working with a team to discover the source of epileptic seizures in a young woman. They were applying electrical currents through surgically implanted electrodes to various regions of her brain, when upon reaching her left temporoparietal junction (TPJ, located roughly above the left ear) she suddenly reported feeling the presence of a shadow person standing behind her. The phantom started imitating her body posture, lying down beneath her when she was on the bed, sitting behind her, and later even attempting to take a test card away from her during a language exercise. While the scientists interpreted the activity as a natural, though mysterious, biological function of the brain, is it possible they were actually discovering gateways of perception into the spirit world that were closed by God following the fall of man? Were Tandy's "ghost" and Blanke's "shadow person" *living unknowns?* If so, is it not troubling that advocates of human-mind-to-machine intelligence may produce permanent conditions similar to Tandy and Blanke's findings, giving rise to simulated or real relationships between humans and "entities"? At the thirteenth European Meeting on Cybernetics and Systems Research at the University of Vienna in Austria, an original paper submitted by Charles Ostman seemed to echo this possibility:

> As this threshold of development is crossed, as an index of our human/Internet symbiosis becoming more pronounced, and irreversible, we begin to develop communication modalities which are quite "nonhuman" by nature, but are "socio-operative" norms of the near future. Our collective development and deployment of complex metasystems of artificial entities and synthetic life-forms, and acceptance of them as an integral component of the operational "culture norm" of the near future, is in fact the precursory developmental increment, as an enabling procedure, to gain effective communicative access to *a contiguous collection of myriad "species" and entity types (synthetic and "real") functioning as process brokeraging agents.*[78]

A similar issue that "pinged" in our memories from past experience with exorcism and the connection between *sound resonance* and contact with supernaturalism has to do with people who claim to have become possessed or "demonized" after attempting to open mind gateways through vibratory chanting at New Age vortices or "Mother Earth" energy sites such as Sedona, Arizona. When we queried www.RaidersNewsNetwork.com resident expert Sue Bradley on this subject, asking if she believed a connection could exist between acoustics, harmonics, sound resonance, and spirit gateways, she e-mailed this lengthy and shocking response:

> Tom and Nita:
>
> From the ancients to the New Age, resonance and harmonics have long been recognized as vehicles of communication and manifestation. Ancient rock outcroppings, sacred temples, and monuments have for millennia been used as gathering places for the so-called spiritually enlightened. Through recent understanding of quantum entanglement and the high energy physics of sound and light, both with adaptable vibratory characteristics, these popular sites for gatherings with ritual chants and offerings, often employing ancient spells and mathematical harmonic codes in various sets of tandem frequencies, may well have measurable and far greater esoteric effects than even recently believed.
>
> Note what New Ager and modern shaman Zacciah Blackburn of *Sacred Sound, Sound the Codes* says he came in contact with at such sites:

It is not mere coincidence many of the ancient stone temples of the world were made with crystalline embedded stones, such as granite, which are known for their properties to pass or store energy.... Through Sacred Sound and awareness practices, the unseen "wisdom keepers" and guardians of these sacred temples have communed with me, and showed me how to hold frequency of awareness in the heart and mind, and combine them into sound codes to create a "key" which opens the "libraries" of these temples of ancient star beings and wisdom keepers to the modern way traveler whom comes with pure intent.[79]

With this in mind, also consider how the word "ear" appears 120 times in Scripture, "ears" 151 times, and is important with regard to *sound connected to spiritual hearing.* First used in Exodus 15:26, the ear is linked to a covenant relationship for those that *hearken* to the voice of the Lord and keep His statutes. The *right ear* is repeatedly described in the Levitical instructions: "Then shalt thou kill the ram, and take of his blood, and put it upon the tip of the right ear of Aaron, and upon the tip of the right ear of his sons" (Exodus 29:20; [Leviticus 8:23 and 24; 14:14, 17, 25, and 28]).

Subsequent references to the ear and hearing are presented as petitions *to* God from His servants as well as *from* God as counsel, forewarning and rebukes.

The ear as a spiritual gateway termed "Ear-Gate" first appeared in English usage through an allegory penned by John Bunyan in 1682. Bunyan's classic, *The Pilgrim's Progress,* was the most widely read and translated book in the English language apart from the Bible: it was also an educational staple and considered to be required reading in the U.S. from colonial times through World War II. While *The Pilgrim's Progress* allegorizes the encounters and obstacles of a man seeking salvation, Bunyan's *The Holy War* or *The Losing and Taking Again of the Town of Mansoul* recounts the cosmic conflict for the souls of mankind with Peretti-like descriptions and precision.

The town of Mansoul, designed in the image of the almighty, *Shaddai,* is the target of the deceptive and malevolent giant, *Diabolus.* Mansoul is a city of five gates: the Ear-Gate, Eye-Gate, Mouth-Gate, Nose-Gate and Feel-Gate. The first and most strategic gate is the first gate breached: the Ear-Gate.

Nineteenth-century theologian, Rev. Robert Maguire, comments on the importance of the Ear-Gate:

> This was the gate of audience, and through this gate the words of the tempter must penetrate, if the temptation is to be successful. Into the ears of our first mother did the wily serpent whisper the glozing words of his seductive wiles and through the Ear-Gate, he assailed her heart and won it. To give audience to the tempter is the next step to yielding up obedience to his will.[80]

One of the two principal powers in Mansoul, *Resistance,* quickly succumbs to an arrow from the army of Diabolus. The promises of Diabolus are familiar: to *enlarge the town* of man-soul, *to augment their freedom* and in the subtlety of pattern identical to Eden, *challenging the prohibition of the Tree of Knowledge* itself.

Dr. Maguire continues to describe this initial incursion at the Ear-Gate with the introduction of Mr. Ill-Pause, another of the diabolical army that visits Mansoul:

> Satan has many mysterious angels who are ready to second their master's temptations and to commend his wily overtures. Thus Ill-Pause persuades the men of Mansoul; and, lo! to the temptation from without (which was utterly powerless in itself), there answers the yielding from within. This is the fatal act; and is straightaway followed by another grave disaster—the death of Innocency, one of the chiefest and most honorable townsmen. His sensitive soul was poisoned by the contact of the breath of the lost.[81]

The Holy War continues with civil war raging within Mansoul and the defeat of the giant Diabolus and his demonic army by the son of Shaddai, Emmanuel, but the allegory perhaps finds more direct application in the twenty-first century than earlier. This is because, more than any other time in history, the seduction of high-tech has taken firm root—and among the most vulnerable of the population. Culturally adrift, this high risk generation, most of whom have never heard the exquisite truths of John Bunyan, has been denied spiritual cultivation through an educational system which values tolerance above absolutes and through social training that elevates technology above heritage.

Full-Fledged Ear-Gate Assault

With the advent of cell phones, iPods, and other "personal devices," the ear-gates of an entire generation have been dangerously compromised. In addition to the obvious physical risks that associate cell phone use and texting while driving, effects have been measured on teenage language abilities and a markedly increased incidence of tinnitus, a chronic "ringing-in-the-ears."

A 2005 ChildWise study found that one in four children under the age of eight had a mobile phone, a figure which increased to 89 percent by the time the child reaches eleven years.

"Teenagers: A Generation Unplugged" is a 2008 study which determined that four out of five teens carry a wireless device (an increase of 40 percent from 2004) and found that their cell phones rank second, only to clothing, in communicating personal social status and popularity, "outranking jewelry, watches and shoes." Additionally, over half (52 percent) view cell phones as a form of entertainment and 80 percent feel that a cell phone provides a sense of security while 36 percent dislike the idea of others knowing their exact location.

While a recent WHO [World Health Organization] study determined that a cell phone-cancer link is inconclusive, the UN [United Nations] did acknowledge that the 2010 examination of thirteen thousand participants found up to 40 percent higher incidence of glioma, a cancerous brain tumor, among the 10 percent that used the mobile phone most. While there is near-unanimous agreement within the scientific community that it is simply too early to accurately project damage caused by radiation, even the most modest estimates acknowledge minimal consequences, the estimated 4.6 billion cell phone users "appear prepared to take the risk" without "firm assurances" that they are safe.[82]

As dire as these incidences for physical damage appear, the psychological and spiritual implications are the significantly more profound—and sinister.

"Thought reading" has come of age. First published in January 2009, CBS revealed technology conducted at Carnegie Mellon University that makes it possible to see what is happening within the brain while people are thinking. Using specialized magnetic resonance, neuro-activity can be recorded by analyzing brain activity.[83]

While mainstream media carefully smudges the science fiction-actual science line, both government and private research groups charge the fields of neuro-fingerprinting, neuro-databases, and abject control neuro-control.

Following the Human Genome Project's mapping of human DNA, the Human Brain Project, HPB, was launched. The international research group hopes to provide a "blueprint of normal brain activity" to the goal of understanding brain function for improved health care, but inherent in the study is the very real possibility of threatening autonomous and unrestricted thought. If in 2002 the BBC was touting wireless sensors that record and generate brain waves and anatomical functions remotely,[84] and in 2008, *Scientific American* reported that scientists can "selectively control brain function by transcranial magnetic stimulation (TMS)" via the pulsing of powerful electromagnetic fields into the brain or a subject's brain circuits,[85] what might be a more current—and sinister—application?

Unbounded Evil

A March 2010 study published in the *Proceedings of the National Academy of Sciences* reported that electro-magnetic currents directed at the right temperoparieto junction (TPJ), located just above and behind the right ear (the same location mentioned above from Exodus 29:20 where the priests were to be anointed that they might hear from God), can impair a person's ability to make moral judgments by inducing a current which disrupts this region of the brain.

By producing "striking evidence" that the right TPJ is "critical for making moral judgments," the lead author, Liane Young, also noted that "under normal circumstances, people are very confident and consistent in these kinds of moral judgments." The researchers believe that transmagnetic stimulation, TMS, interfered with the subject's ability to interpret the intentions of others, suggesting that they are believed to be "morally blameworthy."[86] Subsequent publications have proposed an interest by the U.S. military to use transmagnetic stimulation to enhance soldiers' battle duration by reducing the need to stop for sleep.[87]

With the acknowledged identification, documentation and cataloging of "brain-printing" via wireless devices, and the comparatively recent release of the morally consequential findings of transmagnetic stimulation, the premise of Stephen King's 2006 novel, *Cell,* evokes a frighteningly possible scenario:

> Mobile phones deliver the apocalypse to millions of unsuspecting humans by wiping their brains of any humanity, leaving only aggressive and destructive impulses behind....
>
> What if cell phones didn't cause cancer? What if they did something much worse? What if they turned the user into a zombie killing machine?[88]

Or perhaps just a glance at a keyboard before powering down: The message is clear: CONTROL   ALTER DELETE

From Sue Bradley's chilling e-mail above discussing how the area of the right ear (which was to be anointed for priestly hearing of God in the Old Testament) is now being targeted by electromagnetic currents to illustrate how a person's moral judgment could be impaired, to the work of neurologist Olaf Blanke that produced a "shadow person" by stimulating the left TPJ at the left ear, serious questions arrive about the mysteries of the mind and what God may know that we don't (and therefore why the priests were anointed there) about spiritual gateways existing in these regions. Once again, by interfacing with or manipulating the brain in this way, are we approaching a forbidden unknown?

MIND GATES—FROM NIGHTMARES TO INCEPTION

Another example of how near-horizon neurosciences and human-machine integration may reconfigure human brains to allow borderline (or more than borderline) supernatural activity involves certain video games played before bedtime, which are being shown to allow people to take control of their dreams, to shape the alternate reality of dream worlds in a way that reflects spiritual warfare. According to *LiveScience* senior writer Jeremy Hsu, published studies on the dreams of hard-core gamers by Jayne Gackenbach, a psychologist at Grant MacEwan University in Canada, found that gamers experienced reversed-threat simulation in nightmares, which allowed the dreamer *to become the threatener instead of the threatened.* In other words, a scary nightmare scenario turned into something "fun" for a gamer, allowing the player to assume the role of the aggressor or demon attacker. "They don't run away; they turn and fight back. They're more aggressive than the norms," Gackenbach explained. "Levels of aggression in gamer dreams also included hyper-violence not unlike that of an R-rated movie," and when these dreaming gamers became aggressive, "oh boy, they go off the top."[89]

From learning to influence our private dreams via game-tech to having our dreams infiltrated and manipulated by outside forces, disquieting ideas deepen. In the 2010 movie *Inception* starring Leonardo DiCaprio, industrial spies use a dream machine called PASIV to steal corporate secrets by means of invasion and "extraction" of private information through a victim's dreams. In a second scenario, the film depicts ideas planted in the person's mind (inception) so that the individual perceives them as his or her own, thus allowing the victim to be steered toward particular decisions or actions—a modern upgrade on brainwashing a la the *Manchurian Candidate*. While the film *Inception* is fantasy, it is based in part on near-future technology. Electroencephalograms, functional Magnetic Resonance Imaging (fMRIS), and Computed Tomography (CT) scans are already being used to "read and even influence the brain," points out Aaron Saenz at the Singularity Hub. But could the fundamental science that the film *Inception* examines actually be setting the stage for making it a reality? "We're certainly working towards it," Saenz adds, continuing:

In the next few decades we could have the means to understand, perhaps in rather detailed terms, what a person is thinking. Once that barrier is passed, we may develop the means to influence what someone thinks by directly stimulating their brain. [So] while the mind is still a very mysterious place, it may not remain that way forever.[90]

This trend toward technological mind invasion and mind control is or should be a frightening proposal for most people, especially those who value the concept of *free will*.

That is because most secular neuroscientists view free will as an outdated religious notion related to "a fictional omnipotent divinity" (God) who chooses not to interfere with the choices of individuals, thus leaving them morally accountable for their actions and future judgment. There is even a concerted effort on the part of some neuroscientists to find proof against free will to illustrate that man is little more than an automaton whose decisions are predetermined by a complex mixture of chemical reactions, past events, and even nature, which work together to determine one's course of action. In the 1970s, Prof. Benjamin Libet of the University of California in San Francisco claimed to have discovered proof of this theory through a series of tests in which a "time gap" between a brain's decision to act and the person's awareness of this decision led to the activity being carried out by the individual. His findings ignited a stormy debate regarding the ancient philosophical question of free will, says Naomi Darom for the online edition of *Haaretz* newspaper in Israel. "Are our decisions, the basis for our ostensible free activities, made before we are aware of them? In other words, does the brain ostensibly decide for us? And to what extent do we actually make our decisions consciously?" Prof. Hezi Yeshurun explained how those engaged in the brain research concluded "the question of free will is meaningless, because…the fact that your brain has actually decided in your absence and that I can know what you've decided before you do, paints a picture of an automaton."[91]

To insinuate that a section of the human brain makes decisions ahead of man's independent awareness of them opens a wellspring of opportunity for civil or military arms technology to target that aspect of the brain and to develop methods for "inserting" ideas in minds. DARPA, American Technology Corp., Holosonic Research Labs, and others are working on methods to adapt this science, where thoughts and ideas can be projected or "implanted" in the brain and perceived by the individual as his or her own. A while back, *Wired* magazine reported on DARPA's "sonic projector" as well as troops studying the Long Range Acoustic Device (LRAD) as a modified "Voice of God" weapon:

> It appears that some of the troops in Iraq are using "spoken" (as opposed to "screeching") LRAD to mess with enemy fighters. Islamic terrorists tend to be super-stitious and, of course, very religious. LRAD can put the "word of God" into their heads. If God, in the form of a voice that only you can hear, tells you to surrender, or run away, what are you gonna do?[92]

Wired went on to acknowledge how, beyond directed sound, "it's long been known that microwaves at certain fre-quencies can produce an auditory effect that sounds like it's coming from within someone's head (and there's the nagging question of classified microwave work at Brooks Air Force Base that the Air Force stubbornly refuses to talk about)." It is also reported that the Pentagon tested similar research during the Gulf War of 1991 using a technology called Silent Sound Spread Spectrum (ssss), which evidently led to the surrender of thousands of Iraqi soldiers who began "hearing voices."

People of faith, including church theologians and philos-ophers, should find the idea of using technology to read the minds and manipulate the thoughts of individuals indefensible, as the vanguard of free will is fundamental to our religious and philosophical ethic. To humans, autonomy of thought is the most basic of doctrines in which man is unrestrained by causality or preordained by mystical powers. Yet how these issues—neurosciences, brain-machine interfacing, cybernetics, mind control, and even free will—could actually represent a prophetic confluence of events that soon will combine in an ultimate showdown over the liberty of man may be an unavoidable and *beastly* aspect of end-times prophecy.

CHAPTER ELEVEN

WILL YOU *GRIN* FOR THE MARK
OF THE BEAST?

Can a microscopic tag be implanted in a person's body to track his every movement? There's actual discussion about that. You will rule on that—mark my words—before your tenure is over.

> —U.S. SEN. JOSEPH BIDEN,
> asked during Senate Judiciary Committee
> hearings on the nomination of John Roberts
> to be chief justice of the Supreme Court

Although microchip implantation might be introduced as a voluntary procedure, in time, there will be pressure to make it mandatory. A national identification system via microchip implants could be achieved in two stages. Upon introduction as a voluntary system, the microchip implantation will appear to be palatable. After there is a familiarity with the procedure and a knowledge of its benefits, implantation would be mandatory.

> —DR. ELAINE M. RAMESH, patent attorney for
> Franklin Pierce Law Center

> Now imagine a world in which every newborn baby
> immediately has a little capsule implanted under his
> armpit. Inside are monitors, tiny amounts of hormones,
> a wireless transmitter and receiver…. From birth, no
> moment in a person's life will go unmonitored.
>
> —JOSEPH FARAH, *Whistleblower* magazine

Unless you've been hidden under a rock for the past twenty years, you are probably familiar with the development of radio-frequency identification (RFID) technology that under certain applications is forecast to be connected to future GRIN technologies, especially neurosciences, brain-machine interfacing, and cybernetics.

RFID chips employ tiny integrated circuits for storing and processing information using an antenna for receiving and transmitting the related data. This technology is most commonly applied as a "tag" for tracking inventory with radio waves at companies like Walmart, where consumer goods are embedded with "smart tags" that are read by hand-held scanners for supply chain management.

In recent years, RFID technology has been expanding within public and private firms as a method for verifying and tracking people as well. We first became aware of this trend a while back when chief of police Jack Schmidig of Bergen County, New Jersey, a member of the police force for more than thirty years, received a VeriChip (RFID chip) implant as part of Applied Digital Solution's strategy of enlisting key regional leaders to accelerate adoption of its product.

Kevin H. McLaughlin, VeriChip Corp.'s chief executive officer at the time, said of the event that "high-profile regional leaders are accepting the VeriChip, representing an excellent example of our approach to gaining adoption of the technology" (note that VeriChip Corp. was renamed to PositiveID Corp. on November 10, 2009, through the merger of VeriChip Corp. and Steel Vault Corp.). Through a new and aggressive indoctrination program called "Thought and Opinion Leaders to Play Key Role in Adoption of VeriChip," the company set out to create exponential adoption of its FDA-cleared, human-implantable RFID tag. According to information released by the company, the implantable transceiver "sends and receives data and can be continuously tracked by GPS (Global Positioning Satellite) technology." The transceiver's power supply and actuation system are unlike anything ever created. When implanted within a body, the device is powered electromechanically through the movement of muscles and can be activated either by the "wearer" or by the monitoring facility. In the wake of the terrorist attacks in New York and Washington, an information technology report highlighted the company's additional plans to study implantable chips as a method of tracking terrorists. "We've changed our thinking since September 11 [2001]," a company spokesman said. "Now there's more of a need to monitor evil activities." As a result, PositiveID has been offering the company's current incarnation of implantable RFID as "a tamper-proof means of identification for enhanced e-business security…tracking, locating lost or missing individuals, tracking the location of valuable property [this includes humans], and monitoring the medical conditions of at-risk patients." While PositiveID offers testimony that safeguards have been implemented to ensure privacy in connection with its implantable microchips, some believe privacy is the last thing internal radio transmitters will protect—that in fact the plan to microchip humanity smacks of the biblical mark of the Beast. Has an end-times spirit indeed been pushing for adoption of this technology this generation?

Consider the following:

- According to some Bible scholars, a biblical generation is forty years. This is interesting, given what we documented in our book *Apollyon Rising 2012* concerning the time frame 2012–2013, from which, counting backward forty years, one arrives at the year 1973, the very year *Senior Scholastics* began introducing school kids to the idea of buying and selling in the future using numbers inserted in their foreheads. In the September 20, 1973, feature "Who Is Watching You?" the secular high school journal speculated:

  > All buying and selling in the program will be done by computer. No currency, no change, no checks. In the program, people would receive a number that had been assigned them tattooed in their wrist or forehead. The number is put on by laser beam and cannot be felt. The number in the body is not seen with the naked eye and is as permanent as your fingerprints. All items of consumer goods will be marked with a computer mark. The computer outlet in

the store which picks up the number on the items at the checkstand will also pick up the number in the person's body and automatically total the price and deduct the amount from the person's "Special Drawing Rights" account.

- The following year, the 1974 article, "The Specter of Eugenics," had Charles Frankel documenting Nobel Prize winner Linus Pauling's suggestions that a mark be tattooed on the foot or forehead of every young person. Pauling envisioned a mark denoting genotype.
- In 1980, *U.S. News and World Report* revealed how the federal government was plotting "National Identity Cards" without which no one could work or conduct business.
- The *Denver Post Sun* followed up in 1981, claiming that chip implants would replace the identification cards. The June 21, 1981, story read in part, "The chip is placed in a needle which is affixed to a simple syringe containing an anti-bacterial solution. The needle is capped and ready to forever identify something— or somebody."
- The May 7, 1996, *Chicago Tribune* questioned the technology, wondering aloud if we would be able to trust "Big Brother under our skin?"
- Then, in 1997, applications for patents of subcutaneous implant devices for "a person or an animal" were filed.
- In August 1998, the BBC covered the first-known human microchip implantation.

- That same month, the Sunday Portland *Oregonian* warned that proposed medical identifiers might erode privacy rights by tracking individuals through alpha-numeric health identifier technologies. The startling *Oregonian* feature depicted humans with bar codes in their foreheads.
- Millions of *Today Show* viewers then watched in 2002 when an American family got "chipped" with Applied Digital Solution's VeriChip live from a doctor's office in Boca Raton, Florida.
- In November of the same year, IBM's patent application for "identification and tracking of persons using RFID-tagged items" was recorded.
- Three years later, former secretary of the Health and Human Services department, Tommy Thompson, forged a lucrative partnership with VeriChip Corp. and began encouraging Americans "to get chipped" so that their medical records would be "inside them" in case of emergencies.
- The state of Wisconsin—where Thompson was governor before coming to Washington—promptly drew a line in the sand, passing a law prohibiting employers from mandating that their employees get "chipped." Other states since have passed or are considering similar legislation.
- Despite this, in the last decade, an expanding number of companies and government agencies have started requiring the use of RFID for people identification. Unity Infraprojects, for example, one of the largest civil

contractors in India, tracks its employees with RFID, as does the U.S. Department of Homeland Security for workers involved in baggage handling at airports.

- Since September 11, 2001, the U.S. government has proposed several versions of a national ID card that would use RFID technology.
- Starting in 2006, the U.S. government began requiring passports to include RFID chips.
- Hundreds of Alzheimer's patients have been injected with implantable versions of RFID tags in recent years.
- RFID bracelets are now being placed on newborns at a growing list of hospitals.
- Students are being required in some schools and universities to use biometric ID employing RFID for electronic monitoring.
- Thousands of celebrities and government officials around the world have had RFID radio chips implanted in them so that they can be identified—either for entry at secure sites or for identification if they are kidnapped or killed.
- Others, like Prof. Kevin Warwick (discussed earlier), have been microchipped for purposes of controlling keypads and external devices with the wave of a hand.
- Besides providing internal storage for individual-specific information like health records, banking and industry envisions a cashless society in the near future where all buying and selling could transpire using a version of the subdermal chips and wireless authentication. As mentioned above, in 1973, *Senior Scholastics*

magazine introduced school-age children to the concept of buying and selling using numbers inserted in their forehead. But more recently, *Time* magazine, in its feature story, "The Big Bank Theory and What It Says about the Future of Money," recognized how this type of banking and currency exchange would not require a laser tattoo. Rather, the writer said, "Your daughter can store the money any way she wants—on her laptop, on a debit card, even (in the not-too-distant future) on a chip implanted under her skin."[93]

- In 2007, PositiveID, which owns the Food and Drug Administration-approved VeriChip that electronically transmits patients' health information whenever a scanner is passed over the body, ominously launched "Xmark" as its corporate identity for implantable healthcare products.

- And now, at the time this book is going to the printer, the Department of Homeland Security is working out how to implement the "Real ID Act," with the goal of codifying an international biometric ID system.

The list above continues to accumulate, causing a growing number to wonder if RFID adoption will, for all practical purposes, result in every man, woman, boy, and girl in the developed world having an ID chip inside them (like animals worldwide already do) sometime this century. Students of eschatology (the study of end-times events) find it increasingly difficult to dismiss how this all looks and feels like movement toward fulfilling Revelation 13:16–17: "And he causeth all, both small and great, rich and poor, free and bond, to receive a mark in their right hand, or in their foreheads: And that no man might buy or sell, save he that had the mark, or the name of the beast, or the number of his name."

As newer versions of RFID-like transmitters become even more sophisticated—adding other "prophetic" components such as merging human biological matter with transistors to create living, implantable machines—the authors of this book believe the possibility that the mark of the Beast could arrive through a version of this technology increases. That is one reason we found the recent *Discovery News* report, "Part-Human, Part Machine Transistor Devised," particularly disturbing:

Man and machine can now be linked more intimately than ever. Scientists have embedded a nano-sized transistor inside a cell-like membrane and powered it using the cell's own fuel. The research could lead to new types of man-machine interactions where embedded devices could relay information about the inner workings of proteins inside the cell membrane, and eventually lead to new ways to *read, and even influence, brain or nerve cells.*

"This device is as close to the seamless marriage of biological and electronic structures as anything else that people did before," said Aleksandr Noy, a scientist at the University of California, Merced, who is a co-author on the recent *ACS Nano Letters.* "We can take proteins, real biological machines, and make them part of a working microelectronic circuit."[94]

A similar story ("DNA Logic Gates Herald Injectable Computers") was published by *New Scientist* magazine the same month as the story above, and a few weeks earlier, an article by the *Daily Mail* ("Meet the Nano-Spiders: The DNA Robots that Could One Day Be Walking through Your Body") reported the creation by scientists of microscopic robots made of DNA molecules that can walk, turn, and even create tiny products of their own on a nano-scale assembly line. This is important because a while back, one of the authors (Nita) brought up a point we had never considered. She asked if the biblical mark of the Beast might be a conspiracy employing specific implantable technology only now available. Her theory was gripping. An occult elite operating behind the U.S. government devises a virus that is a crossover between human and animal disease—let's say, an entirely new and highly contagious influenza mutation—and intentionally releases it into the public. A pandemic ensues, and the period between when a person contracts the virus and death is something like ten days. With tens of thousands dead in a few weeks and the rate of death increasing hourly around the globe, a universal cry for a cure goes out. Seemingly miraculously, the government then steps forward with a vaccine. The only catch, the government explains, is that, given the nature of the animal-human flu, the "cure" uses animal DNA and nanobots to rewrite one's genetics so that the person is no longer entirely human. The point made was that those who receive this antidote would become part "beast," and perhaps thus the title, "mark of the Beast." No longer "entirely human" would also mean—according to this outline—that the individual could no longer be "saved" or go to heaven, explaining why the book of Revelation says "whosoever receiveth the mark" is damned forever (while also explaining why the Nephilim, whose DNA was part human and part animal, could not be redeemed). If one imagines the global chaos of such a pandemic, the concept of how the Antichrist "causes all," both small and great, to receive this mark becomes clearer. When looking into the eyes of dying children, parents, or a spouse, it would be incredibly difficult to allow oneself to die or to encourage others to do the same when a "cure" was readily available. Lastly, this scenario would mean that nobody would be allowed to "buy or sell" in the marketplace without the mark-cure due to the need to quarantine all but the inoculated, thus fulfilling all aspects of the mark of the Beast prophecy.

To find out if the science behind this abstract would be as reasonable as it appeared on the surface, we again contacted Sharon Gilbert. This was her troubling response:

Tom and Nita:

What is human? Until recently, most of us would readily respond that *we* are humans. You and I, we might argue, are *Homo sapiens*: erect, bipedal hominids with twenty-three pairs of matched chromosomes and nifty little thumbs capable of apposition to the palm that enable us to grasp the fine tools that our highly developed, bi-lobed brains devise.

Humans, we might argue, sit as rulers of the earth, gazing down from the pinnacle of a pyramid consisting of all plant and animal species. We would remind the listener that natural selection and evolution have developed mankind into a superior thinker and doer, thereby granting us royal privilege, if not infinite responsibility. The

Bible would take this definition much farther, of course, adding that mankind is the only part of God's creation formed by His hands, rather than spoken into existence, and that you and I bear God's unique signature as having been created "in His image" (Genesis 1:27).

Many members of the "illuminated brotherhood of science" would likely demur to the previous statement. These have, in point of fact, redefined *human*. Like Shelley's *Modern Prometheus*, Victor Frankenstein, today's molecular magicians play "god" not by stitching together rotting corpses, but by reforming the very essence of our beings: our DNA.

So-called "postmodern man" began as a literary reference but has evolved into an iconic metaphor representing a collective image of perfected humanity beyond the confines of genetic constraints. Transhumanism, also known as the H+ movement (see www.HPlusMagazine. com, for example) envisions a higher life-form yet, surpassing *Homo sapiens* in favor of *Homo sapiens 2.0*, a bioengineered construct that fuses man's original genome with animal and/or synthetic DNA.

While such claims ring of science fiction, they are indeed science fact. For decades, laboratories have created chimeric combinations of animal, plant, and even human DNA under the guise of medical research. The stated goal is to better man's lot by curing disease, but this benign mask hides an inner, sardonic grin that follows an ancient blueprint to blend God's perfect creature with the seed of fallen angels: "You shall be as gods."

You two speak to the heart of the matter when you

warn of a day when true humans may receive trans-human instructions via an implant or injection. A seemingly innocuous vaccine or identification "chip" can initiate intracellular changes, not only in somatic or "body" cells but also in germ-line cells such as ova and sperm. The former alters the recipient only; the latter alters the recipient's doomed descendents as well.

In my second novel, *The Armageddon Strain*, I present a device called the "BioStrain Chip" that employs nanotechnology to induce genetic changes inside the carrier's body. This miracle chip is advertised as a cure for the H5N1/ebola chimera that is released in the prologue to the book. Of course, if you've read the novel, then you know the BioStrain chip does far more than "cure"—it also kills.

Though a work of fiction, *The Armageddon Strain* raises a chilling question: What limitations lie within the payload of a biochip? Can such a tiny device do more than carry digitized information? Could it actually serve as the *mark of the Beast?* The answer is yes.

DNA (Deoxyribonucleic acid) has become the darling of researchers who specialize in synthetic constructs. The "sticky-end" design of the DNA double-helix makes it ideal for use in computing. Though an infinite number of polyhedra are possible, the most robust and stable of these "building blocks" is called the double crossover (DX). An intriguing name, is it not? The double-cross.

Picture an injectible chip comprised of DNA-DX, containing instructions for a super-soldier. Picture, too, how this DNA framework, if transcribed, might also serve a second, *sinister*, purpose—not only to instruct, but also to *alter*.

Mankind has come perilously far in his search for perfection through chemistry. Although millennia passed with little progress beyond roots, herbs, and alchemical quests for gold from lead, the twentieth century ushered science into the rosy dawn of breathless discovery. Electricity, lighter than air travel, wireless communication, and computing transformed the ponderous pace of the scientific method into a light speed race toward self-destruction.

By the mid-1950s, Watson and Crick had solved the structure of the DNA molecule and the double helix became all the rage. Early gene splicing, and thus transgenics, began in 1952 as a crude, cut-and-paste sort of science cooked up in kitchen blenders and petri dishes—as much accident as inspiration. As knowledge has increased (Daniel 12:4), genetic scientists learned to utilize microbiological "vectors" and sophisticated methods to insert animal or plant genes from one species into another. It's the ultimate "Mr. Potato Head" game, where interchangeable plastic pieces give rise to an infinite number of combinations; only, in genetic splicing, humanity is the unhappy potato.

Vectors provide the means of transport and integration for this brave new science. Think of these vectors as biological trucks that carry genetic building materials and workers into your body's cells. Such "trucks" could be a microsyringe, a bacterium, or a virion (a virus particle). Any entity that can carry genetic information

(the larger the load capacity, the better) and then sur-
reptitiously gain entry into the cell is a potential vector.
Viruses, for example, can be stripped of certain innate
genes that might harm the cell. Not only does this (supposedly) render the viral delivery truck "harmless," it
also clears out space for the cargo.

Once inside the cell, the "workers" take over. Some
of these "workers" are enzymes that cut human genes
at specific sites, while others integrate—or load—the
"cargo" into appropriate reading frames—like microscopic librarians. Once the payload is stored in the cell's
nuclear "library stacks," the new genes can be translated,
copied, and "read" to produce altered or brand-new,
"alien" polymers and proteins.

The resulting hybrid cell is no longer purely human.
If a hybridized skin cell, it may now glow, or perhaps
form scales rather than hair, claws rather than finger-
nails. If a brain cell, the new genetic instructions could
produce an altered neurotransmitter that reduces or
even eliminates the body's need for sleep. Muscle cells
may grow larger and more efficient at using low levels of calcium and oxygen. Retina cells may encode for
receptors that enable the "posthuman being" to perceive
infrared or ultraviolet light frequencies. The hybrid ears
may now sense a wider range of sounds, taste buds a
greater range of chemicals. Altered brains might even
attune to metaphysics and "unseen" gateways, allowing
communication with supernatural realms.

Germ-line alterations, mentioned earlier, form a
terrifying picture of generational development and may

very well already be a reality. Genetic "enhancement" of sperm-producing cells would change human sperm into tiny infiltrators, and any fertilized ovum a living chimera. Science routinely conducts experiments with transgenic mice, rats, chickens, pigs, cows, horses, and many other species. It is naïve to believe humans have been left out of this transgenic equation.

If so many scientists (funded by government entities) believe in the "promise" of genetic alteration and transgenic "enhancement," how then can humanity remain human? We cannot. We will not. Perhaps, *some have not.*

Spiritually, the enemy has ever sought to corrupt God's plan. Originally, fallen angels lay with human women to corrupt the original base pair arrangements. Our genome is filled with "junk DNA" that seemingly encodes for nothing. These "introns" may be the remains of the corrupted genes, and God Himself may have switched them off when fallen angels continued their program, post-Flood. If so, today's scientists might need only to "switch them back on" to resurrect old forms such as Gibborim and Nephilim.

I should point out that not all "trucks" (vectors) deliver their payload immediately. Some operate on a time delay. Cytomegalovirus (CMV) is a common infective agent resident in the cells of many humans today. It "sleeps" in our systems, waiting for a window of opportunity to strike. Recently, genetic specialists began utilizing CMV vectors in transgenic experiments. In 1997, the Fox television program *Millennium* featured an episode in the second season called "Sense and

Antisense" (referring to the two sides of the DNA molecule). In this chilling story, a scientist named Lacuna reveals a genetic truth to Frank Black: "They have the map, the map, they can make us go down any street they want to. Streets that we would never even dream of going down. They flip a switch, we go east. They flip another switch, we go north. And we never know we have been flipped, let alone know how."[95]

In the final days of this current age, humanity may indeed "flip." Paul tells us that Christians will be transformed in a moment (1 Corinthians 15:51–53). Is it possible that the enemy also plans an instantaneous "flip"? Are genetic sleeper agents (idling "trucks") already at work in humanity's DNA, waiting and ready to deploy at the appropriate moment?

Science is ready. Knowledge has been increased. The spiritual players have taken the stage.

All we need is the signal. The sign. The injection. The mark. The moment.

We shall ALL be changed. Some to incorruptible bodies ready to meet the Lord. Others to corrupted genomes ready to serve the Beast.

FROM ANTICHRIST'S MARK TO HIS TRANSHUMAN CHURCH

Perhaps related to the rise of Antichrist and his human-transforming "mark of the Beast" technology is an intriguing aspect of transhumanism that is only now developing into what could be an end-times universalist religion. Is it a coincidence that this comes during the same epoch in which the United States Supreme Court, for the first time in its history, became devoid of Protestant representation with the confirmation of Elena Kagan; a time also in which the Claremont School of Theology analyzing the future of American religion concluded at its 2010 Theology After Google Conference that "technology must be embraced" for Christianity to survive?

Although most transhumanists, especially early on, were secular atheists and would have had little resemblance to prototypical "people of faith," in the last few years, the exclusion of supernaturalism in favor of rational empiricism has softened as the movement's exponential popularity has swelled to include a growing number of Gnostic Christians, Buddhists, Mormons, Islam, Raelianism, and other religious traditions among its devotees. From among these groups, new tentative "churches" arose—the Church of Virus, the Society for Universal Immortalism, Transtopianism, the Church of Mez, the Society for Venturism, the Church of the Fulfillment, Singularitarianism, and others. Today, with somewhere between 25–30 percent of transhumanists considering themselves religious, these separate sects or early "denominations" within transhumanism are coalescing their various religious worldviews around generally fixed creeds involving *spiritual transcendence* as a result of human enhancement. Leaders within the movement, whom we refer to here as *transevangelists,* have been providing religion-specific lectures during conferences to guide these disciples toward a collective (hive) understanding of the mystical compatibility between faith and transhumanism. At Trinity College in Toronto, Canada, for instance, transhumanist Peter

Addy lectured on the fantastic "Mutant Religious Impulses of the Future" during the Faith, Transhumanism, and Hope symposium. At the same meeting, Prof. Mark Walker spoke on "Becoming Godlike," James Hughes offered "Buddhism and Transhumanism: The Technologies of Self-Perfection," Michael LaTorra gave a "Trans-Spirit" speech, nanotechnologist and lay Catholic Tihamer Toth-Fejel presented "Is Catholic Transhumanism Possible?" and Nick Bostrom spoke on "Transhumanism and Religion." (Each of these presentations can be listened to or downloaded at our Web site, www. ForbiddenGate.com.)

Recently, the *New York Times* picked up this meme (contagious idea) in its June 11, 2010, feature titled "Merely Human? That's So Yesterday," speaking of transhumanism and the Singularity as offering "a modern-day, quasi-religious answer to the Fountain of Youth by affirming the notion that, yes indeed, humans—or at least something derived from them—can have it all."[96] In commenting on the *Times* article at his blog, one of our favorite writers, bioethicist Wesley J. Smith, observed the following:

> Here's an interesting irony: Most transhumanists are materialists. But they desire eternal life as much as the religionists that so many materialists disdain. So they invent a material substitute that offers the benefits of faith, without the burden of sin, as they forge a new eschatology that allows them to maintain their über-rationalist credentials as they try to escape the nihilistic despair that raw materialism often engenders. So they tout a corporeal New Jerusalem and prophesy the

coming of the Singularity—roughly equivalent of the Second Coming for Christians—that will...begin a New Age of peace, harmony, and eternal life right here on Terra firma.[97]

In the peer-reviewed *Journal of Evolution and Technology* published by the Institute for Ethics and Emerging Technologies (founded in 2004 by transhumansists Nick Bostrom and James Hughes), the "Apologia for Transhumanist Religion" by Prof. Gregory Jordan lists the many ways transhumanism is emerging as either a new form of religion or a mirror of fundamental human ambitions, desires, longings, shared hopes, and dreams that traditional religions hold in common. In spite of denial by some of its advocates, Jordan concludes that transhumanism may be considered a rising religion because of its numerous parallels to religious themes and values involving godlike beings, the plan for eternal life, the religious sense of awe surrounding its promises, symbolic rituals among its members, an inspirational worldview based on faith, and technology that promises to heal the wounded, restore sight to the blind, and give hearing back to the deaf.

Of the technological Singularity in particular, Jordan writes how some transhumanists especially view the Singularity as a religious event, "a time when human consciousness will expand beyond itself and throughout the universe." Quoting Kurzweil's "The Singularity is Near: When Humans Transcend Biology," Jordan provides:

The matter and energy in our vicinity will become infused with the intelligence, knowledge, creativity, beauty, and emotional intelligence (the ability to love, for example) of our human-machine civilization. Our civilization will expand outward, turning all the dumb matter [normal humans] and energy we encounter into sublimely intelligent—transcendent—matter and energy. So in a sense, we can say that the Singularity will ultimately infuse the world with spirit.

According to these Singularitarians, this expansion of consciousness after the Singularity will also be an approach to the divine:

> Evolution moves toward greater complexity, greater elegance, greater knowledge, greater intelligence, greater beauty, greater creativity, and greater levels of subtle attributes such as love. In every monotheistic tradition God is likewise described as all of these qualities, only without any limitation: infinite knowledge, infinite intelligence, infinite beauty, infinite creativity, infinite love, and so on.... So evolution moves inexorably toward this conception of God.... We can regard, therefore, the freeing of our thinking from the severe limitations of its biological form to be an essentially spiritual undertaking.[98]

Yet while development of a *new* universalist religion appears to be forming among members of transhumanism's enlightenment, conservative scholars will taste the *ancient* origin of its heresy as the incarnation of gnosticism and its disdain for the human body as basically an evil design that is far inferior to what we can make it. "Despite all their rhetoric about enhancing the performance of bodily functions," says Brent Waters, director of the Jerre L. and Mary Joy Stead Center for Ethics and Values, "the posthuman project is nevertheless driven by a hatred and loathing of the body."[99] Transhumanist Prof. Kevin Warwick put it this way: "I was born human. But this was an accident of fate—a condition merely of time and place."

Conversely, in Judeo-Christian faith, the human body is not an ill-designed "meat sack," as transhumanists so often deride. We were made in God's image to be temples of His Holy Spirit. The incarnation of God in the person of Jesus Christ and His bodily resurrection are the centerpieces of the gospel and attest to this magnificent fact. While in our fallen condition human suffering is reality, most traditional Christians believe this struggle makes us stronger and that healing and improvements to the human condition are also to be desired. Throughout history, the church has therefore been at the forefront of disease treatment discovery, institutions for health care, hospitals, and other medical schools and research centers. In other words, we do not champion a philosophy toward techno-dystopianism. *Indeed, what a day it will be when cancer is cured and we all shout "Hallelujah!"*

But in the soul-less posthuman, where DNA is recombined in mockery of the Creator and no man is made in God's image, "there are no essential differences, or absolute demarcations, between bodily existence and computer simulation, cybernetic mechanism and biological organism, robot technology and human goals," says Katherine Hayles, professor of English at the University of California, in her book *How We Became Posthuman.* "Humans can either go gently into that good night, joining the dinosaurs as a species that once ruled the earth but is now obsolete," she says in transhuman contempt of—or outright hostility to—intrinsic human dignity, "or hang on for a while longer by becoming machines themselves. In either case…the age of the human is drawing to a close."[100]

Thus the gauntlet is thrown down and a holy war declared by the new and ungodly apostles of a transhuman faith! We who were created in His image will either adapt and be assimilated to posthuman, or be replaced by Nephilim 2.0 and the revival of their ancient mystery religion. This solidifies how, the more one probes into the ramifications of merging unnatural creations and nonbiological inventions according to the transhumanist scheme of seamlessly recalibrating humanity, a deeper malaise emerges, one that suggests those startling "parallels" between modern technology and ancient Watchers activity may be no coincidence at all—that, in fact, a dark conspiracy is truly unfolding as it did "in the days of Noah."

Consider, in conclusion of this chapter, the thoughtful commentary by Dr. C. Christopher Hook:

> There are several key questions that our churches and theologians will have to address. Is it appropriate for members of the body of Christ to engage in alterations that go beyond therapy and are irreversible? Is it just to do so in a world already deeply marked by inequities? What does it mean that our Lord healed and restored in His ministry—never enhanced? Is it significant that the gifts of the Holy Spirit—wisdom, love, patience, kindness—cannot be manufactured by technology?[101]

CHAPTER TWELVE

THOSE "OTHER" SIGNS
OF THE DAYS OF NOAH

As laboratories incubate new blends of man and
machine.... The path of progress cuts through the four-
way intersection of the moral, medical, religious and
political—and whichever way you turn, you are likely to
run over someone's deeply held beliefs. Venter's bombshell
[the creation of the synthetic life "Synthia"] revived the
oldest of ethical debates, over whether scientists were
playing God or proving he does not exist because someone
re-enacted Genesis in suburban Maryland.

—Nancy Gibbs, *Time* magazine

If Christians are to help shape contemporary culture—
particularly in a setting in which I fear the posthuman
message will prove attractive, if not seductive—then they
must offer an alternative and compelling vision; a counter
theological discourse so to speak.

—Brent Waters, Director of the Jerre L. and
Mary Joy Stead Center for Ethics and Values

Earlier in this book, we pointed out how the English theologian George Hawkins Pember, in his 1876 masterpiece, *Earth's Earliest Ages*, studied the book of Matthew—where Jesus in answering His disciples concerning the signs of His coming and of the end of the world said it would be "as the days of Noah were"—and concluded from it that the most fearful sign of the end times would be the reappearance upon earth "of beings from the Principality of the Air, and their unlawful intercourse with the human race."

We have built on this concept as well, suggesting that parallels between human-modifying technology and what the ancient Watchers did in creating Nephilim may be no coincidence at all; that a dark conspiracy could be unfolding by way of GRIN sciences and transhumanist philosophy that specifically allows the fulfillment of the prophecy "as it was in the days of Noah."

But if indeed Satan has initiated an extraordinary conspiracy to revive species-altering supernaturalism as existed in Noah's day, and assuming there is a gap between that sign and when God removes His own from this planet, the church as the body of Christ and God's representation on earth could play a unique role as the instrument through which the Almighty, on behalf of His creation, will engage this evil. True believers are the salt of the earth and the only social influence identified in Scripture as the power against which the gates of hell cannot prevail. This, friends, unveils good news, because while Nephilim were on earth during (and after) the antediluvian age, this was not the only "sign" related to ancient days. There were other signs too, as illustrated in the Bible, having to do with

God's covenant people and their unequaled ability through faith to turn back Nephilim plans. "As it was in the days of Noah" points to this fact as well.

Consider how King Saul in 1063 BC stared across his tent into the eyes of the unproven and youngest son of Jesse. By chance, the teenager named David had come on a mission for his father to deliver food and gather information regarding the welfare of his brothers. On his arrival, Goliath, the champion of the Philistines, stood up at his camp across the Valley of Elah and once again challenged the armies of Israel to send a warrior out against him. Two times per day for the past forty days the fearsome giant had terrified Saul's army, crying over the steep basin to the ranks of Israel:

"Why set the battle in array? Am I not a Philistine and you servants of Saul? Choose a man from among yourselves and let him come down to me," Goliath challenged. "If he is able to fight with me and to kill me, then we will become your servants; but if I prevail against him and kill him, then you shall become our servants. I defy the ranks of Israel; give me a man that we may decide the outcome of this conflict in a single fight!"

On seeing and hearing this spectacle, David learned how Saul was promising a rich reward to any man who could defeat the nine-foot-tall menace. David's response was one of dismay at the lack of Israel's faith. "Who is this uncircumcised Philistine, that he should defy the armies of the living God?" he asked among the soldiers (1 Samuel 17:26). When Saul heard of it, he sent for the lad. But now, standing here in front of him, unable to fill his armor, the ruddy kid didn't look like much of a killer. Then David told him about slaying a lion and later a bear in defense of his father's sheep, and Saul relented.

With nothing but a staff, a sling, and five smooth stones, David emerged on the battlefield and ran toward Goliath. When the chiseled Philistine saw the fair-skinned youth approaching, he looked around, scoffed, then thundered, "Am I a dog, that you send a boy at me with a stick!?" Cursing in the name of his gods, he sneered, "Come on then, and I will give your flesh as supper to the birds of the air and the beasts of the field."

But David shocked everybody with his retort. "You come at me with a sword and a shield, but I am coming in the name of the LORD of Hosts, the God of the armies of Israel, whom you have defied," he cried. "This day the Lord will deliver you into my hand; and I will smite you, and take your head off, and *your* carcass is the one the birds of the air and the beasts of the field will dine on!" With that, David rushed forward, let the stone go from his sling, and the rest, as they say, is history.

Why is this story important to this book? Because Goliath was a Nephilim, and was defeated by a young servant of God. If the arrival of these beings or the spirit of their sins is the pre-eminent sign of the end times, David defeating one is germane as well. This, too, is an important prophetic symbol.

From a youth to an old man, consider another example. Four hundred twenty-seven years before David slew Goliath, the people of Israel were camped along the southern border of Canaan, the "Promised Land" God had said He would give them. Twelve spies—one from each tribe of Israel—went in to survey the land and found walled cities inhabited by giant Nephilim offspring. Psalm 78:41 records what happened at this discovery. "Yea, they turned back and tempted God, and limited the Holy One of Israel." In other words, like Saul's army later did, the children of Israel trembled at the sight of the sons of Anak, the giants of Nephilim descent. "And there we saw the giants, the sons of Anak, which come of the giants," they uttered in hopeless despair before adding, "and we were in our own sight as grasshoppers, and so we were in their sight" (Numbers 13:32–33). Only two of the spies, Joshua and Caleb, believed in the promises of God. They encouraged the people not to be afraid, to trust in the Lord who would give them victory over the Nephilim. But that generation disagreed, wanted to have Joshua and Caleb stoned, cursed God, and died in the wilderness never having received their inheritance in Canaan. Joshua and Caleb, on the other hand, waited for God's further orders, which came in 1451 BC: "Now therefore arise, go over this Jordan, thou, and all this people, unto the land which I do give to them, even to the children of Israel. Every place that the sole of your foot shall tread upon, that have I given unto you, as I said unto Moses.... There shall not any man be able to stand before thee" (Joshua 1:2–3, 5). Joshua and Caleb trusted God as usual, and this time, at the age of eighty-five, no less, Caleb drove out the sons of Anak that had so terrified the unbelieving spies.

The fact that God's people could prevail over the spirit of the Nephilim in these ways is an ageless reality. It suggests that believers today not only could survive, but could triumph, over the inhuman threat represented by GRIN technology and the transhumanist agenda. This will occur as believers recall specific Bible knowledge and engage in dynamic activity, what we title *those other two signs of the days of Noah*.

THE "SECOND SIGN" OF THE DAYS OF NOAH: PREACHING RIGHTEOUSNESS

While it could certainly be possible to get discouraged by focusing on the Nephilim and the prediction of their return at the end of time, a wonderful portion of Scripture from the same days of Noah adds, "But Noah found grace in the eyes of the Lord." Think about what a marvelous revelation this is: that at the darkest time in earth's history, when the sins of the Watchers had spread like a cancer across continents, infecting all of humanity both genetically and philosophically, "Noah walked with God" (Genesis 6:9). At a time when all flesh was tainted by transhuman genes and every imagination of men's thoughts were only evil continually (Genesis 6:5), one man had not forgotten where to glory, one man walked with God, one man found grace.

Today, as we move into the uncharted waters of a resurrected technological and human-transforming era, the keys to victory for believers will be the same as they were for David, Joshua, Caleb, and Noah—knowing where to glory, what to keep one's focus on, where to place one's faith, and whose champion we can be.

On this point, it is clear that Noah did not buy into the transhuman lies of his day. While the immortals known as Watchers were promising advanced technology to the world in exchange for use of human DNA (Book of Enoch, chapter 8), it must have been obvious to Noah how reminiscent this was of the serpent in the Garden who made similar promises of godlike abilities for those who partook forbidden fruit. Noah assumed leadership instead, independently maintaining his faith and focus in God, not willing to compromise his flesh or that of his family for any temporal therapeutic benefit (lie). Furthermore, Noah did not sit idly by keeping these opinions to himself. In 2 Peter 2:5, we learn he became a "preacher of righteousness" (Greek *kerux:* a herald or "one who announces"). This was true in his use of technology as an "illustrative sermon" while building the Ark (contrasted to the misuse of technology by Watchers), but some scholars believe it was more than this, that he preached audibly, facing the transhuman movement of his day with boldness, publically warning of the dangers of grievous sins related to genetic manipulation incited by invisible agents.

In the letter to the church at Ephesus, Paul states the responsibility of the church in this regard for today, concluding this was by divine intention. "His intent was that now, through the church, the manifold wisdom of God should be made known to the rulers and authorities in the heavenly realms" (Ephesians 3:10). Imagine that. It is our duty as believers to follow Noah's example and make known the manifold wisdom of God until even the angelic powers are aware of it. Was this behind what Brent Waters, whom we quote at the top of this chapter, had in mind when he said, "If Christians are to help shape contemporary culture—particularly in a setting in which I fear the posthuman message will prove attractive, if not seductive—then they must offer an alternative and compelling vision; a counter theological discourse so to speak"?

While "a counter theological discourse" reflective of the everlasting gospel of human redemption through the person of Jesus Christ will be antithetical to the salvation plan of transhumanism, it must address the difficult philosophical and ethical questions raised by modern technology and the portentous move by governments and powers to use biological sciences to remanufacture mankind. The message needs to be relevant and must appeal to the questions and style of a generation raised during the Digital Revolution, an age of personal computing and information-sharing technology that for many of us represents a shift away from the Industrial Revolution's outdated methods of communicating. The need to parse information is changing so rapidly that we expect to hit the knee of the techno-info curve sometime around the year 2012, followed by Singularity and critical mass. As a result, the authors of this book have teamed with a group of ministries and intellectuals and are currently organizing a new national conference, the World Congress on Emerging Threats and Challenges (tentative conference title), the first of which is to be held the third week of July 2011 in Branson, Missouri. More information on this event—and why *you* should be there—will be posted before the end of 2010 at www.ForbiddenGate.com, including how the conference will address, among other things, the need for an international statement on human enhancement and a Christian manifesto on GRIN technology and human dignity.

Although the Vatican in 2008 issued a limited set of instructions on bioethics primarily dealing with in vitro fertilization and stem cell research (*Dignitas Personae* or "the Dignity of the Person") and a handful of Christian scientists, policy makers, and conservative academics have hinted in public commentary on the need for a broader, manifesto-like document on the subject, the church as an institution has failed at any concerted effort to focus on the genetics revolution, the government's interest in human enhancement, the viral transhumanist philosophy capturing the mind of a generation at colleges and universities (not to mention via popular media), and the significant moral and ethical issues raised by these trends. As this book heads to editing, four thousand evangelical leaders from two hundred nations are convening in South Africa to adopt a new manifesto related to missiology and "a statement on Nature." This gathering is organized by Billy Graham's Lausanne Committee for World Evangelism (LCWE) and we pray it will include something significant on bioethics, because other than a nearly decade-old Lausanne "Occasional Paper No. 58," which discussed ways in which bioethics could be used as a tool for evangelism (very important), no documentation we have seen thus far indicates that the new LCWE gathering will debate the moral limits of human-enhancement technologies, which have dramatically evolved since the brief "Occasional Paper No. 58."

While the Vatican's *Dignitas Personae* likewise failed to provide instructions on the greater issue of biological enhancement (as envisioned by transhumans and espoused by agencies of the U.S. and other federal governments as the next step in human evolution), its positional paper did provide an important bird's-eye view on the clash developing between traditional morality and *the quiet adoption of transhumanist philosophy by Christian apologists, who likewise have begun to question what it means to be human and whose competing moral vision could ultimately shape the future of society.*

Immediately following the release of *Dignitas Personae,* Catholic scientist William B. Neaves, in an essay for the *National Catholic Reporter,* reflected the new biblical exegesis, causing reporter Rod Dreher to describe it as clearly illustrating "the type of Christianity that is eager to jettison the old morality and embrace the new." The subtleties behind Neaves' comments included:

> An alternative point of view to the Vatican's, embraced by many Christians, is that personhood [a transhumanist concept] occurs after successful implantation in the mother's uterus, when individual ontological identity is finally established.... If one accepts the viewpoint that personhood begins after implantation, the moral framework guiding the development and application of medical technology to human reproduction and treatment of disease looks very different from that described in *Dignitas Personae.*
>
> In the alternative moral framework, taking a pill to prevent the products of fertilization from implanting in a uterus is morally acceptable. Using IVF [in vitro fertilization] to complete the family circle of couples otherwise unable to have children is an unmitigated good. Encouraging infertile couples with defective gametes to adopt already-produced IVF embryos that will otherwise be discarded is a laudable objective. And using embryonic stem cells to seek cures [creating human embryos for research "parts"] becomes a worthy means of fulfilling the biblical mandate to heal the sick.[102]

Notwithstanding that the discussion by Neaves was limited to the Vatican's position on embryos, his introduction of memes involving personhood and "ensoulment" represents worrisome Christian theological entanglement with transhumanist philosophy, further illustrating the need for a solid manifesto providing a conservative vision for public policy with regard to human experimentation and enhancement.

From Noah to the present hour, making known this "righteous" and manifold wisdom of God in hopes of persuading an age to appreciate the human-affirming virtues of Christian morality can be intrinsic to the Great Commission. There is no middle ground for preachers of righteousness in these matters. Believers are either asleep at the wheel or actively engaged in spiritual warfare for the souls of a generation whose members today are desperately seeking reasons to believe, despite everything they are being told, that the church remains relevant. To fail this responsibility will be to abdicate to a frightening transhuman vision of the future such as was predicted by theologian and Christian apologist C. S. Lewis in *The Abolition of Man*. Lewis foresaw the day when transhumanist and scientific reasoning would win out, permanently undoing mankind through altering the species, ultimately reducing Homo sapiens to utilitarian products. Here is part of what he said:

In order to understand fully what Man's power over Nature, and therefore the power of some men over other men, really means, we must picture the race extended in time from the date of its emergence to that of its extinction. Each generation exercises power over its successors: and each, in so far as it modifies the environment bequeathed to it and rebels against tradition, resists and limits the power of its predecessors. This modifies the picture which is sometimes painted of a progressive emancipation from tradition and a progressive control of natural processes resulting in a continual increase of human power. In reality, of course, if any one age really attains, by eugenics and scientific education, the power to make its descendants what it pleases [transhuman/posthuman], all men who live after it are the patients of that power. They are weaker, not stronger: for though we may have put wonderful machines in their hands we have preordained how they are to use them. And if, as is almost certain, the age which had thus attained maximum power over posterity were also the age most emancipated from tradition, it would be engaged in reducing the power of its predecessors almost as drastically as that of its successors.... The last men, far from being the heirs of power, will be of all men most subject to the dead hand of the great planners and conditioners and will themselves exercise least power upon the future.... The final stage [will have] come when Man by eugenics, by pre-natal conditioning, and by an education and propaganda based on a perfect applied psychology...shall have "taken the thread of life out of the hand of Clotho" [one of the Three Fates in mythology responsible for spinning the thread of human life] and be henceforth free to make our species whatever we wish it to be. The battle will indeed be won. But who, precisely, will have won it?[103]

Lewis foresaw the progressive abandonment of what we would call "moral law" based on Judeo-Christian values giving way to "the dead hand of the great planners and conditioners" who would decide what men should biologically become. The terms "great planners and conditioners" correspond perfectly with modern advocates of transhumanism who esteem their blueprint for the future of the species as the one that will ultimately decide the fate of man. A recent step toward establishing this goal (in addition to all the other "steps" we've documented) occurred when the U.S. National Science Foundation (NSF) and the Human Enhancement Ethics Group (based at California Polytechnic State University, whose advisory board is a wish list of transhumanist academics and institutions worldwide) released its fifty-page report entitled "Ethics of Human Enhancement: 25 Questions & Answers." This government-funded report addressed the definitions, scenarios, anticipated societal disruptions, and policy and law issues that need to be considered en route to becoming posthuman (the full NSF report can be downloaded for free at our Web site: www.ForbiddenGate.com). Some of the topics covered in the new study include:

- What are the policy implications of human enhancement?
- Is the natural-artificial distinction of human enhancement morally significant?
- Does human enhancement raise issues of fairness, access, and equity?

- Will it matter if there is an "enhanced divide" between "new" people classifications?
- How would such a divide make communication difficult between "normals" and the "enhanced"?
- How should the enhancement of children be approached?
- What kind of societal disruptions might arise from human enhancement?
- Should there be any limits on enhancement for military purposes?
- Might enhanced humans count as someone's intellectual property?
- Will we need to rethink the very meaning of "ethics," given the dawn of enhancement?

The "Ethics of Human Enhancement" report was authored by the NSF-funded research team of Dr. Fritz Allhoff (Western Michigan University), Dr. Patrick Lin (California Polytechnic State University), Prof. James Moor (Dartmouth College), and Prof. John Weckert (Center for Applied Philosophy and Public Ethics/Charles Sturt University, Australia) as part of a three-year ethics study on human enhancement and emerging technologies. "No matter where one is aligned on this issue, it is clear that the human enhancement debate is a deeply passionate and personal one, striking at the heart of what it means to be human," explained Dr. Lin in the report. Then, with surprising candor, he added, "Some see it as a way to fulfill or even transcend our potential; others see it as a darker path towards becoming Frankenstein's monster."[104]

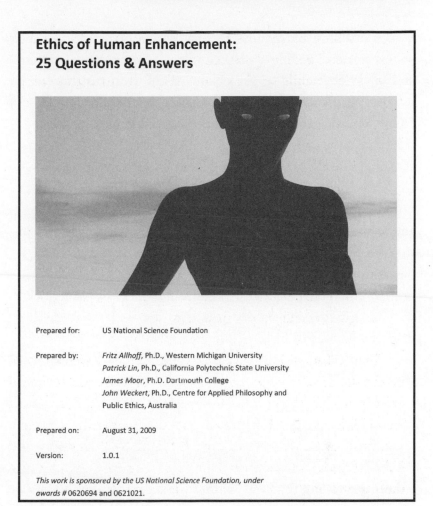

NSF Report: "Ethics of Human Enhancement: 25 Questions & Answers"

Given that the impending human-enhancement revolution raises such profound questions concerning the meaning of life—not to mention threatening to unleash unknown environmental and health-related dangers—the authors of this book hope that by making this information available to the widest possible audience (you can help by telling your pastors and circle of friends to get a copy of the free, thirteen-week teachers' guide based on this subject at www.ForbiddenGate. com and use it to present classes and/or sermons on the considerable subject matter), thinking ministers, policy makers, academics, and the general public will weigh in on this issue while there is still time, get involved in the public debate over human-enhancement technology and transhumanist desires, and make their concerns known. If we fail our generation in this respect (to be, as it were, Noah-like preachers of righteousness), the guidelines for public policy toward morphological human enhancement will be determined in our absence, and we and our children will be forced to live with the decisions made by "the dead hand of the great planners and conditioners." Thank God we still have time to act, if we do so now.

THE THIRD SIGN OF THE DAYS OF NOAH: NOT ALL OF THE ANGELS FELL

According to many Bible scholars, integral to the "signs of the days of Noah" was the fall of the first transhuman technicians—the Watcher angels who altered human genetics through angelic and animal integration. When this mutated DNA began rapidly spreading throughout nature, God instructed Noah, whose family was evidently the last on earth not yet genetically corrupted, to build an ark and to prepare for a Flood that would destroy every living thing. Worldwide extrabiblical texts consistently agree with this Bible story, detailing how the cause of the historic deluge (Great Flood) was in response to "all flesh" having become "corrupted, both man and beast" (see Genesis 6:12). When this Scripture is compared with other ancient texts, it unfolds that the giants of the Old Testament—such as Goliath, whom David slew— were the part-human, part-animal, part-angelic offspring of a supernatural interruption into the divine order of species. The book that contains the clearest historical account of this event is not widely regarded as part of the canon of Scripture (though it is included in the Ethiopian Orthodox Church's canon and the Beta Israel canon). The authorship of this apocryphal text, known as the Book of Enoch, is ascribed to the biblical figure Enoch, the son of Jared, father of Methuselah, and great-grandfather of Noah. While not in most modern versions of the Bible, the Book of Enoch was clearly familiar to the writers of the New Testament and, according to the critically acclaimed 1899 *Encyclopedia Biblica*, influenced their theology. It is quoted as canon or as historical fact by Jude in the New Testament (Jude 1:14–15) and as canon or as fact by Peter in 1 Peter 3. During the discovery of the Dead Sea Scrolls, pre-Maccabean fragments of the Book of Enoch were found, helping scholars verify its antiquity while also illustrating that the ancients held it to be inspired. Many of the early church fathers likewise considered the Book of Enoch to be part of sacred Scriptures, including Justin Martyr, Irenaeus, Origen, Athenagoras, Clement of Alexandria, and Quintus Septimius Florens Tertullianus, (Anglicized *Tertullian*), who offered an explanation in AD 200 for its absence from the Jewish canon, saying it was removed by the Jews because of its prophecies pertaining to Jesus Christ. As the case may be, this ancient book provides the most detailed account of the fall of the Watchers, the angels who fathered the infamous Nephilim. From the sixth chapter of Enoch we read:

> And it came to pass when the children of men had multiplied that in those days were born unto them beautiful and comely daughters. And the angels, the children of the heaven, saw and lusted after them, and said to one another: "Come, let us choose us wives from among the children of men and beget us children." And Semjaza, who was their leader, said unto them: "I fear ye will not indeed agree to do this deed, and I alone shall have to pay the penalty of a great sin." And they all answered him and said: "Let us all swear an oath, and all bind ourselves by mutual imprecations not to abandon this plan but to do this thing." Then sware they all together and bound themselves by mutual imprecations upon it. *And they were in all two hundred; who descended in the days of Jared* on the summit of Mount Hermon, and they called it Mount Hermon, because they had sworn and bound themselves by mutual imprecations upon it. And these are the names of their leaders: Samlazaz, their leader, Araklba, Rameel, Kokablel, Tamlel, Ramlel, Danel, Ezeqeel, Baraqijal, Asael, Armaros, Batarel, Ananel, Zaqlel, Samsapeel, Satarel, Turel, Jomjael, Sariel. These are their chiefs of tens.[105]

We raise the record of the Book of Enoch in particular because, if it is an accurate account, only two hundred of the powerful angel class known as the "Watchers" fell. When added to Revelation 12:3–4, which says, "And there appeared another wonder in heaven; and behold a great red dragon [whose] tail drew the third part of the stars of heaven, and did cast them to the earth," a reference some scholars believe represents one-third of the angels following Lucifer in his fall, the record becomes clear: most angels—including the powerful ones—did not fall. In other words, the third sign "of the days of Noah" is that far more angels remain on our side than those against us. Why is this important to this book? Because angels play an active and historic role in assisting preachers of righteousness in making known the manifold wisdom of God to the world. Thus if "evil angels" or the spirits of Nephilim are at work behind transhumanism, as we believe they are, unfallen and more powerful ones can assist in our counter-mission as emissaries of God. We have supernatural "secret agents" on our side who can go where we cannot and "whisper" ideas and suggestions into the ears of policy makers and legislators at the highest levels of geopolitical influence.

From the Old and New Testament accounts, the responsibility of angels as it relates to such message delivering is obvious. The New Testament word *angelos*, like the Old Testament word *malak*, simply means "messenger." This definition not only implies angels carry dispatches for God, but that they deliver tangible actions. This includes "guidance" to nations, help for the body of Christ, and protection of individuals. Their ministry in this capacity is according to the will of God, not the church's (meaning we do not give them direct orders, God does), and is defined in Scriptures according to four main categories, each of which is important to this book and to our involvement in the revival of targeted spiritual warfare.

1. Angels deliver messages of guidance to nations.

Angels, both good and evil, take part in the spiritual battle for civilization. Throughout the Bible there is clear evidence that angels regularly participate in influencing world governments and in shaping human history, especially as it relates to God's covenant people and prophetic fulfillment. In Exodus 23:20, we read, "Behold, I send an angel before thee, to keep thee in the way, and to bring thee into the place which I have prepared." When God brought Israel out of Egypt, He promised that His angel would go before them and assist them in the development of their nation. In Daniel 12:1, we discover the archangel Michael will continue this relationship with Israel during the Great Tribulation period. "And at that time shall Michael stand up, the great prince which standeth for the children of thy people: and there shall be a time of trouble, such as never was since there was a nation even to that same time." Throughout this seven years of Jacob's Trouble, the book of Revelation depicts angels serving God in shaping the future of nations by dispensing His will and judgments through pouring out vials, sounding trumpets, carrying out functions related to wars, and affecting "natural" phenomena such as earthquakes and storms. This latter role is especially interesting given how, simultaneous to GRIN advances and man's current fascination with becoming creation-altering technology gods, we are witnessing in America and around the world the most bizarre and destructive weather patterns in hundreds of years; in some cases, the most devastating storms on record. When we understand how angels strive with nations by controlling natural phenomena (such as weather), it emerges that God may be saying something to this generation about the message of 2 Chronicles 7:14: "If my people...will humble themselves, and pray, and seek my face, and turn from their wicked ways; then will I hear from heaven...and will heal their land." Does this suggest if we as preachers of righteousness participate in repentance and spiritual warfare, God will send forth the "heavenly host" to assist in guiding the world toward moral clarity on the issues described in this book?

2. Angels deliver messages of direction to individuals.

This first and most recurrent function of angels, message bearing, includes delivery of special instructions from God to individuals concerning the best courses of action. It was an angel that brought God's prophetic message to Mary concerning the immaculate conception of her Son, Jesus (Luke 1:26–38). Earlier, a similar message was delivered by an angel to Zechariah about the birth of his son, John the Baptist (Luke 1:5–25). But after Jesus was born, angels delivered a specific warning to Joseph, instructing him to flee with Mary and Jesus into Egypt. The angel added, "be thou there until I bring thee word: for Herod will seek the young child to destroy him" (Matthew 2:13).

Another example of a message from an angel to an individual giving instructions on timing and movement is found in the book of Acts. Satan had filled Herod's heart with hatred for the Church. James was killed and Peter was imprisoned for preaching the gospel. When the believers understood that Herod was also planning to kill Peter, "prayer was made without ceasing of the church unto God for him" (Acts 12:5).

Peter was in strict confinement, sleeping between two Roman soldiers in chains. During the night, an angel entered the prison and hit Peter on the side. "Arise up quickly," the angel said. "Gird thyself, and bind on thy sandals…and follow me" (Acts 12:7–8). Peter thought he was dreaming as he followed the angel outside past the guards. It was not until he was standing on the street that he realized the *angelos*, the messenger of God, had pronounced God's instructions and delivered him from the Roman prison.

Each of these examples reveals that, as we pray, divine prompting will help in determining the timing and correct course of action each of us will need in the days ahead. A peculiar additional fact to keep in mind concerning angels delivering such messages is how often they are perceived as "heavenly beings" only after their departure. This was the case in Judges 6:11–24, with the angel that appeared to Gideon; and in Hebrews 13:2, it adds the important caveat: "Be not forgetful to entertain strangers: for thereby some have entertained angels unawares." Entertaining angels without being aware that's what they are is possible, because while angels can appear brilliant or even frightening, they usually manifest in simple human form. As we move toward a dystopian future, it would be interesting to know how many times we may encounter these mysterious "strangers" and how often the "person" who delivers God's special words of counsel at just the right moment might actually be an *angel on assignment.*

3. Angels deliver messages of strength and encouragement.

In the tenth chapter of the book of Daniel, the prophet had been praying and fasting for three weeks—conducting spiritual warfare for the future of Israel—when, as he stood on the banks of the Tigris River, the angel Gabriel appeared before him. Daniel fell on his face trembling, overcome by the extent of his fast and by the glorious presence of the angel. He said, "How can the servant of this my lord talk with this my lord? for as for me, straightway there remained no strength in me, neither is there breath left in me" (Daniel 10:17). Then the angel touched him, saying, "O man greatly beloved, fear not: peace be unto thee, be strong, yea, be strong" (Daniel 10:19), and Daniel immediately received strength and energy to continue supernatural combat.

Psalm 34:7 is a beautiful verse about this, written from the warrior's perspective. It says, "The angel of the LORD encampeth round about them that fear him, and delivereth them." It was an angel that ministered such strength and deliverance to Elijah in 1 Kings, chapter 19, when he was running for his life and trying to escape the wicked queen Jezebel. In the New Testament, we find angels ministering to Jesus in similar fashion following His wilderness experience (Mark 1:13). Thankfully, such ministry is not limited to great prophets or to Jesus exclusively, for as Paul taught, these are ministering spirits, sent forth to deliver messages of strength and encouragement to all of God's children (Hebrews 1:14). In other words, they will be there for us too as we advance in our mission.

4. Angels deliver messages of protection for preachers of righteousness.

In the Scriptures, we read how angels were sent to protect Jesus. "For He shall give His angels charge over thee, to keep thee in all thy ways. They shall bear thee up in their hands, lest thou dash thy foot against a stone" (Psalm 91:11–12). Such verses reflect the ancient (and we believe accurate) Jewish belief that God assigns protective angels to those who belong to Him.

The writers of the early church, including Origen and Eusebius, believed that every person is accompanied by a personal guardian angel. The followers of Christ evidently held this view as well, for when Peter stood outside knocking on the door at Mary's house, they said, "It is his angel" (Acts 12:15). Angels watching over children is depicted in Matthew 18:10, and in Daniel 6:1–23, it appears this is also true for adults. After a sleepless night of fasting, King Darius ran to the lion's den where Daniel had been thrown. "O Daniel, servant of the living God," he cried, "is thy God, whom thou servest continually, able to deliver thee from the lions?" Daniel answered, "O king, live for ever. My God has sent His angel, and hath shut the lions' mouths" (Daniel 6:20–22).

Another example of angels protecting the servant of God is found in 2 Kings 6:13–17. The king of Aram hated Elisha and sent spies to track him down. When they found Elisha in the city of Dothan, they surrounded him with a great army. "And when the servant of the man of God was risen early, and gone forth, behold, an host compassed the city both with horses and chariots" (2 Kings 6:15). On seeing this multitude, the servant of Elisha cried out in panic, "Alas, my master! How shall we do?" And Elisha answered, "Fear not: for they that be with us are more than they that be with them" (2 Kings 6:15–16). Elisha prayed that God would open his servant's eyes and allow him to see the angelic realm. "And the LORD opened the eyes of the young man; and he saw; and, behold, the mountain was full of horses and chariots of fire round about Elisha" (2 Kings 6:17).

During spiritual warfare, we can thus pray for God to surround our homes in this way and provide our families with angelic shelter. Volumes of testimonies have been given over the verity of such requests. In an earlier chapter, we related the story of a possessed young man and his attempt to attack us. We have always believed the "something" that came between us and him that day was a guardian angel.

THE RELATIONSHIP BETWEEN PRAYER AND PRINCIPALITIES

While the church does not give direct orders to angels, it is obvious from the biblical examples above that both good and evil supernaturalism responds to effective intercession by saints. Robert E. Lee (general of the Army of Northern Virginia and famed southern preacher) once wrote of this, saying, "intercessory prayer is our mightiest weapon and the supreme call for all Christians today."[106] Lee found this important because in 2 Chronicles 7:14, the intercessory role of God's people is directly tied to the "healing" of the nation. This is partly due to interdiction of enemy angels on behalf of persons, cities, states, nations, and even generations that can occur during intercessory prayer. John Knox was so well known for this type of prayer that the queen of Scotland, "Bloody Mary" (who burned the Protestant reformers at the stake during the Marian Exile), confessed she feared his prayers more than an army of soldiers. It is this kind of spiritual activity, when issued from a sincere and repentant heart, that radiates God's authority and turns back evil supernaturalism. Every verse in the Bible dealing with spiritual warfare confirms this divine symmetry between God's authority and overcoming evil as predicated upon the church's responsiveness as evangelists of mankind. Jesus commissioned Paul to preach to the Gentiles and to "turn them from darkness to light, and from the power of Satan unto God" (Acts 26:18a). The Bible subsequently reveals that it is the believer's responsibility to "ask" before God will respond, to bind and release on earth for heaven to do the same, and that part and parcel of the Great Commission is the duty of the church to cast out demons and to tread over the power of the enemy. Apparently when we do, we send shock waves through the heavenlies! Note how in Nehemiah 9:6, the prophet spoke of more than one heaven: he saw the heavens and the "heaven of heavens." These were not peripheral heavens as taught in Mormonism, but heavenly divisions as Paul referred to in 2 Corinthians 12:2, saying, "I knew a man in Christ above fourteen years ago, (whether in the body, I cannot tell; or whether out of the body, I cannot tell: God knoweth;) such an one [was] caught up to the third heaven." Some scholars believe when Paul referred to this third heaven, he was echoing his formal education as a Pharisee concerning three heavens that included a domain of air (the *kosmos*) or height, controlled by Satan—Beelzeboul, "lord of the height." In pharisaical thought, the first heaven was simply the place where the birds fly, anything removed from and not attached to the surface of the earth. On the other end of the spectrum and of a different substance was the third heaven—the dwelling place of God. This was the place from which angelic spheres spread outward. Between this third heaven, "where dwells the throne room of God," and the first heaven, where the birds fly, was a war zone called the "second heaven." This was the *kosmos*—the Hebrew equivalent of the Persian *Ahriman-abad*—the place where Satan abides as the prince of the power of the "air" (Greek *aer:* the lower air, circumambient; see Ephesians 2:2), a sort of gasket heaven, the domain of Satan encompassing the surface of the earth. From here, *kosmokrators* could overshadow the ages of men and intrude upon and attempt to influence their philosophy and affairs.

A particularly interesting mystery about the kosmos has to do with the ancient belief that Satan's minions could close this space above specific areas (strongholds) so that prayers from the saints would not be able to penetrate through to God. Some say this concept is allegorical, but that it illustrates how when believers pray, their intercession is literally opposed—both going to, and answers returning from, God. The effectual, fervent prayers of the righteous (James 5:16) are the battering rams that push through all such demonic opposition en route to and from the third heaven. Was this illustrated in the tenth chapter of Daniel, when the prophet prayed for twenty-one days until the angel broke through and delivered God's answer? It would seem so, as the persistence of our prayers, when they are prayed "according to His will," creates activity within the second and third heavens. In turn, the heavenly responses affect every level of spiritual and physical society. Daniel prayed until he pushed a hole through walls of demonic opposition and the heavens opened with spiritual revelations. In 1 Kings 18, Elijah continued in prayer until the heavens opened and the rains fell. The disciples interceded until their prayers penetrated the heavens and the glory of Pentecost came rushing down from the throne of God. Jacob prayed and the heavens opened. Angels ascended and descended. Elisha prayed and his servant beheld the heavens opened and the angelic host standing upon the mountains to help them.

If modern believers pray as eagerly, can we expect similar supernatural authority over the looming threat of Nephilimism via GRIN technology and the transhuman agenda?

A HAUNTING LESSON FROM THE YALU RIVER

As one considers the role of prayer in spiritual warfare, there is what we call the Yalu River Dilemma. From 1950–53, America fought one of her most bloody and forgotten battles, the Korean War, a conflict in which the dictator of North Korea, Kim Il Sung, obtained military help from the USSR dictator, Joseph Stalin. During this time, the Chinese army, on November 26, 1950, surprised Gen. Douglas MacArthur by crossing the Yalu River in great force. Hitting the exposed flanks of MacArthur's forces, the Chinese stunned the allies and forced them back. By Christmas the same year, the United Nations forces were once again fighting below the thirty-eighth parallel.

It was this point that would lead to irreconcilable differences between President Harry S. Truman and General MacArthur. Truman—thoroughly frightened by China's action and fearing the possibility of a world war—moved to limit the confrontation, while MacArthur pressed to bomb the bridges at Yalu and expand the war into China proper. Truman refused and decided to allow only the Korean halves of the Yalu bridges to be bombed. By March of 1951, Truman announced his "limited war" policy. The compromise so infuriated MacArthur that he released his "Military Appraisal," an amazing document that amounted to an ultimatum to the Chinese and to President Truman. This led to Truman firing MacArthur. "By this act," the president said, "MacArthur left me no choice—I could no longer tolerate his insubordination." MacArthur was ordered to return home, relieved of duty. Afterward, MacArthur famously addressed the Congress, saying, "There is no substitute for victory!"

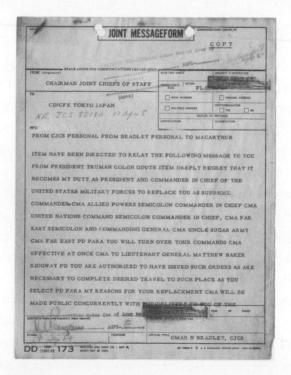

A 1951 telegram conveys President Truman's decision to relieve Douglas MacArthur of his commands. (RG 319, Records of the Army Staff)

Douglas MacArthur wanted to end the Korean War by total military victory in Asia. Truman chose to continue a limited engagement. In the spirit realm, we face this same type of dilemma. As a local church or as individuals, we pray. When short-term victories come, we may slack off, only to later discover the same problems resurfacing. This principle is critical for believers to understand. A limited war policy or passive approach to prayer can only result in the enemy simply retreating behind its own Yalu River, there to regroup, strategize, and attack again when prayer has ceased. But here is the good news: Whether it is the issue of transhumanism and the deepening challenge to maintain our humanity as God made us, or private issues currently faced by the reader, God has given the church what the U.S. government refused to give MacArthur during the Korean War: the power to move beyond the protective bridges of our enemy's stronghold. God allows the contrite believer to invade the opponent's headquarters through the power of prayer, to identify and bind the ruling prince through the authority of Jesus' name, and to permanently destroy the fortress walls of nefarious warlords; or, as the military would say, "to offer them no quarter."

Of course, some will argue this is easier said than done. When looking at the awesome scope of government and academic interests in GRIN technology and the planned rollout of industrialized techno-sapiens, we as individuals may feel small or powerless, as though our singular prayers or input will be of little effect. The Tea Party movement in the United States illustrates this is not true. A nation is simply a multitude of persons. Each time an individual takes a righteous stand, we move one person closer to victory. In fact, every notable spiritual awakening began with the individual. The Reformation started with the convictions of Martin Luther. Paul stood alone at Ephesus, a city ruled by an unsurpassed religious and political machine, yet he started a church there that ultimately released the minds of men and women from the deception of Diana worship and brought the downfall of a cult that had flourished for hundreds of years. When Charles Finney launched his evangelism effort, he took onto his team a man named Nash, who made prayer his only role. When Finney preached, Nash stayed behind and prayed, and guess what? As many as fifty thousand people per week accepted Jesus as Lord. Jonathan Edwards, George Whitefield, Catherine Booth, Gilbert Tennent, Shubal Stearns, Fanny Crosby, Daniel Marshall, Billy Sunday, Maria Woodworth-Etter, and numerous others proved one cannot underestimate the power of a single dedicated believer.

Having said that, the past also reveals what happens when individuals do nothing, or worse, when they become corrupt and tyrannical. Students of history have looked with interest at the French Revolution, which was marked by death and torture under Maximilien Robespierre, and have compared it to the Revolutionary War in America that eventually resulted in unprecedented cultural and monetary success. While citizens after the war in America were rejoicing in newfound freedoms, in Paris more than twenty thousand people died in the guillotine. The years to follow in France witnessed a reign of terror leading to totalitarianism and the rise of an antichrist figure, Napoleon. Why were the American and French Revolutions followed by such contrasting conclusions? The difference was that in America the pilgrim influence had created strong Christian sentiments, while in France the movement was anti-God. The forces behind the French Revolution were out to eliminate God as the enemy of France. They placed a statue of a nude woman upon the altar in the church of Notre Dame and proclaimed the God of Christianity dead. Soon after, the French government collapsed.

Conversely, when we understand how during the American Revolution a small number of mostly agrarian Americans stood up for something that mattered and held tightly to a Christian faith that could not be stamped out by the fires of revolution, we comprehend where the strength of those generations that followed came from, including the so-called Greatest Generation, the children of the pioneers who overcame the Great Depression, who won World War II, and who outperformed their competitors during the Industrial Revolution. Those who followed them built on the same success until finally the United States emerged as "a shining city on a hill," a beacon of hope and inspiration to the rest of the world—what President Ronald Reagan in his January 11, 1989, farewell speech called "a tall, proud city built on rocks stronger than oceans, windswept, God-blessed, and teeming with people of all kinds living in harmony and peace, a city with free ports that hummed with commerce and creativity, and if there had to be city walls, the walls had doors and the doors were open to anyone with the will and the heart to get here."[107]

WHOSE VISION WILL PREVAIL?

Ronald Reagan's depiction of America is sweet, but (as we have documented) a worrying trend is darkening the horizon and threatening to undo this dream and similar big ideas in countries around the world. Recent polling shows a generation disinterested in the faith of their fathers and even less attracted to Judeo-Christian definitions about sin and repentance. Society now wants a God that makes them happy and who only comes around when needed. This new widespread movement even has a name: it is titled "Moralistic Therapeutic Deism" (dubbed so by researchers during a National Study of Youth and Religion at the University of North Carolina). It defines what has become the "Christianity" of choice among modern teens and their parents. Like the deistic God of the freemasons and eighteenth-century philosophers, "This undemanding deity is more interested in solving our problems and in making people happy," concludes Dr. Albert Mohler Jr. for the *Christian Post*. "In short, [this] God is something like a combination Divine Butler and Cosmic Therapist: he is always on call, takes care of any problems that arise, professionally helps his people to feel better about themselves, and does not become too personally involved in the process."

In continuing his troubling dissertation, Mohler unknowingly describes elements of transhumanism:

This radical transformation of Christian theology and Christian belief replaces the sovereignty of God with the sovereignty of the self [a central transhumanist value]. In this therapeutic age, human problems are reduced to pathologies in need of a treatment plan. Sin is simply excluded from the picture, and doctrines as central as the wrath and justice of God are discarded as out of step with the times and unhelpful to the project of self-actualization.

All this means is that teenagers have been listening carefully. They have been observing their parents in the larger culture with diligence and insight. They understand just how little their parents really believe and just how much many of their churches and Christian institutions have accommodated themselves to the dominant culture. They sense the degree to which theological conviction has been sacrificed on the altar of individualism and a relativistic understanding of truth. They have learned from their elders that self-improvement [another important theme of transhumanism] is the one great moral imperative to which all are accountable, and they have observed the fact that the highest aspiration of those who shape this culture is to find happiness, security, and meaning in life. [We thus] face a succession of generations who have transformed Christianity into something that bears no resemblance to the faith revealed in the Bible. The faith "once delivered to the saints" is no longer even known, not only by American teenagers, but by most of their parents. [108]

Thus, like a ship adrift at sea, a gilded age arises in which intellectual achievements and human-transforming technologies are valued supreme. And no wonder. For more than five decades, hundreds of millions of dollars in public funds have poured into transhumanist goals; media outlets have denigrated traditional values; the highest courts in the land have ruled with imperious decree against the free expression of Christianity; evangelicals have been disinvited to the National Day of Prayer at the Pentagon; and finally, according to the current president of the United States, Barack Hussein Obama, America is no longer a Christian nation.

The net result is the dawn of a generation without sacred moorings, an era in which people are sufficiently prepared to accept the nightmarish transhuman vision unfolding around us. The question is, is it too late to reverse these trends and set this age on track toward moral and spiritual recovery? We must believe that it is not too late—that if, like Noah, David, Joshua, and Caleb, we stand up to the infernal power operating just beyond the range of normal vision, it will yet be possible to illustrate the living dynamic against which the gates of hell cannot prevail.

But make no mistake about it: The gods of chaos are coming. They are poised to redefine what it means to be human, and to remove anyone or anything that stands in their way. The church must prepare for this now, both physically and spiritually, as the threat is real and spreading like cancer.

To help believers get ready for what is unfolding, we are providing free of charge two more books in portable document format (.pdf) that teach about the armor we have as saints, how to fast and pray, how to engage pagan deities in spiritual warfare, and numerous related subjects. At the same Web site, you can download the free thirteen-week teacher's guide, watch videos, download government reports referred to in this book, and more.

Here is what we highly recommend readers do:

1. Download the FREE, thirteen-week teacher's guide based on this book (available at www.ForbiddenGate.com) and use it during classes and sermons to instruct others on

transhumanism. The teachers guide is a powerful supplement for this work and contains *additional information and resources.*

2. Download the FREE, 207-page .pdf version of our 1998 book, *Spiritual Warfare: The Invisible Invasion"* (available at www.ForbiddenGate.com) to learn more about spiritual warfare, the armor we have as saints, how to fast and pray, and numerous related subjects.

3. Download the FREE, 191-page .pdf version of our 1999 book, *The Gods Who Walk among Us* (available at www. ForbiddenGate.com), to learn more about the role of pagan "gods" and their relationship to spiritual warfare.

4. Plan to attend the "World Congress on Emerging Threats and Challenges" (tentative conference title) to be held the third week of July 2011 in Branson, Missouri. More information on this event—and why *you* should be there—will be posted before the end of 2010 at www.ForbiddenGate.com

5. Stay attuned to developments within transhumanism and related fields of science by visiting www.Raiders NewsNetwork.com on a daily basis. This is the world's leading conservative Web site on such issues and will help you stay informed as things develop.

6. Download FREE guides at www.SurvivorMall.com that will help you with physical preparedness. Because GRIN technology portends natural threats as well as supernatural, we are giving away hundreds of pages from reports and booklets on how to survive earthquakes, storms, floods, terrorism, chemical contamination, nuclear fallout, and dozens of other emergency situations. These booklets and reports can be printed out and placed on a table in a church foyer,

handed to neighbors and given out during classes—or better yet, taught as a class on preparedness and tied in with the mandates of Scripture (or used as supplements during classes based on this book).

7. For churches or groups interested in inviting the authors to present a one-day seminar on the content of this book, please make contact through the Web site www.Raiders NewsNetwork.com.

Also NEW from Tom and Nita Horn!

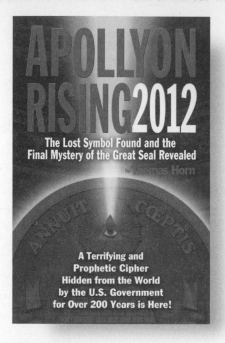

APOLLYON RISING 2012: The Lost Symbol Found and the Final Mystery of the Great Seal Revealed

THE PUBLISHER'S #1 BEST-SELLING BOOK FOR OVER A YEAR!

From the lips of U.S. congressmen and senators to syndicated shows like the History Channel and the top ten talk radio shows and news sources across the nation, the revelations in Tom Horn's new book, *Apollyon Rising 2012: The Lost Symbol Found and the Final Mystery of the Great Seal Revealed,* have created nonstop shock waves since its release. In this book, the author welcomes you to learn the secrets of the true Lost Symbol (what Dan Brown was looking for and did not find), the forbidden knowledge of the Vatican and Washington DC, and the two-hundred-year-old cipher hidden in plain sight at the U.S. Capitol Dome and on the Great Seal of the United States. You are about to embark upon the discovery of a lifetime, with a countdown toward the year 2012 that is unlike anything you have heard or read anywhere before.

"Tom, I've been following your career for a long time. You have emerged as the leading expert in this field and a great intellect." —MELANIE MORGAN, ABC anchor with award-winning columnist John McCaslin for *America's Morning News*, the nationally syndicated show in partnership with the *Washington Times*

"I've been reading your new book, Tom, and Apollyon Rising 2012 *is a must-read for every serious believer."* —DR. CHUCK MISSLER, CEO, Koinonia House on *Raiders Live! News Talk Radio*

"I'm speechless! Tom Horn's Apollyon Rising [Is] *Shocking! Terrifying! Provocative! Edgy! Dangerous! Dare I say it could be the best book I have ever read!?"* —BOB ULRICH, for Prophecy in the News

"Skeptics can stick their heads in the sand, but Horn presents the research. Wishing his claims away won't make them go away. Horn, a key figure in the modern Bible prophecy movement, has compiled enough detail to merit serious consideration. Compelling!" —JIM FLETCHER, WorldNetDaily

Available at www.SurvivorMall.com

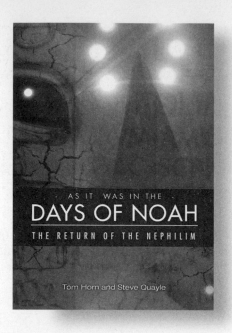

As It Was in the Days of Noah:
The Return of the Nephilim

As It Was in The Days of Noah: The Return of the Nephilim has been called "The Best-Ever Series" by popular radio personalities Tom Horn and Steve Quayle. This is a fascinating and sometimes frightening exposé on little-known passages from the Bible and apocryphal texts, which speak of an alien agenda, great deception giving rise to the Antichrist, and—in the last two parts of this series—the most incredible information ever revealed over the airwaves about the return of the giants in the last days. Tom's newest revelation from the Book of Enoch left Steve Quayle speechless for several seconds and led to newshounds seeking additional information and a feature editorial at WorldNetDaily, the world's #1 online news site.

Available at www.SurvivorMall.com

CONSPIRACY THEORY

S P E C I A L   E D I T I O N

Tom Horn and Spencer Bennett

Based on Tom and Nita Horn's book, *The Ahriman Gate,* and Tom Horn's new book, *Nephilim Stargates: The Year 2012 and the Return of the Watchers,* this six-hour investigative interview between reporter and actor Spencer Bennett and Tom Horn discusses in detail the subject of end-times prophecy and its relationship with biotechnology, UFOs, nephilim, and speculation about the return of the Watchers in the year 2012. Do ancient texts reveal advanced transgenic science was used to create the mysterious beings known in the Bible as nephilim?

Do holy books point to a return of these beings when science once again breaches species barriers, as is happening now in laboratories around the world? Is the timing of this science with the invasion of Iraq and global tension over Iran and Israel something more than is visible to the human eye? Listen to this incredible six-CD series and prepare yourself for what most people are unaware of. A time prophesied by the ancients is at hand when the Watchers of lore may be about to return!

Special Edition
6-Hour CD Set

Available at
www.SurvivorMall.com

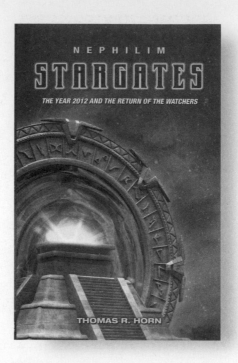

Nephilim Stargates: The Year 2012 and the Return of the Watchers

Something alarming has been happening since the dawn of time, which has been recorded in the history, holy books, and mythos of every great civilization. Ancient rabbinical authorities including Septuagint translators and early church fathers understood it. Sumerians, Assyrians, Egyptians, Greeks, the Hindus, the American Indians, and virtually all other civilizations wrote about it. Beings of super intelligence sometimes referred to as "gods" descend through openings of sky, earth, and sea to interact with this planet's creatures. According to Tom Horn, prophecy says they will return... and at a time much sooner than most people realize.

Available at www.SurvivorMall.com

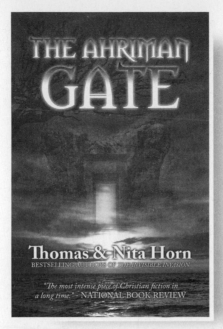

The Ahriman Gate: Some Gates Should Not Be Opened

Joe Ryback, a twenty-six-year-old marine whose lieutenant colonel father was murdered under mysterious circumstances, stumbles upon a cover-up that reaches to the highest levels of U.S. government and military agencies. Suddenly too deep to turn back, he struggles to contain the nightmarish forces closing around him and his family. As a mind-boggling phantasm brings him face to face with genetically modified creatures and spiritual-alien forces, a sinister plan unfolds at Montero—a government-funded research laboratory—that could usher in the coming of Antichrist and the end of the world. With dynamic plot twists, mesmerizing ideas, and unchained high-tech weaponry, *The Ahriman Gate* moves the reader feverishly toward disclosure of shadow governments involved with transgenic research, extraterrestrial vehicles, crypto-archaeology, and ghastly genetic research, convening in a nightmare scenario that takes the breath away.

Available at www.SurvivorMall.com

Notes

1. Gregory A. Boyd, *God at War: The Bible and Spiritual Conflict* (Downer's Grove, IL: InterVarsity, 1997) 19, 55.
2. Philip J. King, Michael David Coogan, J. Cheryl Exum, Lawrence E. Stager, *Scripture and Other Artifacts: Essays on the Bible and Archaeology in Honor of Philip J. King* (Westminster: John Knox, 1994) 121.
3. Lucius Apuleius, *The Golden Asse*, Book 11 (1566) emphasis added.
4. Hymns of Homer, XXX, Chapter 11, 1–19.
5. Thomas and Nita Horn, *The Ahriman Gate* (Crane, MO: Defender, 2005) 63–64.
6. Mircea Eliade and Willard R. Trask, *Yoga: Immortality and Freedom* (Princeton, NJ: Princeton, 1970) 221–222.
7. Gary Lachman, *Politics and the Occult: The Left, the Right, and the Radically Unseen* (Wheaton, IL: Theosophical, 2008) 97–98.
8. Hermann Rauschning, *Hitler m'a dit* (Paris, 1939).
9. Samantha Smith, "Signs and Wonders Phenomenon," *Eagle Forum* (vol. 18, no. 3) 20.
10. Carolyn R. Staffer, "Dr. Leslie Gray, Bridge between Two Realities," *Shaman's Drum* (Fall 1987) 25.
11. Raymond Moody with Paul Perry, *Reunions* (New York: Villard, 1993) 54–62.
12. C. Claiborne Ray, "Science Q & A: Dancing Angels," *New York Times* (11/11/97) http://www.nytimes.com/learning/students/scienceqa/archive/971111.html.
13. "Spanish Exorcist Addresses Claims of Satanic Influence in Vatican," *Catholic News Agency,* http://www.catholicnewsagency.com/news/spanish_exorcist_addresses_claims_of_satanic_influence_in_vatican/.

14. David Wilkerson, "Witchcraft in the Church," *Believers Web*, http://www.believersweb.org/view.cfm?ID=735.

15. Thomas Horn, "New Testament Theology, According to the Vampire Lestat," *Raiders News Network* (2/1/10) http://www.raidersnewsnetwork.com/vampires.htm.

16. Chip Ingram, *The Invisible War* (Grand Rapids, MI: Baker, 2006) 133.

17. Hugo de Garis, *The Artilect War: Cosmists vs. Terrans: A Bitter Controversy Concerning Whether Humanity Should Build Godlike Massively Intelligent Machines* (Palm Springs, CA: 2005) 11–12, 15, 84.

18. Theodore Kaczynski, "Industrial Society and Its Future," Wikisource, http://en.wikisource.org/wiki/Industrial_Society_and_Its_Future.

19. Joe Garreau, *Radical Evolution: The Promise and Peril of Enhancing Our Minds, Our Bodies—and What It Means to Be Human* (New York: Broadway, 2005) 71–72.

20. Ray Kurzweil, *The Singularity is Near* (New York: Penguin, 2006) 7–8.

21. Abou Farman, "The Intelligent Universe," *Maison Neuve* (8/ 2/10) http://maisonneuve.org/pressroom/article/2010/aug/2/intelligent-universe/.

22. Kurzweil, 9.

23. "The Coming Technological Singularity," presented at the VISION-21 Symposium sponsored by NASA Lewis Research Center and the Ohio Aerospace Institute (3/30–31/93).

24. Jerome C. Glenn, "The State of the Future" (7/14/10) www.kurzwcilai.net/the-state-of-the-future, emphasis added.

25. Ibid, emphasis added.

26. Case Western Reserve University, "Case Law School Receives $773,000 NIH Grant to Develop Guidelines for Genetic Enhancement Research: Professor Max Mehlman to Lead Team of Law Professors, Physicians, and Bioethicists in Two-Year Project" (April 28, 2006).

27. Jane Picken, "Medical Marvels," *The Evening Chronicle* (April 13, 2007).

28. Joseph Infranco, "President Barack Obama Warped and Twisted Science with Embryonic Stem Cell Order," *LifeNews* (4/13/09) http://www.lifenews.com/bio2823.html.

29. Nick Bostrom, "Transhumanist Values," www.nickbostrom.com.

30. "Facing the Challenges of Transhumanism: Religion, Science, Technology," *Arizona State University*, http://transhumanism.asu.edu/.

31. http://lach.web.arizona.edu/Sophia/.

32. Leon R. Kass, *Life, Liberty, and the Defense of Dignity: The Challenge for Bioethics* (New York: Encounter, 10/25/02).

33. Rick Weiss, "Of Mice, Men, and In-Between," *MSNBC* (11/20/04) http://www.msnbc.msn.com/id/6534243/.

34. http://news.yahoo.com/s/cq/20090315/pl_cq_politics/politics3075228.

35. *American Journal of Law and Medicine*, vol. 28, nos. 2 and 3 (2002), 162.

36. As quoted by Margaret McLean, PHD, "Redesigning Humans: The Final Frontier," http://www.elca.org/What-We-Believe/Social-Issues/Journal-of-Lutheran-Ethics/Book-Reviews/Redesigning-Humans-by-Gregory-Stock/Redesigning-Humans-The-Final-Frontier.aspx.

37. "The Coming Technological Singularity," presented at the VISION-21 Symposium sponsored by NASA Lewis Research Center and the Ohio Aerospace Institute (3/30–31/93).

38. Noah Shachtman, "Top Pentagon Scientists Fear Brain-Modified Foes," *Wired* (6/9/08) http://www.wired.com/dangerroom/2008/06/jason-warns-of/.

39. Nigel M. de S. Cameron, *Human Dignity in the Biotech Century* (Downers Grove, IL: InterVarsity, 2004) 75.

40. Ibid., 87, emphasis added.

41. Mihail Roco, *Converging Technologies for Improving Human Performance* (U.S. National Science Foundation and Department of Commerce, 2002) 6.

42. http://www.newamerica.net/events/2010/warring_futures_a_future_tense_event.

43. Chris Floyd, "Monsters, Inc.: The Pentagon Plan to Create Mutant 'Super-Soldiers,'" *CounterPunch* (1/13/03).

44. Garreau, *Radical Evolution:* 269–270.
45. Katie Drummond, "Holy Acronym, Darpa! 'Batman & Robin' to Master Biology, Outdo Evolution," *Wired* (7/6/10) http://www.wired.com/dangerroom/2010/07/holy-acronym-darpa-batman-robin-to-master-biology-outdo-evolution/.
46. Katie Drummond, "Darpa's News Plans: Crowdsource Intel, Edit DNA," *Wired* (2/2/10) http://www.wired.com/dangerroom/2010/02/darpas-new-plans-crowdsource-intel-immunize-nets-edit-dna/.
47. Katie Drummond, "Pentagon Looks to Breed Immortal 'Synthetic Organisms,' Molecular Kill-Switch Included," *Wired* (2/5/10) http://www.wired.com/dangerroom/2010/02/pentagon-looks-to-breed-immortal-synthetic-organisms-molecular-kill-switch-included/.
48. *Institute for Responsible Technology,* http://www.responsibletechnology.org/GMFree/Home/index.cfm.
49. Waclaw Szybalski, *In Vivo and in Vitro Initiation of Transcription,* 405. In A. Kohn and A. Shatkay (eds.), *Control of Gene Expression,* 23–24, and Discussion 404–405 (Szybalski's concept of Synthetic Biology), 411–412, 415–417 (New York: Plenum, 1974).
50. "First Self-Replicating Synthetic Bacterial Cell," *J. Craig Venter Institute,* http://www.jcvi.org/cms/research/projects/first-self-replicating-synthetic-bacterial-cell.
51. Peter E. Nielsen, "Triple Helix: Designing a New Molecule of Life," *Scientific American* (12/08) http://www.scientificamerican.com/article.cfm?id=triple-helix-designing-a-new-molecule&ec=su_triplehelix.
52. Charles W. Colson, *Human Dignity in the Biotech Century* (Downers Grove, IL: InterVarsity, 2004) 8.
53. C. Christopher Hook, *Human Dignity in the Biotech Century* (Downers Grove, IL: InterVarsity, 2004) 80–81.
54. Garreau, *Radical Evolution,* 116.
55. Francis Fukuyama, *Our Posthuman Future: Consequences of the Biotechnology Revolution* (New York: Picador, 2002) 6.
56. Garreau, 106.
57. Ibid., 113–114.

58. "Carried Away with Convergence," *New Atlantis* (Summer 2003) 102–105, http://www.thenewatlantis. com/publications/carried-away-with-convergence.
59. Ibid.
60. Bill Joy, "Why the Future Doesn't Need Us," *Wired* (April 2000) http://www.wired.com/wired/archive/8.04/joy.html), emphasis added.
61. Mark Walker, "Ship of Fools: Why Transhumanism is the Best Bet to Prevent the Extinction of Civilization," Metanexus Institute (2/5/09) http://www.metanexus.net/magazine/tabid/68/id/10682/ Default.aspx.
62. Gary Stearman, "The Extraterrestrial Question," *Prophecy in the News* (March 2010) 10.
63. Hendrik Poinar, "Recipe for a Resurrection," *National Geographic* (May 2009) http://ngm.nationalgeographic. com/2009/05/cloned-species/Mueller-text).
64. Chuck Missler and Mark Eastman, *Alien Encounters* (Coeur d'Alene, ID: Koinonia House, 1997) 275.
65. Louis Pauwells and Jacques Bergier, *The Dawn of Magic*, first published in France under the title *Le Matin des Magiciens*, (Paris: Editions Gallimard) 68.
66. Annette Yoshiko Reed, *Fallen Angels and the History of Judaism and Christianity: The Reception of Enochic Literature* (Cambridge, 2005) 214.
67. Ashlee Vance, "The Lifeboat Foundation: Battling Asteroids, Nanobots and A.I." *New York Times* (7/20/10) http://bits.blogs. nytimes.com/2010/07/20/the-lifeboat-foundation-battling-asteroids-nanobots-and-a-i/.
68. Ian Sample, "Global Disaster: Is Humanity Prepared for the Worst?" *Observer* (7/25/10) http://www.guardian. co.uk/science/2010/jul/25/disaster-risk-assessment-science.
69. Ibid.
70. Rory Cellan-Jones, "First Human 'Infected with Computer Virus,'" *BBC News* (5/27/10) http://www.bbc. co.uk/news/10158517.
71. Hook, 92.

72. Ibid., 93.
73. Mihail Roco and William Sims Bainbridge, ed. *Converging Technologies for Improving Human Performance* (New York: Kluwer Academic, 2003) emphasis in original).
74. Garreau, 7–8.
75. Robert Jeffress, *The Divine Defense: Six Simple Strategies for Winning Your Greatest Battles* (Colorado Springs, CO: WaterBrook, 2006) 78.
76. John Horgon, "We're Cracking the Neural Code, the Brain's Secret Language," *Adbusters* (1/25/06) https://www.adbusters.org/the_magazine/63/Were_Cracking_the_Neural_Code_the_Brains_Secret_Language.html.
77. "Brain-Computer Interface Allows Person-to-Person Communication Through Power Of Thought," *ScienceDaily* (10/6/09) http://www.sciencedaily.com/releases/2009/10/091006102637.htm.
78. Charles Ostman, *The Internet as an Organism: Emergent Human / Internet Symbiosis* (Vienna, Austria: Thirteenth European Meeting on Cybernetics and Systems Research at the University of Vienna, April 9–12, 1996) emphasis added.
79. Sounding the Codes (2007) http://www.thecenteroflight.net.
80. Robert Maguire, Charles J. Doe, *Commentary on John Bunyan's The Holy War* (2009) 11.
81. Ibid., 7.
82. Frank Jordas, "Study on Cell Phone Link to Cancer Inconclusive," *Associated Press* (2010) http://abcnews.go.com/print?id=10668283.
83. "How Technology May Soon 'Read' Your Mind," *CBS 60 Minutes* (June 2009) http://www.cbsnews.com/stories/2008/12/31/60minutes/main4694713.shtml.
84. "Remote Control Brain Sensor," BBC (November 2002) http://news.bbc.co.uk/2/hi/health/2361987.stm.
85. R. Douglas Fields, "Mind Control by Cell Phone," *Scientific American* (May 2008) http://www.scientificamerican.com/article.cfm?id=mind-control-by-cell.
86. Liane Young, Joan Albert Camprodon, et al, "Disruption of the Right Temporo-Parietal Junction with Transcranial Magnetic

Stimulation Reduces the Role of Beliefs in Moral Judgments," Proceedings of the National Academy of Sciences (March 2010) http://www.eurekalert.org/pub_releases/2010-03/miot-mjc032510.php.

87. Mark Baard, "EM Field, Behind Right Ear, Suspends Morality," *Sci-Tech Heretic* (March 2009) http://heretic.blastmagazine.com/2010/03/em-field-behind-right-ear-suspends-morality.

88. *Stephen King, Cell (New York: Simon and Shuster, 2006).*

89. Jeremy Hsu, "Video Gamers Can Control Dreams, Study Suggests," *LiveScience* (5/25/10) http://www.livescience.com/culture/video-games-control-dreams-100525.html.

90. Aaron Saenz, "Is the Movie 'Inception' Getting Closer to Reality?" (7/15/10) http://singularityhub.com/2010/07/15/is-the-movie-inception-getting-closer-to-reality-video/.

91. Naomi Darom, "Will Scientists Soon Be Able to Read Our Minds?" *Haaretz*, http://www.haaretz.com/magazine/week-s-end/will-scientists-soon-be-able-to-read-our-minds-1.291310.

92. Sharon Weinberger, "The 'Voice of God' Weapon Returns," *Wired* (12/21/07) http://www.wired.com/dangerroom/2007/12/the-voice-of-go/.

93. Joshua Ramo, "The Big Bank Theory," *Time* (4/27/98) http://www.time.com/time/printout/0,8816,988228,00.html.

94. Eric Bland, "Part-Human, Part-Machine Transistor Devised," *Discovery News* (6/2/10) http://news.discovery.com/tech/transistor-cell-membrane-machine.html, emphasis added.

95. *Millennium,* "Sense and Antisense," Fox (original air date 10/3/97).

96. Ashlee Vance, "Merely Human? That's So Yesterday," *New York Times* (6/11/10) http://www.nytimes.com/2010/06/13/business/13sing.html?_r=1.

97. Wesley J. Smith, "Pitching the New Transhumanism Religion in the NYT," *First Things* (6/14/10) http://www.firstthings.com/blogs/secondhandsmoke/2010/06/14/pitching-the-new-transhumanism-religion-in-the-nyt/.

98. Gregory Jordan , "Apologia for Transhumanist Religion," *Journal of Evolution and Technology, Published by the Institute for Ethics and Emerging Technologies* (2005) http://jetpress.org/volume15/jordan2.html.

99. Brent Waters, "The Future of the Human Species (Part 1)," http://www.cbhd.org/content/future-human-species.

100. As quoted by C. Christopher Hook in "The Techno Sapiens Are Coming," *Christianity Today* (January 2004) http://www.christianitytoday.com/ct/2004/january/1.36.html.

101. Ibid.

102. Rod Dreher, "Vatican Bioethics Document and Competing Moral Visions," *BeliefNet* (12/12/08) http://blog.beliefnet.com/crunchycon/2008/12/vatican-bioethics-document-and.html.

103. C. S. Lewis, *The Abolition of Man,* http://www.columbia.edu/cu/augustine/arch/lewis/abolition3.htm.

104. "Ethics of Human Enhancement," *Human Enhancement Ethics Group* http://www.humanenhance.com/category/news-and-events/press-releases/.

105. Book of Enoch 6:1–8, (Oxford: The Clarendon Press) emphasis added.

106. Deborah McComber, "Robert E. Lee," *Berean Bible Heritage Church,* http://bereanbibleheritage.org/extraordinary/lee_robert.php.

107. "City Upon a Hill," *Wikipedia,* http://en.wikipedia.org/wiki/City_upon_a_Hill.

108. Dr. Albert Mohler Jr., "Moralistic Therapeutic Deism—the New American Religion," Christian Post (4/18/05) http://www.christianpost.com/article/20050418/moralistic-therapeutic-deism-the-new-american-religion/pageall.html.